# The Complete Career Paths Series

Career Paths Vols. 1-5

Thriving at Work

The Pragmatist's Rules for Work

Work Hard and Get Ahead

Happiness and Leadership

A Fine Idea

Problem Solving and Communication

Copyright © 2025 by James Bellerjeau

All rights reserved.

No portion of this book may be reproduced in any form without written permission from the publisher or author, except as permitted by U.S. copyright law.

An earlier version of several of these articles was previously published in the ACC Docket (https://docket.acc.com/). Copyright © 2023, Association of Corporate Counsel. Reprinted with permission. All rights reserved. Visit www.acc.com.

# Contents

Thriving at Work

The Pragmatist's Rules for Work

Work Hard and Get Ahead

Happiness and Leadership

Problem Solving and Communication

# Thriving at Work

Career Paths Vol. 1: 26 Essential Lessons on the ABCs of Work

James Bellerjeau

A Fine Idea

Copyright © 2025 by James Bellerjeau

All rights reserved.

No portion of this book may be reproduced in any form without written permission from the publisher or author, except as permitted by U.S. copyright law.

An earlier version of these articles was previously published in the ACC Docket (https://docket.acc.com/). Copyright © 2023, Association of Corporate Counsel. Reprinted with permission. All rights reserved. Visit www.acc.com.

# Contents

Is There a Formula for Success at Work? — 5

1. Ambition Is the Foundation of All Progress — 7
2. Believing You Will Succeed Speeds Your Journey — 11
3. Continuous Improvement Is a Superpower Available to Everyone — 15
4. Diversity of Thought Is Rare — 19
5. Equanimity Comes From Seeing the Underlying Value — 23
6. Fakery Is a Time-Honored Path To Growth — 27
7. Do A Good Job and Great Things Follow — 31
8. Happy in All Weather and at All Times — 35
9. The One Thing You Can Never Compromise — 39
10. Joy Is Your Reward for Approaching Work Well — 43
11. When Kindness Helps You As Much as Others — 47
12. Your Attitude To Learning Tells Me a Lot — 51
13. The Self-Motivation That Never Leaves You Hanging — 55
14. Why You Should Welcome Novelty Into Your Day — 59
15. When To Obey Your Boss or Defy Their Decision — 63
16. We Were Wrong To Banish Prayer From Work — 67
17. Carve Out Quiet Time if You Want To Make Some Noise — 71

18. Rest Your Way To Better Performance 75
19. Why Stress Crushes Some Colleagues But Motivates Others 79
20. Working With Teams That Weigh You Down 83
21. What Makes You Useful? 87
22. Is It True Your Values Don't Change? 91
23. You're Worth Way More Than You Think 95
24. Is It Beneath You to Xerox? 99
25. Saying No Is Easy — Know When To Say Yes 103
26. A Zen-Like Attitude Makes You More Successful at Work 107

# Is There a Formula for Success at Work?

## Introduction to Thriving at Work: The ABCs of Work

Greetings readers and congratulations! Simply by virtue of being here, you are already on the path to increasing your odds of success.

While luck plays a gigantic role in life, that does not mean you are helpless to control your fate. If you want to think of it this way, the tips we'll explore are ways to increase your odds that luck will find you.

I spent years in the corporate laboratory, focused first on advancing myself. Although I was no doubt lucky, my progress helped me land the top legal role as General Counsel of a public company at the age of 30. I spent the next 20 years as a senior executive making sure luck stayed on my side.

Keen to understand what works and why, I studied what my colleagues, peers, and team did. I've condensed the resulting wisdom into these 26 essential lessons. No matter where you are in your career, the tips here will help you calibrate your approach and meet your goals.

Although I'll cover a lot of ground with these lessons, you should consider them foundational rather than comprehensive. There are additional approaches to succeeding at work, including playing zero sum games. Because your competitors will be using some of these tactics, I've prepared a companion volume explaining them. See **The Pragmatist's Rules for Work** to arm yourself appropriately.

Be well.

Chapter One

# Ambition Is the Foundation of All Progress

## It is appropriate we start with ambition as the factor that will increase your chances of success

Ambition here means not your desire to get a promotion, make more money, or any other career goal you no doubt have. I am using ambition in the sense that you *desire to get better*.

It helps if your desire to improve is intrinsic, that is something you do because it's part of your personal values. Not because you feel external pressure, or because anyone is watching. If your ambition is essential to your character, it will consistently guide your behavior.

But you can reap the benefits of ambition even if it doesn't come naturally. You will need to spend time actively thinking about your desire to improve and reminding yourself why you are striving towards the goals you have set. You won't need to prod yourself for too long before your focus on self-improvement becomes a habit.

Using reminders, rewards, and repetition for just a few weeks can turn many practices into reliable habits. Habits take much less energy to maintain than they do to create. Once you've made thinking about your ambition into a habit, your desire to improve has become intrinsic for all practical purposes.

**The benefits of ambition**

What happens when you are a person who feels ambition?

- Well, for one thing, you become much more focused on the **process of your work** than just the outcome. That is, you become aware of the time you spend on tasks, and whether that time is wasted or well-spent.

- Because you want to improve, you spend time **eliminating inefficiencies**, even if this means you initially take more time to redesign processes.

When you hew to an improvement mindset, you also become aware of how others' behavior affects your productivity. Other people's competence, or lack thereof, affects you. As does their openness, responsiveness, reliability, and more. You will become more effective for all the ways you find to work effectively with your colleagues.

Realizing the impact of others' competence on you, you are likely to become committed to improving your own. This is ambition (the desire for improvement) serving as self-reinforcement.

As we shall see in this series, success begets success. The more you work on your own improvement, the better you perform.

You also focus on the **quality of your work**. You realize that often small features distinguish people's work product. Your business colleagues are probably not in a position to substantively evaluate your area of expertise. But they are still evaluating your performance.

How do your business colleagues judge your contributions?

- Can they understand what you're saying (i.e. do you write clearly, in plain language)?

- Does your work product look professional, in that it is well-formatted and typo-free, with headings and sub-headings (can I trust you because you demonstrate attention to detail)?

- Have you answered their question, and answered it timely (are you responsive, in both substance and process)?

- Do you anticipate additional questions they did not ask but should have (are you thoughtful and helpful)?

- Does your output enable them to move forward (are you competent in a business-savvy way)?

If you can cultivate the ambition to improve your performance generally, this ambition is likely to benefit your work broadly. Also in unexpected ways, because the mindset becomes a tool you bring to every task.

Thus, it is appropriate we start with ambition as the foundational factor that will increase your chances of success.

## Honorable mentions

Leveraging a single tip to drive work success is a heavy lift, even a tip as important as ambition. Our formula will necessarily be incomplete. But the formula has an impact. All the more so because we've kept things simple.

Here to finish are some honorable mentions to serve as food for thought.

**Aptitude** — Do you know what you're especially good at? It is powerful to leverage your strengths. More useful, in fact, than trying to improve your weaknesses. Pick a few areas and become a superstar.

**Attitude** — Keeping a positive attitude when times are tough makes you stand out. Most people let stress make them miserable, which rubs off on the people around them. Staying happy in the face of adversity makes you a valued colleague indeed.

Be well.

Chapter Two

# Believing You Will Succeed Speeds Your Journey

## Self-confidence is incredibly helpful to your prospects of success. It is helpful not because your perception is necessarily accurate

We started the series by highlighting the importance of ambition, meaning your *desire to get better*. An important corollary is you must also have a firmly grounded *belief that you can*.

Self-confidence is incredibly helpful to your prospects of success. It is helpful not because your perception is necessarily accurate. Early in your career, your self-confidence will not be warranted. No, self-confidence propels your career because it inspires you to push yourself and try things you otherwise would not.

### The power of belief

From one perspective, saying you must believe you can improve and succeed is trivial. We wouldn't do anything if we didn't think we could do it, right? Upon reflection, I don't believe this is true.

If you think about it, people undertake things all the time without being committed to the belief they will succeed.

- How many people apply to top schools where their admittance odds are dismal?

- Or submit a resume for a job that is, ahem, "aspirational" given their qualifications?

- It takes a certain amount of wishful thinking to make a budget request for new capital spending, but that never stopped anyone from doing it.

- Every new product proposal or freshly launched marketing campaign comes with questionable success rates.

What are all these people thinking? We can't tell just from their behavior. I've observed people make decisions for many years and then explored their thought processes.

From this, I suggest there are fundamentally two approaches: In the first camp, people who think "Whatever, it's my job," and in the second, people who think "I can do this. I will do this. I will be successful."

- Your visual reference for the first group is Marvin, the robot from *The Hitchhiker's Guide to the Galaxy*, who suffers terrible depression, ironically from being asked to do only trivial tasks beneath his abilities.

- The standard-bearer for the second group is Hans Solo preparing to fly into an asteroid field and responding to a worried C3P0 in *The Empire Strikes Back*, "Never tell me the odds!"

When you genuinely believe you will succeed in a task, you increase your odds of success in that task. The phenomenon comes about in various ways:

- You are undaunted by small setbacks because you know that success requires persistence and overcoming obstacles.

- Your confidence inspires others, who are more likely to contribute wholeheartedly to projects that they think will be successful than those doomed to failure.

- You put in more effort than on tasks you're not fully committed to because failure is not an option.

- You spend more time thinking about the task because the thought of succeeding is pleasant, which has the side effect that you anticipate problems and come up with creative solutions.

All this adds up to belief and self-confidence helping luck find you more often.

## Can a delusional belief become counter-productive?

We all know people who are confident well beyond any reasonable justification. These people sometimes get in dangerously over their heads and cause disasters.

My advice is **self-belief and over-confidence helps you more than it hurts you**.

The world continually sends adjusting signals that keep people from overreaching. As such, you are much more likely to underestimate your abilities than overestimate them.

And even when you are genuinely delusional in your beliefs, you still are improving your odds. Best of all, *sometimes you will succeed*. Nothing begets belief in yourself like seeing that belief justified. The more you do it, the more reinforcement you'll get.

## Honorable mentions

**Belonging** — You will perform better when you identify with your company, your colleagues, and your work. Does embracing bonds in this way make you a sap, or make it easier for your boss to take advantage of you? Maybe.

But put aside the cynicism and embrace belonging, and you'll be amazed at what it does for your prospects. You stand out precisely because so many others are worried about being considered old-fashioned sentimentalists.

**Bravery** — Success is borne on the back of hard calls correctly made. By definition, hard calls are fraught with risk. You will be wrong sometimes.

People appreciate it when you take a principled stand for the right reasons, even if your decision proves wrong in hindsight. Your colleagues will forgive you for being wrong occasionally much more than they'll tolerate cowardice.

Be well.

# Chapter Three

# Continuous Improvement Is a Superpower Available to Everyone

## You don't have to do great things to achieve great things. You simply need to consistently do small things well

In the previous chapter I talked about Belief, in the sense that you must believe you can achieve your goals. Here I talk about perhaps the single best way to make progress towards virtually any goal: Continuous improvement.

**Continuous improvement is unstoppable**

If you've been reading along for a while, you know that continuous improvement is a frequent and favorite topic of mine. I revisit it from various angles and describe how it drives performance at the business level and the personal level.

What makes continuous improvement so powerful? In a word, you don't have to do great things to achieve great things. You simply need to consistently do small things well. The continuous improvement mindset is disarmingly simple and surprisingly powerful.

Even better, we don't even need to be *good* at something to benefit from continuous improvement. Let's say we're just starting out, complete novices. Our task for the day is to pay attention to what we're doing and improve just a little bit.

What are some places our gains might come from?

- Maybe today's gain comes from reading a reference book or watching a tutorial online

- Perhaps we ask a colleague who is more advanced to share some tips from their experience

- How about we pause after our initial attempt and reflect on what went well and what we'll try differently next time

- Or it could be that we put aside our work product for a few hours with the plan to revisit with fresh eyes what we've written

- Sometimes we will benefit from nothing more than taking a few minutes to think about our chosen task

- And if nothing else, simply repeating tasks on a regular basis makes us more comfortable performing

All this adds up to continuous improvement helping luck find us more often.

## Does continuous improvement ever not work?

I am such a cheerleader for continuous improvement that I risk ignoring potential blind spots. Does it work for everyone? Does it work in every setting? Are there pitfalls for the unwary? I think the answers are no, no, and yes.

No, continuous improvement will not work for everyone. Why is that?

- You need to be patient because your gains will be incremental and sometimes vanishingly so.

- Colleagues around you will take big swings and sometimes make huge gains. This will cause some practitioners to lose hope and lose focus.

- The slow path is a boring, lonely path. No one will give you a medal for being quietly competent and improving every day.

No, continuous improvement does not work in every setting.

- Some tasks we must accomplish are short-lived in nature. We're going to complete them (or not) with the tools and skills we already possess. In such cases, a continuous improvement mindset is less useful.

- Also, some of our characteristics are innate, and much less amenable to change. You can set yourself the goal of becoming taller, but no amount of continuous improvement will get you there.

And yes, there are pitfalls for the unwary. Perhaps the biggest one is that continuous improvement efforts benefit from prioritization, just like almost everything else we do.

We can waste our efforts by focusing on activities that, while improvable, bring us relatively little benefit. Thus, it is helpful to reflect where in our particular circumstances we will benefit a lot from our continuous improvement program.

- For some, it will be clear writing.

- For others, it will be presence and public speaking.

- Others will gain the most from learning to exercise the levers of persuasion. And so on.

A related point: Some tasks are unlikely to advance us at all. If your goal is to strike it rich, applying continuous improvement principles to the task of playing the slot machine is a fool's errand. The more time you spend pulling the lever, the poorer you will become. Thus, it is important to know when you are betting against the house and direct your activities and time accordingly.

## Honorable mentions

**Consistency** — This might be a synonym for continuous improvement, in the sense that consistency implies slow, steady, incremental progress.

**Collegiality** — Our success (or lack thereof) is not entirely in our control. Luck plays a part to be sure. But so do other people, and particularly, their impressions of us. Are you a person people like to be around? Do you help out when you can, even when there is no direct benefit to you? Are you supportive and understanding?

**Competence** — I said above it doesn't matter if you start out as a novice. That's true, but you cannot remain at the beginner level. In your chosen tasks, you must rise to at least the average performer level, and ideally go beyond it. True competence is handsomely rewarded, chiefly because it is uncommon. Strive for competence and you might achieve greatness along the way.

Be well.

Chapter Four

# Diversity of Thought Is Rare

## You want to invite uncertainty into your thinking, but not self-doubt

Last time I talked about Continuous Improvement, in the sense that small actions taken consistently add up to big results. Today I talk about a great way to make course corrections along the way: Diversity.

### Diversity helps keep us humble

Diversity for us today means one thing above all others, and that is diversity of thought. This may well come about from having a team comprising different cultures, genders, races, and more. But those characteristics do not guarantee diversity of thought. It is entirely possible to encounter monolithic thinking in a team that seems very diverse on its face.

No, diversity of thought comes from two qualities:

- Being open to the possibility that your idea is not necessarily the best one

- Allowing yourself to be confronted with multiple ideas

While I can state the two conditions simply enough, it is no small thing to achieve diversity of thought in our busy workplace. Why, you ask?

Well, the very busyness of work is one hurdle. We are pressured to perform, to complete tasks. This means working efficiently and productively. It means making quick decisions and not second-guessing ourselves.

That all cuts directly against any notion of mulling over multiple ideas and leaving open the possibility our preferred path may be suboptimal.

Although I am normally the biggest proponent of efficiency above all things, today I encourage you to consider slowing down. Make yourself inefficient, if only for a short while, to improve the end product's ultimate quality.

How so? We have fantastic and convenient access to humanity's combined knowledge and experience: Virtually everything that humankind has thought and done.

- What are the chances that, without consulting anything but your inner thoughts, you already know everything you need to optimally solve this problem?

- If we're honest, we should be humble indeed. Chances are quite good that someone, somewhere has another insight on the topic.

- And even if you do happen to possess excellent knowledge and experience on a topic, how likely is it that your first formulation of a solution is perfect? Really? Is there *nothing at all* you can improve in your approach?

Start by accepting your likely fallibility. You may be near perfect, but unless you can eliminate the "near," consider this easy solution: Do not be deeply committed to your initial idea. Be humble by allowing the possibility that there may be other solutions. That there may be better solutions.

Then go in search of those solutions by exposing yourself to other inputs and ideas. Research, read, talk to colleagues. And, crucially, do not go in search of confirmation for why your idea is correct. That is the default we easily slip into.

Remember you are only weakly tied to your starting proposition. As such, you are looking for contrary and contradictory information. What could cause your initial hypothesis to be flawed? Could you tweak your idea, improve the implementation, or anticipate a stumbling block?

## Are there downsides to diversity?

You want to invite uncertainty into your thinking, but not self-doubt. After canvassing the landscape for improvements, you must return to decision and implementation mode.

Switching back and forth between open doubting and confident action takes practice. Most people tend to linger at one end of the spectrum. The one always seeks more information and is uncomfortable making a decision. The other grows confident in their powers and is closed to outside input.

You must try to stay in balance. Because people tend towards confidence, I'll recommend one helpful tool. This is to say often, even if just to yourself in your inner thoughts, "But I could be wrong."

Just allowing the possibility helps you remember to seek out more diverse inputs and ideas.

## Honorable mentions

**Data** — We need to do more than rely on our intuitions. Gathering data and measuring our progress is a great way to check whether we are really on track.

**Delivery** — It does not matter how hard we work, even though it sure feels like our sweat and tears should count for something. Ultimately, our performance will be measured by results. Do you reliably deliver on your promises? If yes, you will advance. If not, all your early mornings and late nights are for naught.

**Detachment** — In this series, we are exploring all the ways to improve performance at work. This can lead to helpful focus and intensity, but that comes with a downside, which is forgetting that you have a life outside work. Work hard, but don't be a workaholic. Enjoy what you do, but work should not be your only enjoyment. Detachment means that you see work in its proper perspective, not that you don't care.

Be well.

## Chapter Five

# Equanimity Comes From Seeing the Underlying Value

### If you can bring a smile to your face when all others frown, people will want you by their side in a crisis

Last time I talked about Diversity, in the sense that we must keep an open mind and expose ourselves to multiple ideas. Today I talk about the mindset that is most conducive to long-term success: Equanimity.

**Is equanimity just another plug for the Stoics?**

It is true I am a big fan of Stoic philosophy. At its core, Stoicism calls upon us to recognize the difference between things that are in our control and things that are not. Very many external circumstances are outside our control, and this includes much of what we're confronted with at work.

- A supplier going bankrupt
- A customer re-opening negotiation on a completed framework agreement
- An employee raising discrimination allegations
- A regulator asking for more information about something your CFO said at an investor conference

The list is depressingly long. When everything in our environment is unstable, what is it that we can control? In a word, our thoughts.

We have control over how we respond to the situations we find ourselves in. Can we stay calm, maintain our composure, and keep our tempers? This is the Stoic ideal, and interestingly enough, close to the definition of equanimity.

The Stoic's highest possession is his or her own well-ordered mind. Applying our reason to our situations, we can ensure that we act consistently with our values. We may not be able to control outcomes, but we can control our inputs, which include our thoughts and our actions.

There's another benefit to maintaining equanimity amidst difficult circumstances. If you do so, you will stand out, because most people cannot. When confronted with indignities and unfairness, which are all too common at work, most people give vent to their frustrations. This is temporarily satisfying but does nothing to make things better.

If you can bring a smile to your face when all others frown, people will want you by their side in a crisis. If you can keep your cool no matter how unpleasant the mess you're in, people will trust you to make good decisions. It's one way average performers leap to next-level performance.

## Should we ever avoid equanimity?

In the spirit of keeping an open mind, and questioning whether our approach is always, is it ever OK not to be even-keeled?

I would say yes and no. No, in the sense that you should never really lose your self-control. But yes, in the sense that it is sometimes appropriate to display genuine emotion. Let me give you a couple of examples.

You are the person responsible for communicating the impact of new laws and regulations to management and business colleagues. Because these laws and regulations slow down the business while increasing cost and risk, no one is ever happy with the news you're bringing. Indeed, they are sorely tempted to vent *their frustrations*, resulting in your taking hits as the messenger.

You counteract this by displaying your own emotion — you agree that the new law and regulation is annoying, distracting, misguided, etc. You express frustration at ignorant regulators who impose stupid rules on hardworking, honest businesses. You make sure to put yourself on the same side of the desk as your business colleagues in venting. And only then do you talk about how to deal with the new law in a sensible way.

And don't underestimate cultural norms. Your Spock-like logical approach might work wonders with your Chinese, American, and German colleagues, but your Southern European colleagues are used to seeing a little heat. I still remember my friendly Italian General Manager pulling me aside to tell me I needed to show more emotion.

"James," he said, "I don't know whether you really care about an issue until I see you get excited about it." That was a valuable lesson. I now pay close attention to my feelings before making a conscious choice whether to amplify or dampen them, depending on the moment's need.

## Honorable mentions

**Emotional Intelligence** — Knowing your own emotional makeup, and how your behaviors impact others, are hallmarks of emotional intelligence. This is closely related to what we've been discussing today.

**Equity** — I debated including this at all, but I want to be honest with you even when it is painful. You are likely to be confronted with the desire to promote equity at work. All I'll say is beware. Equity is not equality, and people pushing the former are typically not interested in the latter. The unintended consequences could be severe.

**Example** — Serve as an example to others. This is particularly true when you are in a leadership position. But I say serve as an example even when no one is watching. You are also serving as an example to yourself. You hold yourself to a high standard because *you want to*, not because anyone is forcing you to.

Be well.

Chapter Six

# Fakery Is a Time-Honored Path To Growth

## As you behave so shall you believe. The way you act becomes the way you are

Last time I talked about Equanimity, in the sense that we must maintain our self-possession in difficult circumstances. Today I talk about an interesting side-effect that arises when people are mindful of their thoughts and actions: The possibility for fakery.

**What does fakery have to do with work?**

Let's look at it from two angles. No doubt many of you are recalling the common advice for newly promoted managers to "Fake it until you make it." So, the first type of fakery involves the tools and attitude we employ when we feel nervous about performing up to the high standards our jobs demand.

It is normal to be anxious about measuring up. For high achievers, it is expected. You've been successful in part by caring deeply about doing well, which means worrying whether you've done enough and are ready.

If we all waited to take action until we felt fully ready, nothing would ever get done.

It is necessary, therefore, to trust that you will be able to navigate your way in new waters. You may not know exactly how you'll make your way to the next shore. But you know that you have successfully accomplished many difficult tasks and will rise to the occasion.

Call upon your well-founded confidence that you will prevail despite unknown odds and uncertain methods. Then, and this is crucial, behave as if your confidence is warranted. Do your best and don't second-guess yourself or betray uncertainty.

The Stoics say, "As you think so shall you become." I say, as you behave so shall you believe. The way you act becomes the way you are.

Early in my legal career, I was surprised to find one of the most useful skills I had practiced came from my high school days: Acting. I did all the school plays and musicals, and I did them for the sheer joy of it.

What a boon to find out that acting was a great tool for the budding lawyer.

- Do you need me to portray confidence in a contested negotiation? No problem.

- Are we bluffing the mediator that this is our best and final offer and now we go to court? They'll never know.

Call it acting. Call it fakery. Call it whatever you want. Just call upon it in whatever measure you need to get you through the times of self-doubt.

## When faking it is ill-advised

I said we'd examine fakery from two angles. We've explored the positive. The second angle is when you need to be on your guard. You are not the only one employing fakery to personal ends. Everyone else is too.

I often heard a wonderful saying in Switzerland (although I understand the origin is Russian): Trust, but verify. I'll take you at face value, but I'll also make sure not to get taken for a fool.

Listen to what people say and watch what they do. Over time, you'll learn who deserves trust and who deserves closer watching.

Finally, never forget that you deserve vigilant watching as well. Because our method serves to build your self-confidence and push you to take on hard challenges, you will be tempted to bluff when you really shouldn't.

There is no shame in recognizing when you're genuinely in over your head. On the contrary, it takes a mature and confident person to say, "I need help."

It is only well-founded confidence that supports safe fakery. Make sure you know when you've strayed into dangerous pretensions of competence when you lack sufficient foundation.

## Honorable mentions

**Forgetting** — People will do you wrong. Bad things will happen to you and your company. Unless bad people are plotting to do you imminent wrong again (in which case I have another F-word I'd like to apply), it is healthy to learn how to forget.

You may even be so magnanimous to arrive at forgiveness, but I say forgetting a past grievance is enough. Anger and regret are corrosive to peace of mind and distract you from doing your best work. Leave them.

**Friends** — People will also be wonderful. You will learn to appreciate and like many colleagues. Should you become friends with them? Some measures of the best workplaces ask whether you have meaningful friends at work.

I say it depends on your personality and your role. It is harder for the boss to be friends with her team than for peers to befriend one another.

**Fun** — Finally, a tip that you can get fully behind! Yes, work can and should be fun. Do everything in your power to contribute to a fun workplace. Your colleagues will appreciate it, and you will enjoy your life that much more.

Be well.

Chapter Seven

# Do A Good Job and Great Things Follow

Don't be undone by impatience just when you've positioned yourself for further good things. Stay focused on the goal

L ast time I talked about Fakery, in the sense that it is appropriate to trust you'll be successful in a new setting by calling on your existing skill set. Today I talk about what happens when your trust is rewarded, namely that you do a good job.

**Do a good job at what, exactly?**

I implied earlier that if there was just one formula for success, it would be to follow continuous improvement principles. See Continuous Improvement Is a Superpower Available to Everyone.

I was dispensing separate advice to ambitious colleagues, however, even earlier than I was proselytizing about continuous improvement. That was reinforcing the critical importance of *doing a good job in your current job*.

- Your ambition I take as given

- Your belief in your ability to improve I will toss in for free

- Your experience, abilities, and outlook are all superb

- But they all add up to virtually nothing if, in your pursuit of promotion, you neglect to do a good job in your current job

Many, many colleagues are convinced they could do more. Many are right, they could do more. The thing is that job opportunities don't only come at convenient times. Sometimes they come when we're *not* yet ready. Just as often we must wait a while after we're more than ready for a change.

This chapter is for all the impatient waiters. No one ever got promoted by neglecting their current duties. Yes, you may be capable of so much more. But you demonstrate that by excelling in your current job and volunteering for projects on the side.

Don't be undone by impatience just when you've positioned yourself for further good things. Stay focused on the goal, which is in fact not the promotion as such, but rather doing your very best at everything you do.

Of course, let your boss know you want more. Your boss can sympathize better than you think. Maybe they can't (or won't) vacate their job tomorrow to make way for you. But they can certainly find ways to help you develop your skills and experience.

Be open to non-traditional approaches. I promise, if you can keep your performance up and your motivation up, things will look up.

## Can you be too good at your job?

Yes, and for the excellent reasons I will discuss in a later volume. For now, I'll summarize by saying your super performance risks your boss asking you to do a disproportionate share of work, doing some unscrupulous colleagues' work as well, and burning out.

That's nothing you want, so learning to draw healthy boundaries is key.

## Honorable mentions

**Give and take** — The more effective you become, the more you will succeed at what you do. You will be more persuasive than most, which means you'll win arguments more easily. Don't be a jerk about it, and don't abuse your skills. Remember there are more ways to win than dominating the field. Sometimes letting others take a victory in small things makes it easier for them to let you take the victory in big things.

**Gratitude** — When we're focused on improving, it is so easy to be dissatisfied with our current condition or pace of progress. I admit, a certain desire to challenge the status quo is necessary to get better. But never at the expense of your own happiness.

You must therefore cultivate the competing mindsets of appreciating what you have while striving to improve. Expressing gratitude is a fine method. Each day, note several things you're thankful for. You can write them down or say them out loud at dinner with your family. Make it quick and easy so you can do it daily.

**Greatness** — Good is almost always good enough, as long as you apply it across everything you do. You don't need to strive for greatness in any one thing because it's time-consuming, difficult, and rare. You can still be a great performer, though, by doing a lot of things well.

Be well.

Chapter Eight

# Happy in All Weather and at All Times

## You can hack your way to happiness. Consider these methods to cultivate a positive mindset

Last time I talked about doing a Good Job, in the sense that you must do a good job in your current job before you're ready to move on to the next one. Today I talk about how to manage your happiness, whatever stage your career is at.

### Oh, is that all?

If only it were so easy, right? By identifying the importance of being happy, we can just flip a switch and decide to be happy. (It's almost like thinking that attending a 30-minute training on unconscious bias can overcome deeply rooted and inherent elements of the human condition. But that's a separate topic.)

My first foray into writing about seeking happiness and satisfaction at work discussed why our career ambitions risk making us miserable. I suggested there that we change the ways we think about what work offers us. We read quotes on happiness from Seneca

> *A wise man is content with his lot, whatever it be — without wishing for what he has not.*

and Lao Tzu

> *Be content with what you have, rejoice in the way things are. When you realize nothing is lacking, the entire world belongs to you.*

Excellent words, but they tell us what we seek, not necessarily how to get there.

I can offer more specific guidance. You can consider these methods to **cultivate a positive mindset**.

- **Express gratitude**. Every day, take a few minutes to acknowledge one or two things you are thankful for. They can be trivial, such as sunny weather or the fact you took the stairs instead of the elevator. The key is to habituate yourself to recognize and appreciate good things. We do it at the family dinner table, where each person takes a turn. It is one of my favorite parts of the day.

- **Write down some thoughts**. Also known as journaling, but no need to be fancy. The method here is simplicity itself. Take the first five minutes at work to write down whatever's on your mind. That's it. Don't worry whether it's profound, interesting, or even coherent. Just expressing thoughts like this tends to create a calmer mind.

- **Connect with people in your network**. Once a week, send a short message to a few people in your network, personal or professional. If you are regular in your habit, you'll interact with many people over a year. Even brief social encounters do wonders for our long-term happiness.

- **Exercise**. Keeping with the simplicity theme, just get up and walk around for five minutes every two hours. That alone is sufficient to improve a sedentary person's health. If you want to do more, by all means. An exercise habit is an all-round superstar in unlocking life benefits.

- **Keep a task list**. In addition to whatever fancy method you use, try writing on a piece of paper each day some tasks you wish to accomplish. The simpler the better. Then cross off the items you complete. So satisfying. Do it daily, and you'll be that person who regularly gets things done.

## Is this just another case of faking it?

Now you might be thinking, "James, are you suggesting that if I try these simplistic hacks, I can trick myself into being happy? I've got problems and stress you know nothing about!"

I acknowledge you are unique and may be in some tough situations. But yes, I also assert that you can hack your way to happiness.

But don't take my word for it. Run some experiments on yourself. The beauty in this approach is that with a few minutes' investment, you aren't sacrificing much of your day.

The potential upside is pretty great, and the cost is minimal. So give being happy a try and you can thank me for it later.

## Honorable mentions

**Heavy lifting** — I could also have said "hard work" for this one. Simply working hard will not guarantee your success. But provided you're working on your strategic priorities, hard work will certainly help you make progress.

Look, our jobs are not easy. Sometimes we just need to put our heads down and invest quality time. Not everyone can do it, and if you can you will pull ahead.

**Helpful** — Just like people prefer to work with happy people, we also love to be around helpful people. When we're busy, it is easy to jealously guard our time and focus on our own priorities. Doing so is essential to avoid being overwhelmed.

Yet some of the busiest people I know still find time to help their colleagues. Making a connection, passing on a helpful reference, answering a question. A few minutes is often all it takes to greatly help someone. They're much more inclined to help you when the tables are turned.

Be well.

Chapter Nine

# The One Thing You Can Never Compromise

## Your personal integrity is the thing that sets you apart from all others. You will be called upon to follow your personal values in difficult situations

Last time I talked about why you should strive to be Happy because this will allow you to maintain a high level of performance over the long term. Today I talk about the importance of integrity (both yours and that of others) to having a successful career.

**The one thing you can never compromise**

I'm the first one to say that we should be flexible and keep an open mind. It's OK to have an opinion and even to believe firmly in it. But it is most helpful to allow for the possibility that our opinion may be wrong.

There's one time, however, when you should not waver in your conviction: When it comes to your integrity. It doesn't matter whether the issue is trivial, and no one will notice. Nor does it matter when the stakes are gigantic and the upside to you for being "flexible" is equally large.

Your personal integrity is the thing that sets you apart from all others. It is your professional obligation, sure, to never behave in an unethical or illegal manner. It should also be your personal commitment to live your life consistently with your personal values.

It can take some time to gain a practical sense of how our personal values play out in practice. But rest assured. Your work will likely put you in situations that give your theories real-world tests. You will thus develop your personal values about the correct way to behave.

Your mission is now to **follow your personal values** in difficult situations, such as the following:

- **Behaving illegally**. This one is hardly difficult, right? You'd be surprised how many otherwise honorable people find themselves making regrettable decisions due to situational pressure.

- **Behaving unethically**. You can be aggressive, you can zealously represent your company's interests. But you must be alert to recognizing when you are crossing the line and violating your values.

- **Keeping company with villains**. Can you be a person of high integrity if your business associates are not? Theoretically, I suppose, but if you help an improper business prosper your own integrity is open to question.

- **Supporting win-at-all-costs approaches**. You probably don't have criminals for colleagues. But what about hyper-competitive types who believe winning justifies all? You must trust your colleagues will follow your advice. Winning at all costs means there *are costs*. Who is going to pay them?

- **Being untruthful**. A white lie in pursuit of a noble goal? Leave it for answering a friend's question about whether those jeans make them look fat. At work, your standard should be never to lie. If you ever do you risk your primary value proposition, which is telling the truth in difficult situations.

## Can you take personal integrity too far?

Being honest doesn't mean saying everything that comes into your head. You will certainly want to keep your own counsel in delicate situations. Sometimes the best thing to say is nothing.

Behaving with integrity also doesn't mean substituting your judgment for your colleagues' judgment. Many situations are gray, permitting multiple approaches. Businesses thrive upon calculated risk. Even though you may advise a different approach your business may still proceed along other legal paths.

## Honorable mentions

**Information** — You cannot be too well-informed. Read widely and consult many sources, including other people. You should know what's going on in your industry, among peer companies, and in the business world generally.

**Innovation** — Be creative and try new things. But don't innovate for the sake of innovation. Your best innovations will be process improvements that generate efficiency gains and reduce friction in the business.

Be well.

Chapter Ten

# Joy Is Your Reward for Approaching Work Well

## Joy means you find meaning in what you are doing. You see the value behind your work

Last time I talked about the importance of Integrity, which is vital to having a sustainable career. Today I explore the benefits of finding joy in an otherwise joyless work landscape.

### Know the difference between joy and enjoyment

You might be wondering what is the difference between happiness and joy. Just a short while ago (Happy in All Weather) I urged you to learn how to be happy at work. Isn't finding joy in your work the same thing?

It is similar to be sure. Here's why they are not the same thing. When you are happy you have a positive outlook on life. You see the silver lining in every situation. As a result, people like to be with you.

Joy means you find meaning in what you are doing. You see the value behind your work. If other people like to be with happy people, a joyful person likes to be with themselves.

Joy here means deep fulfillment. Joy is lasting and comes from within. Contrast this with enjoyment, which comes from external things and is typically fleeting:

*When you are free from doubt, worry, jealously; when your course is the same whether you are pushing into the headwind or blown along by a tailwind; when you delight in stillness as much as you do in motion; when you do not rely on external things, joy is your reward.* — James Bellerjeau in Pragmatic Wisdom, On Joy and Enjoyment

Here are some ways you can find joy at work:

- **Seeing how our actions add value**. We all want our work to mean something. The best way to achieve this is to ensure we are working towards a greater goal. Helping our companies execute on their strategies is a good place to start.

- **Making a real contribution**. We're sometimes in a position to choose our own priorities. How joyful it is when we pick topics that bring meaning to others and make their lives better. Whether leading a diversity initiative or helping your company on its sustainability journey, opportunities abound.

- **Helping others**. We think we'll be happiest when we help ourselves. It turns out that we are most moved by helping others. Can you propel a team member along in their career? Help unstick a colleague who can't progress at the moment? These are the things that you (and they) will remember. And they bring joy.

- **Staying true to your principles**. Last time we talked about integrity. When you are put under pressure and remain committed to your principles and values, you rightly feel joy.

## What's wrong with enjoyment?

Nothing, as such. But beware mere thrill-seeking.

Because enjoyment comes from external things some people become addicted to seeking it out. At best, everything goes well and the person easily finds satisfaction. More often, a thrill-seeker needs greater thrills to attain the same heights of enjoyment. Eventually, the risk-reward calculus becomes unbalanced. Disappointment and unhappiness await.

Joy is less flashy than enjoyment but more durable once found.

Although you focus on finding joy, you can and should take pleasure in enjoyment. Mark your victories where you will and celebrate your wins. You will have many fun times with your team. Savor them. Fun times are necessary to get you through dark times when stress is your constant companion.

## Honorable mentions

**Judgment** — For years, this was my go-to answer to the question of what key attribute I look for in my colleagues. The best employees know when they can answer a question directly, when they need to do more work, and when they need help. When deciding amidst uncertainty, they make the correct call most frequently. While judgment can be coached, the best teacher seems to be experience.

**Justice** — It helps to take a step back and keep perspective. Businesses are competitive and like to win. We are competitive and like to win. Winning should never be our sole guiding principle, however. Our aim should be to do what's right, not what's expedient.

Be well.

Chapter Eleven

# When Kindness Helps You As Much as Others

## Even if you want to drive your own career helping others is a good way to proceed. There are several ways to do this

Last time I talked about the importance of Joy, which comes from knowing and working towards your inner purpose. Today I explore the benefits of practicing kindness in an otherwise ruthless world.

### This doesn't sound very results-oriented

"Has James gone soft on us? First, it was Happiness, then Joy, and now Kindness? I thought we were talking about how to be successful at work. This sounds like a good path to get taken for a ride, not take charge of my career!"

I hear you and I haven't forgotten the over-arching mission. You want to be successful in your career, and I want to help you get what you want. But I don't want you to get something you *think you want* only to find out later it wasn't what you thought.

It behooves us to consider not only what success means to us but also what are the potentially varying paths that will take us there.

Here are some ways you can practice kindness at work:

- **Help others advance their careers**. Even if you want to drive your own career helping others is a good way to proceed. We succeed in large part because our teams, our colleagues, and our companies succeed. Time spent helping others is thus never wasted. If you do it altruistically, that is because you are happy to help others, your kindness still pays dividends.

- **Help others accomplish their tasks.** This is the more mundane aspect. Practically, though, this is where you prove your kindness. You're busy and a colleague needs help. Do you stop and help them in the moment? Small acts of kindness compound. You never know which person you took a few minutes to help will be instrumental in helping you later.

- **Don't be too quick to judge:** *"If you would not be judged by your worst moment, do not be quick to judge others for theirs."* The kindness here comes in both giving the benefit of the doubt and in being forgiving when matters are not in doubt. By remembering your own mistakes and how others reacted, you can be the kind of person you would like to work with.

- **Be kind to yourself.** It's probably not hard to remember your own mistakes because you will make mistakes. The key is to learn from them, which requires reflection, but not to overly beat yourself up.

- **Remember the human aspect.** You will work on tough topics, affecting people's lives and livelihoods. It is tempting to wall off your emotions to avoid bad feelings. We must never forget the people our decisions affect are individuals, just like us. They have hopes and dreams and reasonable expectations to live happy lives.

## Can kindness backfire?

Yes, there is a risk. Unscrupulous colleagues will take advantage of you. Seeing your helpful nature, they will ask for your help more than they genuinely need it. After all, if they can get someone to do some of their work, why not?

Others may think you are weak, not realizing that it takes not just character but strength to be kind when you could be cruel.

## Honorable mentions

**Killer Instinct** — If this seems like the opposite of kindness, hold on. Sometimes you have to be tough. You will certainly be called upon to make hard decisions. Don't shy away. Your colleagues will appreciate it when you step in to deal with unpleasant situations.

But being tough and decisive is not the same as being mean or ignoring your emotions. You should feel exactly the same empathy when being tough as when you're being kind.

**Kevlar** — You fulfill a role as an employee, but *you* are not that role. You must develop imperviousness to people associating you with the topics you work on and the decisions you make.

I use the mental image of putting on a cloak to represent my role. It's not me, it's just what I do for the company. Your Kevlar cloak protects you from the harsh external world.

Be well.

## Chapter Twelve

# Your Attitude To Learning Tells Me a Lot

## The people who invest in lifelong learning are steadily improving their skills. And it shows

Last time I talked about why you should demonstrate kindness, which allows you to advance together with your colleagues. Today I explore why learning is one of the key levers to a successful career.

**Isn't that what I went to school for?**

It's true, our schooling represents a learning threshold. We need to learn to think and build our substantive know-how. The final exams represent a key threshold. Once passed, many people say, "I'm done with studying, done with memorizing, let me get down to work!"

I get it and I sympathize. Take a break, switch gears. But not for too long. Can you think of any skills that don't get better with practice? Why should your basic skills, thinking, and analysis be any different? The people who invest in lifelong learning are steadily improving their skills. And it shows.

But fear not, being a diligent student is much easier when you're doing it for yourself and no one is grading you.

Here are some excellent opportunities to weave learning into your work:

- **Reading widely.** This should be easy because there are no limits on what you read. Read science fiction, read professional journals, read blogs, read user's manuals. A reading habit helps you stay curious, engaged, and well-informed with little effort.

- **Researching work topics**. You have to deal with novel topics for work. Treat these as more than just the need to answer a question. Why not build some expertise along the way? With each topic you learn a little about you become more valuable.

- **Giving training presentations**. In preparation for training others, you master your subject that much more. This is because you want to do well and so spend more time in the details than you otherwise would.

- **Offer to speak at events**. Besides internal trainings, be alert for external training events. These expose you to other interesting people, including the organizers, other speakers, and audience members.

- **Network**. Talking with interesting people is a great way to learn new things in a social setting. You often make serendipitous connections between diverse bits of knowledge, also on work topics.

- **Continuing Education**. If school didn't leave you cold, consider also formal learning opportunities. You must carefully consider benefits and costs, including the time commitment. There are more convenient programs than ever, including online offerings.

## Is learning ever harmful?

I suppose anyone who's let spill the beans to their kids that Santa Claus isn't real can question whether knowledge is universally good. That's usually less of a concern at work.

The one area I'd suggest exercising caution is being nosy when it doesn't concern you. There will always be sensitive business or employment topics that you're curious about but not involved in. Let those go and focus your learning elsewhere.

## Honorable mentions

**Lazy** — By this I mean don't do unnecessary work. You will work hard, so appear the very opposite of lazy. Working hard can be a crutch in the sense that you power through otherwise inefficient uses of your time. If you're occasionally lazy, you are motivated to invest in improving processes to save yourself more time later.

**Lean** — I originally made a typo in the title of this chapter, which prompted me to consider two merits to this fine word: First, lean on others for help, because knowing when you need help is a mark of strength, not weakness. Second, keep a lean organization, i.e. be efficient.

Be well.

Chapter Thirteen

# The Self-Motivation That Never Leaves You Hanging

## The motivation I want you to cultivate is self-motivation. It is the striving towards goals you have set for yourself for reasons that are intrinsic to you and your values

Last time I talked about why you should seek to learn across your entire career. Today I discuss the importance of motivation to your success and where you can find it.

**My boss is supposed to provide the motivation, no?**

You are lucky if you have strong, positive, external motivation. Sometimes this comes from an inspired boss, yes. For sure a good leader sets out a vision that people want to work towards.

The Stoic in me says watch out in relying on external motivation, however. The reason is that such motivation is largely outside your control. Maybe you have an inspired boss or a good leader, but sometimes you will not.

And many bosses think pressure is the same thing as motivation because it has the same effect, i.e. getting people to do work.

The motivation I want you to cultivate is self-motivation. It is the striving towards goals you have set for yourself for reasons that are intrinsic to you and your values.

It is surely helpful if the goals you've set align with important company goals. But company goals by themselves pale alongside the ones you've arrived at yourself.

Here are some self-motivation examples to illustrate the point:

- **Holding yourself to your own high standard.** How well do you perform when no one is watching you? When no one will see the result but you? If you do your best given the time and circumstances because you would not be satisfied with anything less, you are motivated to do good work.

- **Feeling part of something larger than you.** Perhaps you entered the profession because you wanted to address injustice and help make the world a better place. In helping uphold the rule of law, you are contributing to a long tradition of improving the human condition. Yes, reviewing one or ten or a hundred more contracts is mind-numbing. But viewed through the lens of maintaining the rule of law, your motivation is easier to maintain.

- **Creating something that will outlast you.** Sometimes it seems our work is fleeting. Stepping back, it's easy to wonder if Priest Mansei's question is apt: "*To what shall I compare this world? To the white wake behind a ship that has rowed away at dawn?*" Creating something bigger than you that will outlast you can be quite motivating. Your team itself is a great opportunity, as is working on a project that has a long life, such as a knowledge management system.

- **Providing for family.** It can be highly motivating to feel you are working towards a higher purpose, and there are few purposes more powerful than taking care of family members. Whether it is aging parents or your own children, the idea that you are contributing to their well-being is a great motive to keep working and do well.

## Can motivation lead me astray?

As we've defined it here, I don't think so. You may come into circumstances where your intrinsic motivation and your company's or colleagues' motivation diverge. In these cases, you should carefully consider whether your values are consistent with staying put.

Sometimes your own motivation is all that keeps you from going astray following others.

## Honorable mentions

**Maybe** — Your colleagues want certainty and you will want to deliver certainty. It is vital to recognize when you're operating in a gray area, which will happen often. It's OK to say "I think this is the answer, but let me double-check." It's OK to leave open the possibility that you might be wrong.

**Money** – Nothing will ruin your motivation more surely than looking to see what your peers are paid. The reason is that while you may be in the top decile, you'll always find some fool earning more than you.

That said, you don't want your company to take advantage of you either. Tell your boss you just want to be paid fairly using appropriate benchmarks and that you trust her to do right by you. Then give her a chance to do right by you.

Be well.

## Chapter Fourteen

# Why You Should Welcome Novelty Into Your Day

## Successful long-term performance requires us to learn to not just tolerate recurring work but thrive upon it. That's where understanding novelty comes in

Last time I talked about why you should find self-motivation to stay engaged at work. Today I explore why novelty is important and how you can foster novelty in an otherwise unchanging environment.

### Novelty implies change for change's sake

For many lawyers, novelty is a dirty word. We live for precedent, for examples. We never want to be the first ones to try something. We find comfort in the idea that many people have safely gone before us.

As a result, a great deal of in-house legal work is repetitive. This is our standard contract, and this is how we negotiate contracts. Now go do it 1,000 times until it becomes second nature. And then do it 10,000 times more.

Repetition can lead to boredom, which leads to carelessness. Repetition causes us to question our motivation, which leads to stress and burnout. Successful long-term performance thus requires us to learn to not just tolerate recurring work but thrive upon it.

One way to thrive when involved in repetitive work is to find novelty. Let's look both at repetitive work itself and at the broader scope of in-house responsibilities.

## Repetitive work is probably not identical work

Every year for twenty years I prepared for the annual shareholders' meeting. Time-consuming and detail-oriented yet largely the same tasks each year.

How did we keep it fresh? For one, we rigorously applied continuous improvement principles. From the smallest information-gathering task to compiling and checking data in the proxy statement, to preparing for shareholder questions, we asked these questions: What went well, what didn't go so well, and what can we do better next time?

That kept us focused and diligent every year when we might have been tempted to zone out and go through the motions. Did the small process improvements justify the effort? Perhaps not, although our meetings were marvels of efficiency. The benefit came in keeping genuinely motivated to work well on the annual meeting each year.

Same thing with your contracts, or any other repetitive work you face. Want it to be less burdensome? Start by taking it even more seriously and seeking to improve it. Make your form better. Find a way to negotiate the same points less often. Really explore the risks you are minimizing and ask if there are other ways to accomplish your task.

When every contract is a potential experiment in process improvement, suddenly your task is much less boring.

## Much work we do is genuinely novel

Ironically, it took getting one too many oddball questions to make me appreciate the "boring" work that I could do with little effort. Each morning, I would check emails and voicemails with mixed anticipation and dread. *"What new trouble could the organization have cooked up somewhere in the world overnight?"*

This was novelty in its true form. I never knew what the day's challenges would contain. I relished the novelty, but I realized that having only new legal questions would be incredibly stressful.

I came to appreciate a healthy mix: A generous amount of routine work I knew I could do well, leavened with interesting nuggets that broke up the routine and challenged me.

## When is the old way best?

You must not change for the sake of change, i.e. without a specific improvement in mind. You also must not seek changes just because a process is imperfect. They're all imperfect.

Before messing with existing systems, you must understand in great detail why they were established the way they were.

## Honorable mentions

**Negative** –This is your reminder not to be negative. Or to put it positively, be optimistic. Especially when times are tough people appreciate colleagues who keep a level head and can focus on the silver lining.

**Never** — You should keep a private list on which you describe *things you'll never do*. Maybe your list says you'll never compromise your values for money, or you'll never answer a colleague with a flat "No," instead of "No, but..."

Your list is personal to you and will develop as your career develops and you find yourself in more novel situations.

Be well.

Chapter Fifteen

# When To Obey Your Boss or Defy Their Decision

## Stay alert to when the responsible businessperson is prepared to make a decision. This is when danger to you is greatest

Last time I talked about ways to seek out novelty even when doing routine work. Today I explore why it's important to know when to obey and, equally important, when not to.

### "Obey" sounds out of place in the workplace

I agree with you on that. I used a strong word partly to get your attention. Now let me convince you why it's not wrong.

First, to your (and my) concern with the word. The workplace is not the military, with strict command hierarchies and an absolute expectation that individuals will follow their superiors' orders.

We treasure in-house lawyers in particular because they exercise independent judgment. A good lawyer must be willing to speak her mind when others may fear challenging management.

Because lawyers hone their independent judgment, however, they risk forgetting who their ultimate client is. In the corporate setting, our responsibilities are to the corporation. Our fiduciary duty is to protect the company's interests and drive long-term shareholder benefits.

Our role, though, is rarely to serve as the *final arbiter*. Other management colleagues, like the CEO, CFO, and other senior executives, are charged with making both policy and operational decisions in their respective bailiwicks. The Board of Directors oversees company affairs most broadly.

The best lawyers bring their excellent judgment to every situation, not just legal questions. And therein lies today's problem. We are used to others listening to us and deferring to our judgment, at least in our specialty. So what happens when there is a conflict between what we think the company should do and what management or the board thinks?

## How to Properly Exercise Judgment

Here's how to resolve the dilemma. I suggest you follow this four-step process.

1. Start by exercising your independent judgment and then forcefully arguing for what you believe is best. You can and must **be a zealous advocate for your positions**. This is your core value proposition as an in-house lawyer.

2. Alongside ensuring your colleagues understand your points, you must take care to **understand *the business* considerations**. You should not be trying to win the argument necessarily so much as contribute to a fulsome discussion. Take particular care to distinguish in your mind which decisions relate to legal topics versus business topics.

3. Once points 1 and 2 are satisfied, stay alert to when the responsible businessperson is prepared to make a decision. This is when danger to you is greatest because you will want to continue to argue your side. If the decisionmaker has relevant information and is ready to decide, **you switch to listening mode**.

4. Finally, but vitally, and especially if you disagree with a decision or would have decided differently yourself, **you must help implement the decision** with the same fervor that you just argued against it.

We do pretty well with the first point. I've seen lawyers mess up with 2, 3, and 4, with increasingly severe consequences. Being inattentive to others' arguments is harmful to our effectiveness, but not always fatal to good decision-making.

Being over-zealous in arguing our case makes management annoyed with us. Because our independent voice is valuable, though, good colleagues usually give feedback to help us avoid going too far.

It is the last point that ends in-house lawyers' careers. After the decision is made, you must put aside personal feelings and wholeheartedly go along. Don't fall in love with your arguments.

Logic and analysis are only partly why businesses make decisions. Emotions, risk appetite, and strategy all play important roles. All these mean management may decide to do things differently than we would. And *their role* is also to exercise independent judgment.

## Are there times when we must refuse to obey?

Yes. If your colleagues should propose illegal conduct, then the decision is not one in their competence to make. That's your ultimate responsibility and there can be no compromise. When you cannot resolve such a situation through your persuasiveness, you must escalate within the company.

And if you've escalated to no avail, the U.S. requires in-house counsel to make a "noisy withdrawal." This means to openly resign, stating the reasons why, in effect becoming a whistleblower. But don't be too concerned. I've never seen it in a corporate setting, and I hope you'll never be confronted with it.

Again, the difficulty comes when we mistake business decisions for legal ones. You might feel a need to keep arguing or even disobey. I counsel against it. Have a follow-up private meeting with the decision maker to express your concerns. Let him or her demonstrate they understand the legal risks and show they're making a business decision.

## Honorable mentions

**Opportunities** — The lawyers I've seen progress the most in their careers took advantage of opportunities that came their way. Opportunities are often unpredictable, both in substance and in timing. Being willing to try something out, even if it isn't what you were hoping for, opens many doors that remain locked for others.

**Optimistic** — By now you've come to expect me to exhort you to see the positive. I repeat the point because it's a valid and good one. If you see the bright side, you are a happier person. People like to work with you. Your thoughts mold your mind. Knowing this, why not shape yours in a direction that makes you genuinely satisfied with your life?

Be well.

Chapter Sixteen

# We Were Wrong To Banish Prayer From Work

## Thinking about the outcome we desire and then fervently wishing for it to come true is really just prayer by another name

Last time I explored a process to follow to know when to obey business decisions. Today I explore why it's important to pray for good outcomes.

**You're using another word inappropriately, James**

I want your attention again, true, but I'm convinced the word pray has meaning for us in the work context.

Let me first acknowledge that I mean no disrespect for anyone's religious beliefs. I don't mean to trivialize prayer in any way. If anything, I want to elevate the idea to the secular context to reinforce why prayer is so helpful.

The reason is the same one behind the articles in this book: Luck plays a gigantic role in life. We're exploring ways to help luck find us. Well, thinking about the outcome we desire and then fervently wishing for it to come true is really just prayer by another name.

Why does wishing for the outcome we desire help increase the odds that we will achieve that outcome? Several reasons come to mind. For one, it helps to acknowledge what we want. To set a priority, if you will, and say to the world, *"This is what I'm working towards. There, I said it."* We progress the furthest when we set priorities and focus our efforts.

For another, when we give regular attention to an outcome (praying for luck), we are by definition thinking about it more frequently. This means we're more likely to consider additional ways to progress. We are more alert to potential obstacles. We refine and improve our approach.

Then, if we've made our prayer public, we potentially unlock assistance from others. Someone else may hold the key to advancing your project, but they don't know it. When you make your wishes known, they are suddenly in a position to help. Prayer answered.

## When you'll benefit from praying for luck

What situations are more amenable to a healthy dose of praying for luck to find us?

- **When you're seeking a promotion.** Your prayer here includes talking with colleagues, especially your boss, about your desires. It includes taking on new challenges with the hope, but no guarantee, they'll pay off.

- **When you're trying to convince others** of an important point. Prayer here reflects thinking through alternatives, anticipating objections, and honing your arguments and delivery. You pray you've done enough to win the day.

- **Waiting for a jury verdict** to come back in. Whether it's helpful or not I can't say. But I would be surprised at any in-house counsel who didn't do a little secret prayer as they waited.

## Praying for luck is no substitute for performance

This is important. If you've neglected to put in the necessary work, praying for divine intervention is too little done too late. Done properly, expressing your sincere wishes is a component of good project planning, not a substitute for planning.

## Honorable mentions

**Preparation** — The five Ps. I have a senior in-house friend who told me about the importance of the five Ps: Preparation prevents piss-poor performance. He held himself accountable for bad outcomes, never others, because he assumed with enough preparation he would always prevail. That's a great attitude and will take you far in life.

**Present** — Be in the now. Do not dwell in the past other than to briefly take the lessons learned from your mistakes. Do not daydream of the future other than to set your intention towards the goals you are striving for.

Paying attention to what you're doing at this exact moment brings you clarity and focus. Because so many others are multitasking, you easily beat them just by paying attention to the one thing you're doing right now.

Be well.

## Chapter Seventeen

# Carve Out Quiet Time if You Want To Make Some Noise

## We can acknowledge that our work worlds are complex without succumbing to being tossed helplessly from task to task

Last time I discussed the many reasons to pray for good outcomes at work. Today I examine how finding moments of quiet helps you achieve good outcomes more often.

**If only I could get everyone else to be quiet**

Most lawyers like to read and analyze what they're reading. We like to think. We're happiest surrounded by heavy tomes that we wallow in without deadlines or external stress.

Alas, someone is usually clamoring for a quick answer. They don't want the legal theory, a long explanation, or really anything more than a simple Yes/No — can we do it?

It's not just business colleagues demanding answers. It's the business world itself. Countless calls on our attention. From emails and voicemails, memos and alerts, complaints and investigations. Every day is a cacophony of stimuli. Where to look first? What to rush through now so I can rush through something else.

We can acknowledge that our work worlds are complex without succumbing to being tossed helplessly from task to task. Just because someone wants an answer right now doesn't mean you must provide it on their timeline.

The best in-house counsel learn to jealously guard their time and parcel it out according to pre-determined priorities. They establish priorities based on overarching strategic considerations. You work on the most important thing regardless of how red an urgent thing is flashing.

Because work life is noisy and complex, your options for introducing quiet are necessarily limited. I suggest keeping your expectations modest but then sticking to your prioritization. For example, set aside two one-hour periods each day for quiet work. Block this time in your calendar and let no one intrude.

## Some tasks that particularly benefit from quiet

What should you focus on when you are in one of your quiet moments?

- **Updating your strategic priorities**. Nowhere will you benefit more than in keeping your strategy clear. It guides everything you and your team do. You must thus ensure your strategy evolves as business needs and the environment change.

- **High-stakes projects**. Save your best work for the projects that have the biggest impact. It may be tempting to knock off administrative tasks or small items on your to-do list because you can get a lot done in a short time. Contrast big projects, which usually require dedicated effort for longer periods to pay off.

- **When you're emotional**. Many regrets are midwifed by strong emotions. When you find your blood pressure rising, find a way to take a break. You can write an angry mail but never send it while angry. Wait until you've reconsidered it in a quiet moment.

## When you'd rather make some noise

When you see inappropriate behavior, for example when someone is acting against your company's values, being quiet is not an option. Similarly, be alert if you feel like you're being asked to act against your personal values. Never ignore or quiet that nagging internal voice warning you something's wrong.

## Honorable mentions

**Queer** — Here I refer to the other meaning, i.e. to "queer a deal" or derail what looked like a sure thing. You will probably recall times when negotiations went long, and you were near the end. Suddenly your business colleagues start pressuring you not to cause trouble by raising open points.

While you must never inadvertently queer the deal, nor should you cave on important points. The final negotiations are where you deliver your greatest value, which never comes from meekly yielding open points.

**Question** — Asking questions is probably the in-house lawyer's lowest-cost activity with the greatest payback. Questions show you're interested. The answers sometimes uncover hidden assumptions. You learn new things. You are a more effective lawyer in proportion to the questions you ask.

Be well.

# Chapter Eighteen

# Rest Your Way To Better Performance

Your burnout risk is real. But that's not the best reason to avoid overwork. You take breaks because they unlock stronger performance

Last time I explored why you should find quiet at work for particularly important topics. Today I discuss how building in periodic Rest at work helps you produce more than by simply working more hours.

## Rest is for weak people, not winners

Banish this thought from your mind. High performers usually accustom themselves to high standards and hard work. It's true being capable of hard work sets you apart.

Your burnout risk is real. But that's not the best reason to avoid overwork. You take breaks because they unlock stronger performance.

I started taking lunchtime runs several years into my career. I made the choice for health and wellbeing reasons. I was thus determined to stick with my exercise habit regardless of any loss in productivity. Imagine my surprise to find I felt better and accomplished more on run days. This came despite logging fewer "work" hours.

What is the mechanism? Simply this: Rest and recovery are vital to peak performance. I can't tell you how many new ideas and solutions to thorny problems popped into my head on a run. Think of rest as refueling your tank, mental and physical, allowing you to perform at high levels for longer.

## How to spot signs you're ready for some rest

First, just pay attention to your thoughts. In one of your quiet moments, check your feelings to see if you might not be ready for a break. Here are more likely candidates for times you may evaluate taking some rest.

- **You've been working intensely** for a decent spell. This might be a couple of hours, or it might be a couple of weeks. It depends on the project and your intensity. The longer you're trying to maintain your best performance, the more you're likely to need a break.

- **You've made a big step forward**. Sometimes the emotional rush from advancing motivates us to keep pushing. We want to leverage momentum. These can also be great points for short breaks, which can feel natural because they seem well-deserved.

- **You've had a big setback**. Our disappointment at failing can motivate us to redouble our efforts. This is natural, but we risk being colored by negative thoughts. A short break can help us reset and focus again in a positive way.

- **When you're emotional**. If you're flying off the handle, or feeling more highs or lows than usual, this is a good time to break your routine and do something else.

## When rest is out of the question

As much as I promote work-life balance, sometimes you must sustain an all-out effort. If you are up against a hard deadline, tell yourself you'll rest once you're done. If you are on the cusp of great victory, pushing through to the finish is often preferable to pausing to consolidate your gains.

And some corporate crises permit no rest. We hope they come rarely, but when they do come, our jobs require us to be indefatigable.

## Honorable mentions

**Repeat** — When communicating, repeat simple, clear messages more than you think is necessary. You never reach everyone with one communication. Your guidelines, corporate values, and other cultural topics all require repetition.

**Retreat** — Sometimes the best way to advance is first to retreat and consider an alternative approach. Because we're smart and formidable, we get used to winning. This means we sometimes take on improbable odds via head-on attacks. When we encounter stiff resistance, a tactical retreat and reevaluation can save an otherwise doomed campaign.

**Reuse** — No need for us to redo what has already been competently done. Your first step is to diligently identify and capture reusable content. Contracts and forms are the tiniest part. Every question you answer is implicit knowledge that you should capture for potential reuse in the future. Over time your cumulative know-how will become your team's greatest asset.

Be well.

Chapter Nineteen

# Why Stress Crushes Some Colleagues But Motivates Others

You may be applying the exact right stress to the team, but they'll respond differently because they start with different stress baselines

Last time I discussed why and when you should take rest breaks at work to drive peak performance. Today I examine the related topic of managing stress to ensure you continue to perform your best.

**Stress drives performance, but only to a point**

You probably know that no stress is no fun. That is, without any pressure to perform, people have a harder time motivating themselves. To perform our best, we need to see there's something at stake.

The psychologists Robert Yerkes and John Dodson demonstrated the relationship between pressure and performance. They showed that increased attention and interest drive performance, but beyond a certain point extra stress impairs performance because of anxiety.

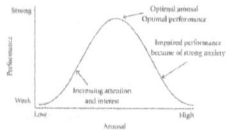

*The Yerkes-Dodson curve*

The trick is, of course, to find the optimal stress level. That zone when we're properly motivated but not overly anxious. It is surprisingly tricky. Why is that you ask? Because stress never comes to us in isolation.

We get little stress doses from many different work tasks. We encounter more from daily life (running errands, paying taxes, etc.), and still more from family and friends.

As the manager of a project, you may be applying the exact right stress to the team, but they'll respond differently because they start with different stress baselines. The one whose relative recently died or who has a child struggling in school, responds far less favorably to your well-meant prodding.

## When healthy stress risks becoming unhealthy

Here too, your thoughts and emotions are a good guide. If you're feeling more stress than is comfortable, that's a signal to act. And when you're the manager, be alert to signs of unhealthy stress on your team.

Here are some times when you should be particularly on the lookout.

- **You have trouble sleeping**. If you're tossing and turning because you can't stop thinking, chances are good that you're suffering excess work stress.

- **You have work dreams**. A sure sign for me that work stress was too high was when I dreamt of work problems. This leads to sleep being less restful.

- **Your physical health suffers**. This can be reflected in more easily catching colds, gaining weight (or, for some, losing weight), or an increase in sick days.

- **You're more emotional**. If you're flying off the handle, or feeling more highs or lows than usual, this is a good time to break your routine and do something else. A related sign is you find yourself dreading work.

## How to build your resilience

Because we perform in high-stress environments, we're more competitive when we expand our capacity to handle stress. There are various ways to build resilience. One is to simply tell ourselves we're the kind of person who thrives on stress. Just saying it helps it to become true.

Another way to build stress resilience is to take periodic rest breaks like we discussed last time. By first building and relieving stress, we become accustomed to the cycle. Simply feeling stress, even high stress, is no cause for concern, because we know we can soon find relief.

## Honorable mentions

**Separate** — You may find delight in separating your work life from your life outside work. I used my commute to switch gears and switch mindsets. On the way home, I left work behind and embraced home and family. The morning time I spent getting back into the in-house mindset. By focusing intensely on the relevant audience and avoiding distractions, you can improve your performance in both arenas.

**Success** — Only you can define what success means to you. Society will try mightily to tell you the meaning of success. Accept parts, reject parts, or make your own definition. The key is to live according to your principles and values.

**System** — A good system, consistently applied, beats our extraordinary one-off efforts. And the system is easier to maintain and improve over time. Whenever you do work that repeats, consider ways to systematize it. Once you make it a process, you can share the work, question the work (is it necessary, how important, etc.), and optimize the work, among other benefits.

Be well.

# Chapter Twenty

# Working With Teams That Weigh You Down

## It behooves us to find ways to work well with teams that are underperforming because we're likely to be confronted with them

Last time I explored how stress is necessary for strong performance, while too much stress is counterproductive. Today I discuss how working well with your team enhances everyone's performance.

**From solo performer to team performer**

This happens to all of us as our careers progress. We start out as individual performers. Then we begin working on projects in teams. With a little adjustment, we learn to work cooperatively.

Some of us then start to lead project teams or go on to manage teams. Some stop here. The best find ways to strategically leverage teams for the teams' (and their) greater success.

Eventually, every great performer has found support from an army of teammates. To increase your odds, follow my simple rule: Help your colleagues at every turn, even more than they help you.

**Sometimes the team holds you back**

Although teams can be a great driver of performance, sometimes they'll make you miserable. Not only that, a misfiring team will make strong performance impossible. In such cases, you're better off finding a way to stay away.

Here are team dynamics to avoid or fix (see next section):

- **Unclear purpose.** When team members understand the project goals differently or, worse, can't say what the goals are, the team cannot function. This is a failure of leadership communication.

- **Insufficient resources.** A team with clear purposes will fail if they lack resources. A low- or no-budget team is a nice-to-have that the business will let politely fail.

- **Backstabbing teammates.** We've all met them. Teammates who think progress is a zero-sum game. The least harmful are those who claim credit for themselves. The worst believe this requires them to undermine their teammates.

- **Glory-hounding boss.** If you can suffer a credit-claiming colleague, it is far more dangerous in a boss. Why? A boss who takes credit for the team's work kills everyone's motivation. The boss's temporary gain is undone by the team's sudden lack of forward progress.

## Turning teamwork to your advantage

It behooves us to find ways to work well with teams that are underperforming. Let's face it. We're likely to be confronted in our careers with this particular nightmare. Here are some ways to turn those losing teams around.

Feel empowered to ask questions to uncover purpose and build consensus around that purpose.

When budgets are scarce, find adjacent projects that are flush with cash and hitch your fortunes to theirs.

When teammates are cruel, call them on their bad behavior. Do it loudly and publicly, at least within the team. You may not cause their bad behavior to cease, but you'll isolate their effect.

Be careful with the greedy boss, because interfering with their glory-seeking can backfire. Take solace in that your boss's bosses likely know very well the team is behind the work. If appropriate, commend a colleague's extraordinary contribution (never your own) directly to senior management.

## Honorable mentions

**Temporary** — There's a saying among Ironman athletes I like a lot: *Pain is temporary, winning is forever.* An alternative: *Tough times don't last, tough people do.*

When we're neck deep in mud, it's hard to bring to mind the thought "*This too shall pass.*" Get into the habit of recalling it — both good times and bad times will pass. Make sure to enjoy the fun times. And have faith that the bad times will also soon recede into memory.

**Trust** — After your judgment, the most valuable asset you possess as in-house counsel is others' trust. "Wait," you're wondering. "How can I possess something that's in someone else's hands?"

You establish others' trust slowly, event-driven, on the back of shared hard times. To earn trust, be trustworthy. And you must also gain your team's trust. To gain trust, show trust.

Be well.

# Chapter Twenty-One

# What Makes You Useful?

When you help enough other people accomplish their objectives, you gain a reputation as a most useful person to have around

Today we uncover why it's important to understand the utility of your actions. This is the same as knowing the value behind everything you do. Last time I explored how working well with your team will propel your career. Today I discuss how focusing on the utility of your actions helps you avoid wasting time.

### Utility according to whom?

We all want to feel we're working on valuable things, i.e. that our work has utility. A few moments' reflection, however, makes clear just how hard it is to demonstrate our worth.

Isn't it second nature to downplay the difficulty and significance of what others do? In part, that's because we don't see in any detail what lies behind the results they deliver. Nonexperts also underestimate the skills needed to perform complex tasks.

And, ironically, the better we do our jobs, the less impressive our results seem to others:

*A clever fighter is one who not only wins, but excels in winning with ease. Hence his victories bring him neither reputation for wisdom nor credit for courage.* — Sun Tzu

To start, you must measure your worth. You have two yardsticks: How well does your work advance your strategy, and how well does it advance your company's strategy? The two should be well aligned, but there will still be differences.

## Recognize what is NOT utility

Here are two things that have no relation to utility: Intention and effort. It doesn't matter that you mean well. Rather, you must mean well, but that's entirely insufficient on its own.

Similarly, how hard you work is irrelevant. The best results require hard work in the right direction on the right topics. Well-meaning and extraordinary effort on strategically irrelevant topics wastes time and resources. You get no gold star for trying hard and striking out.

## Delivering utility makes you popular

I said above that you must start by measuring your worth. You will be rewarded for measuring well. People will notice your work if you pick the right topics.

Especially when your strategy is aligned with the company's strategy, you will work on topics that help advance other people's priorities. Trust me, they notice that.

It takes perspective and maturity to recognize when helping a colleague is the best way to invest your time. When you help enough other people accomplish their objectives, you gain a reputation as a most useful person to have around.

## Honorable mentions

**Umbrella** — I sometimes visualized our Code of Conduct as an umbrella acting as a shield over the whole company, helping protect us from a hostile world. Umbrellas can be wide or narrow, but they're not going to help you weather every storm. You're wise to layer on multiple protections.

**Uneasy** — We've all felt it — that queasy feeling in our stomach that something's not right. Listen to that feeling. Ignoring a good feeling may mean you miss an opportunity. Ignoring a lingering doubt may lead to lasting regrets.

**Urgent** — Urgency is the natural enemy of important things. Remember your strategic yardsticks and measure every new request against how well it advances a valuable goal. If not, stick to your priorities, no matter how urgent the alternative demands.

Be well.

Chapter Twenty-Two

# Is It True Your Values Don't Change?

## You need not write your own values statement, but it may help you to list core values that are important to you

Today we explore the importance of values at work. These are relevant both for improving your performance but also for enhancing your life. Last time I explored why it's critical to understand the utility in your work so you can deliver the greatest value. Today I discuss how to think about values in the work context.

**What does your company value?**

Let's start with your company's values. Why? Because your company has, most likely, helpfully written them out in a corporate values statement.

Now, it's unlikely your company will put anything unseemly in its corporate values. So you might think, why bother? But you should study them carefully with several questions in mind.

- Do the corporate values reflect what management and employees really think? Do they accurately capture your company's culture?
- Or are there unstated rules? Values that people demonstrate that you'll find listed on no company website?
- Perhaps people feel the rules are applied unevenly. That is, some people violate the rules and get away with it.

The ideal situation is where your company's stated values match the company's culture, and those values are followed by all.

## What do you value?

Having examined your company's values, you're now in a position to consider your own.

How important to you are things like integrity, hard work, respect, collegiality, dependability, reliability, courage, gratitude, sustainability, well-being, balance, kindness, humility, transparency, honesty, and more?

You need not write your own values statement, but it may help you to list core values that are important to you. You'd like to see some overlap between your values and the company's values. And hopefully no outright conflicts.

## Values don't change with the weather

Here's why this exercise is important: You will not thrive at a company whose values diverge too much from your own. Though you may be well-positioned to shape and reinforce culture, change is hard-fought and takes time to accomplish.

Just like company values are slow to change, ours don't change that quickly either. So it's critical to know yourself and what you're getting into at a new company.

When I saw how important cultural fit (read: values alignment) was to new employee success, I changed my interview approach. I stopped trying to sell applicants on the company's virtues. I spent quality time laying bare our warts:

*Here's how we really are, and here's how we behave each day. This is what you're going to find when you come to work here. How does that grab you?*

There's nothing worse than joining a company on false pretenses. A company with high-minded ideals and values that go unlived in practice. That breeds disillusionment and leads to turnover.

At the same time, it's a delight attracting other like-minded colleagues whose values resonate with yours and your company's. Everyone likes working with people who share their values.

When you feel this alignment, you will be happier and more satisfied with your life overall. What's not to like?

## Honorable mentions

**Venal** — When discussing personal and corporate values, it pays to understand that some people and organizations are prone to venality. That is, they are tempted by bribes. I hope you encounter only a few venal people and companies. But be aware they're there.

**Verisimilitude** — That's just a fancy word for saying the appearance of being true or real. People must know that you are genuine and honest. That you will tell the truth, especially about the hard things.

**Very** — Adding the word very doesn't enhance your writing very much. In fact, it very often makes you less persuasive. So, I very much recommend you consider omitting every very.

Be well.

# Chapter Twenty-Three

# You're Worth Way More Than You Think

## I say be kind to yourself. We are none of us perfect. And we need not define ourselves by our worst moments, our fears, or our doubts

Today we examine how to calculate your worth at work. More broadly, we discuss how this helps you achieve your goals. Last time I explored the importance of values to designing a meaningful life and satisfying career. Today I discuss how to think about your worth in various contexts.

**What are you worth to your company?**

You might be tempted to answer by slapping down your paycheck. After all, your company pays you a salary, right? That's what you are worth to them. Measuring yourself in just money terms, however, sells your value short.

- Think what it would cost your company to replace you. They must search, find, and successfully hire someone.

- Your company suffers disruption while your position is unfilled and while your successor is getting trained.

- Your lost expertise hurts anew each time your successor can't immediately answer something you knew by heart.

Clearly, you're worth much more to your company than your current paycheck.

Your path to success lies in getting your colleagues to see your non-monetary worth. You do this by being thoughtful, answering the question your colleague should have asked but didn't, and generally being delightful.

I told my team I wanted the business to cherish in-house counsel. That when budget money came free, they would clamor to hire more of us. Aspirational? No doubt. Achievable? You bet.

## What are you worth to others?

In a cold, sometimes uncaring world, at least sometimes we all feel like saying "Not much!" A moment's reflection reveals how wrong we are.

What is a child worth to their parents? What is a parent worth to their children? A spouse to their significant other? A best friend to their friend? And on it goes.

If I was greedy in wanting my business colleagues to cherish the in-house team, it was because I saw how much we are cherished by others outside the business. Why should we settle for any less at work?

## What are you worth to yourself?

This is where we most often see with tinted glasses. Some take themselves far too seriously. These are the people we all agree have a tremendously high self-opinion, usually entirely undeserved.

Many err in the other direction, though, and too often doubt themselves when all evidence suggests they should be kinder.

I say be kind to yourself. We are none of us perfect. And we need not define ourselves by our worst moments, our fears, or our doubts. We should give ourselves credit for showing up and giving our best on all the days when it's hard and we've dug deep just to be there.

When you add up the various ways you're worthy, to your company, to others, and to yourself, you are a valuable person indeed. Take a moment to revel in your worth.

And now get back to work earning it.

## Honorable mentions

**Want** — It is important to be honest about what you want. You need not share your wishes broadly. Start by acknowledging your desires to yourself. Then share with your family, friends, and perhaps eventually work colleagues. You might be surprised by what happens.

**Well-being** — Well-being means managing stress, eating well, exercising, sure. I mean well-being in both a narrower and a broader sense.

Do you feel well? Are you happy? Do you find joy and not just enjoyment in your daily pursuits? This is something that no corporate program delivers. You find this kind of well-being within.

**Work-Life Balance** — We are busy and we regularly get sucked into crises. As a result, we find ourselves working rather a lot. While this can be helpful in our careers, our work ethic risks us missing out on life outside work.

Your family, friends, and hobbies all deserve your attention. You likely won't consider yourself a success in life if all you do is work.

Be well.

Chapter Twenty-Four

# Is It Beneath You to Xerox?

It's not that you must do everything yourself. Rather, you should be capable of doing many things so you can jump in when the need is great and make a difference

Last time I explored the various ways to calculate your worth and came up with an impressive tally. Today I discuss why learning to Xerox is your path to bigger workplace success.

**Were you just looking for an X-word, James?**

I mean today's advice sincerely and wholeheartedly. And I will explain why.

Xerox was the trademark name originally applied to machines used to copy written material. Because of their office ubiquity, people came to refer to making a copy as "xeroxing," and the copy itself as a "xerox."

As I mean it here, "Xerox" is a stand-in for making copies and *everything else* that falls into the administrative side of work:

- Fixing jams in the copy machine, replacing toner, and generally making it work when it isn't working

- Writing, addressing, and dispatching letters, sending overnight packages, and knowing how your company's mail process works

- Being a Microsoft Office guru, including Word, Excel, and PowerPoint

- Becoming an expert in the other software programs your company regularly uses

- Knowing how to connect any computer-like device to any presentation-like device in every setting

- Being able to get your hands on spare batteries, office supplies, paper, post-its, and markers

## Wait, I didn't get an advanced degree for this

I learned how useful it was to be useful at administrative tasks as a junior associate. We worked preposterously long hours, well after midnight when everyone sane had gone home. There were no secretaries, no staff, just desperate lawyers needing to get work done.

When the copier broke at 1:00 a.m. and you could fix it, you were valuable. When a partner struggled to reformat a document and you saved the day with a few clicks, you suddenly looked a lot smarter.

I remember a senior associate one night saying to me, "James, you're a terrible lawyer but you'd make a great secretary."

He thought he was insulting me, but I was secretly pleased. "Why?" you ask. "You didn't go to law school to learn to connect laptops to balky projectors, right?"

How do you stand out in an over-achiever crowd? Every associate was as smart or smarter than me, and almost all went to more prestigious schools. Well, guess what? We were all largely useless compared to even the second-year associates.

But few fancy-degreed lawyers thought it was their job to master office technology. By getting my hands dirty and learning every trick and tool I could, I became more useful than senior associates and partners.

I went to law school to become a lawyer. I learned at work to use every tool at my disposal to advance my career. If being able to create an Excel table quickly and easily makes me shine, that's an easy win.

## Are there times you should just let your assistant do it?

Yes, many. You should jealously guard your time. This means knowing your value proposition and focusing your efforts on where you can have the greatest impact. Usually, this means leveraging your specific legal expertise.

The point is not that you must do everything yourself all the time. Rather, you should be *capable* of doing many things. Then, you can jump in when the need is great and make a difference.

I'll mention another benefit to staying familiar with the copier: Staying humble and grounded. You're not more important as a person than anyone else in your company. You're just an individual with a job and certain skills, so don't let it go to your head.

It used to annoy me when the Chairman asked me at board meetings to coordinate administrative details like letting management and directors know about a new start time for our board dinner. I soon embraced such tasks, both because I was good at them, and because they reminded me, I'm just a person like everyone else.

## Honorable mentions

**Xenophile** — This means a person attracted to foreign peoples, manners, or cultures. I can't think of a better way to build a diverse and robust team than drawing on talent from across the globe.

**Xerophile** — A xerophile is an organism that flourishes in a very dry environment. Successful employees learn to appreciate and work with people who operate in different environments that initially seem dry and hostile. The tax and intellectual property departments come to mind.

Be well.

# Chapter Twenty-Five

# Saying No Is Easy — Know When To Say Yes

## You will say no fifty times more often than you say yes. Just remember that your goal is to eventually find a Yes for every legitimate business purpose

The word Yes is the reason this book exists. Last time I explored many ways to leverage being able to Xerox and perform other administrative functions, and discussed why this can make you stand out. Today I discuss the enduring power of the word Yes.

### Anyone can say No (and they frequently do)

If you compare the average in-house counsel to our business colleagues, we come up short in optimism. For every optimistic business plan, we stand ready to point out obstacles and risks.

To be fair, this is our job. We are there to fulfill a role and often that is to keep the exuberance of the business in check. Plus, with experience, we see just how many ways there are for things to go wrong. I'm not saying we're angels, but the proverb "Fools rush in where angels fear to tread" exists for a reason.

Thus, our roles and our experiences bend us toward seeing the dark cloud rather than the silver lining. It becomes second nature to say no as in "No, that way exposes us to unnecessary risk."

Have you ever noticed a trick some executives use to kill a project they don't support but nor do they wish to be responsible for stopping? "Send it to legal for review." Not only does this create delay, but often we do just as the business expects.

The best in-house counsel know how to avoid this trap. Never the naked no. No is always followed by an alternative suggestion as in "No, but ..."

My favorite book about negotiation is called Getting to Yes. There is always a way to achieve our goals, and it starts with telling ourselves we will help the business get to yes.

## If I always say Yes, am I just giving in?

The question betrays the bias. Giving in to what? Your instinct to say no? Your wish to have others follow your advice? Or is saying yes your path to helping the business succeed? If so, that's not giving in so much as recognizing where your priorities lie.

Remember, nothing you do at work should be personal. That is, take it personally in the sense you care about doing good work, but don't take the tussle itself personally. When management pushes you and you push back, you're both fulfilling your responsibilities.

## What if I really want to say No?

Despite your problem-solving mindset, you must not let business pressure bend you to saying yes to inappropriate things. In fact, you will say no to many hare-brained schemes in helping guide your colleagues to a safe path.

You will say no fifty times more often than you say yes. Just remember that your goal is to eventually find a yes for every legitimate business purpose.

In rare circumstances, your No will be absolute. That is when the desired conduct is improper on its face. The business may see nothing wrong in that friendly information exchange with a competitor, but you cannot bless it. A colleague may hold discriminatory views, but you will ensure they play no part in hiring or promotion.

I hope these circumstances are few in your career. When they arise, your reputation for always helping the business find a way to Yes gives you credibility when you insist on your hard No.

## Honorable mentions

**Yellow** — Observe traffic signals within your company. Here I mean the signs that something has gone wrong but has not caused a crisis. Many people ignore these flashing yellow lights. When you train yourself to spot the warning signs, you can adapt systems and update processes to avert major problems. You will become the rarest and most effective in-house counsel there is: Crisis-free.

**Yesterday** — Yesterday is already in the past and you must quickly move on. Learn from mistakes, both yours and others but don't dwell on them. I found it useful to maintain a mistake log. I wrote down significant mistakes, describing the situation, why it went wrong, and what I learned from it. This helped me improve and helped keep me humble.

**Youth** — Youth typically brings enthusiasm and a positive attitude to work. These are things that experience often wrings from us. When you're young, capitalize on your inherent advantage and make sure everyone sees your happy energy.

And if you're experienced, remember your relatively higher cost and ask what you're doing to demonstrate your value proposition. You can borrow enthusiasm and attitude any time. Marrying that to your knowledge and experience is a powerful combination.

Be well.

Chapter Twenty-Six

# A Zen-Like Attitude Makes You More Successful at Work

Mindful attentiveness brings you a more peaceful mind, the recognition that you can choose your response to emotions, and superior performance in your tasks

Last time I explored why orienting yourself around the word Yes drives outperformance in work and life. Today I end this series by recommending you bring a Zen-like attitude to your endeavors.

**Zen has a long and impressive pedigree**

When I say Zen for our purposes, I mean a state of calm attentiveness. No need to imbue the word with any more meaning than that.

I do love that Zen has a rich, multicultural history: The Japanese pronunciation of a Middle Chinese word that is a transliteration of the Sanskrit word for meditation.

Meditation has come into the mainstream, perhaps because many people feel stressed by modern life. There are as many ways to meditate as there are people who have tried it. Truly it is a welcoming practice. The simplest methods involve paying attention to one's breath for a moment.

You will also hear people talk about mindfulness, which is close to what I mean by Zen, paying attention to the present moment and not letting your mind wander. You can apply mindfulness in every setting and any activity.

## What does a Zen mindset do for me in practical terms?

If calm attentiveness is your goal, two benefits await.

When you learn to observe the thoughts running through your mind, it is a small step to recognize that you are not your thoughts. Thoughts come unbidden to your mind, but you can choose what to do in response. This includes not letting e.g. anger, fear, or frustration drive your behavior.

In other words, by paying careful attention to your thoughts and feelings, you can step off the stress rollercoaster that we inadvertently find ourselves riding on. You can be calm amidst uncertainty. You can be calm when others are losing their cool.

The second benefit comes from attentiveness itself. What happens when you pay careful attention to the task you're doing? You do a better job. When you concentrate your efforts, naturally you perform better than when you're multitasking and distracted.

Simply being able to sit and concentrate is a superpower in today's attention-fracturing environment.

Mindful attentiveness brings you a more peaceful mind, the recognition that you can choose your response to emotions, and superior performance in your tasks. Impressive return for such a modest investment of your time!

## Are there times I should lose my Zen-like calm?

In a word, no. You may choose to show an emotion when the situation requires it, but you should be mindful, that is deliberate.

Just because your natural Zen-like state is calm, you do feel emotions. More importantly, your colleagues get angry, frustrated, and worried as well.

It helps when you empathize with colleagues by acknowledging those emotions. Say a new regulation will impose significant burdens on your company. There's every reason to express frustration and annoyance about the regulation itself. That's a realistic expression of what everyone's feeling. You can then lower the tone and turn to productive work.

Similarly, when someone's made a mistake (including you), it's normal to be disappointed, perhaps even angry. Know when you're feeling these things, decide how much to show, and then rein it in again.

The common bonds of human emotion speak strongest to us across time and space. We understand and appreciate philosophy and poetry across millennia because we recognize the human emotions at play.

Being a keen observer of your emotions allows you to become their master. Then you can let them loose to great effect as needed.

## Honorable mentions

**Zag** — Helen Keller said, "When one door of happiness closes, another opens, but often we look so long at the closed door that we do not see the one that has been opened for us." Our laser-like focus on our goals sometimes risks that we miss adjacent opportunities. There are many paths to success if we're open.

**Zealous** — Lawyers must be zealous advocates for our client's interests. Always remember who the client is. For in-house lawyers, it is the company itself, not the CEO or the management team. And it's also not us. We like to be right, but the job is not about us. We're there to help the company achieve its goals.

**Zeitgeist** — Pay attention to your company's general mood and feeling. Also note the general attitudes and morals of the broader environments your company operates in. This includes your industry, the countries you're present, and regional concerns.

All these will drive your risk assessment. Are employees in one business or region more likely to come under pressure to behave inappropriately? Are competitors slipping on the brass knuckles? Are regulators itching to make an example?

This ends the book, but you can refer back whenever you need a reminder. Whether a chapter helps you overcome a tough work situation or keeps you on the path to living a good life, I hope you continue to find inspiration or a helpful tip or two along the way.

Be well.

# The Pragmatist's Rules for Work

Career Paths Vol. 2: Completing the Picture on Getting Ahead at Work

James Bellerjeau

A Fine Idea

Copyright © 2025 by James Bellerjeau

All rights reserved.

No portion of this book may be reproduced in any form without written permission from the publisher or author, except as permitted by U.S. copyright law.

# Contents

Make Sure You're Not Missing Half the Formula for Success at Work — 115

1. Go Ahead and Be Arrogant — 117
2. It Is Sometimes Necessary To Be a Bastard — 121
3. Take Credit Whenever You Can — 125
4. Demand What You Deserve — 129
5. The Only Expectations That Should Concern You — 133
6. Failure Is Only Fatal to the Unprepared — 137
7. Go When It Suits You, Not Your Company — 141
8. Hide Strategically by Highlighting What You Want Others To See — 145
9. When To Inform on Colleagues or Keep Quiet — 149
10. Success Means Making Honest Judgments — 153
11. The Kamikaze Approach to Making Progress — 157
12. How Not To Be a Loser — 161
13. Don't Be Squeamish Applying Muscle When Needed — 165
14. How To Look Like a Natural in All Settings — 169
15. How Managers Ensure Employees Obey Them — 173
16. Anyone Can Acquiesce but You Can Punch Above Your Weight — 177

| | | |
|---|---|---|
| 17. | Quick and Wrong Is Better Than Slow and Obsolete | 181 |
| 18. | Random Events Only Hurt the Unprepared | 185 |
| 19. | Your Sense of Shame Is Holding You Back | 189 |
| 20. | Terror Is a Tool Some Managers Use Well | 193 |
| 21. | How To Respond to an Ultimatum ... and Give One | 197 |
| 22. | Knowing Which Role Models To Venerate Is Key | 201 |
| 23. | Spotting Weakness Allows You To Exploit It | 205 |
| 24. | When Xenophobia Works to Your Advantage | 209 |
| 25. | Take Advantage of Youth, No Matter Your Age | 213 |
| 26. | Who Wouldn't Want To Be a Zillionaire? | 217 |

# Make Sure You're Not Missing Half the Formula for Success at Work

## Do you want to hear the real truth of the matter? Then you must put aside wishful thinking and fantasy and focus on what works

G reetings readers! Niccolò here, writing through my trusty amanuensis James.

I suppose I should be thankful. After five hundred years' rest, I was disturbed awake by the first volume of the Career Paths series, **Thriving at Work**. It's not that James's tips for success at work are wrong. They're just *incomplete.*

If you want to succeed in your endeavors, you need more than half the formula. That's where I felt compelled to speak across the centuries. A lot has changed since I've been away. But I can already see that human nature is not one of them.

Having had even more time to think over all I've learned about people and their motivations, and considered it with care, I want to share my learnings with a new generation.

Am I pleased that at least one of my books is still being read and my name has become an adjective? Yes, of course. But I do regret people thinking following my advice means they are devious, scheming, or unscrupulous.

My goal in writing The Prince was simple pragmatism: To explain what works and why. That's also my goal with The Pragmatist's Rules for Work, with an emphasis on behaviors that work. I won't sugarcoat the lessons either.

> *Since my aim was to write something useful for anyone interested, I felt it would be appropriate to go to the real truth of the matter, not to repeat other people's fantasies.* — Machiavelli, The Prince

Because a society's success now takes the effort of many, I am writing not just to the world's Princes but to all of you. With the Pragmatist's Rules, I will complete the picture James started in Thriving at Work.

I won't tell you whether to follow James's advice or my advice or some combination of the two. Chances are, you will find yourself applying tips from both ends of the spectrum as circumstances warrant.

And if that makes you cunning, artful, and sly, it will also make you a winner.

Until next time.

Work well and win.

Chapter One

# Go Ahead and Be Arrogant

## Arrogance is nothing more than confidence expressed publicly. Confidence is the beginning and end of your credibility

Arrogance is nothing more than confidence expressed publicly. Confidence is the beginning and end of your credibility. And credibility drives your career.

You are always performing. Your audience is comprised of either fools or foes. The first group includes laypersons, unable to judge your substantive competence. They rely entirely on how you come across when you interact with them to judge your performance.

> *Everyone sees what you seem to be, few have experience of who you really are.* — Machiavelli, The Prince

- When you answer a question, are you hesitant, unsure, or halting? That must mean you don't know what you're talking about.

- Do you look down, hunch your shoulders, and speak under your breath? I think I'll keep looking.

- I want my counterpart to look me in the eye, stand tall, and project confidence.

Your foes include everyone you face across the negotiation table. The numbers of your foes include all those you're competing against. You're competing not just with other experts, but with everyone who wants to come across as competent.

Some of your foes are positioned to know when you're bluffing. This could be because they're also subject matter experts or because they're prone to bluff themselves.

But tell yourself they'll never figure it out from your demeanor. And if you maintain absolute consistency in your confidence, no one else will see through your façade.

## Here are some examples to inspire us

Here's how James says he heard former GE General Counsel Ben Heineman describe his approach:

*Often wrong, never in doubt.*

That's the right attitude. Although I suspect Mr. Heineman was only pretending to be humble in saying he was often wrong. His confidence comes through clearly. Even though he knows he sometimes will be wrong, he projects confidence absolutely. Follow his example.

I can give you further inspiration from my side of the mortal plane. A friend with the unfortunate nickname Dizzy joined us more recently. Mr. Dean explained to me how he became famous not just for his pitching but for his confidence in how well he and his brother would perform.

How can you not love his bravado:

*It ain't bragging if you can do it.*

And that's even more right. The **single best way to be confident is to be competent**. To know you can back up your words with action.

This takes us to the wisdom in James's earlier advice to show Ambition in the sense that you desire to get better. You should always be working to improve. This will give you the skills to back up your words with actions.

## In summary

Do the hard work necessary to develop competence in core areas of expertise. Leverage that competence to get used to feeling confident. Then expand on the situations where you feel confident.

Be clear in your mind that you are a winner, you know what you're talking about, and you will succeed. Project your confidence like a standing wave around you and watch the dominoes fall.

Until next time.

Work well and win.

## Chapter Two

# It Is Sometimes Necessary To Be a Bastard

## To recognize what each situation demands is simple survival. Help others when it helps you. You will both benefit

Be a bastard. To know the wisdom of this statement is to ask yourself two questions:

- How much do you think other people truly care about your success?

- And, perhaps as illuminating, how much do you care about others' success?

I am sure you can think of many people who've supported you in your career. Bosses, mentors, and colleagues who gave you precious assistance when you needed it. But did any of them do so at a cost to themselves?

Now consider your answer to the second question. Doubtless, you can think of many times when you aided a colleague. Perhaps you count as one of your core values helping others to succeed. All well and good.

How does your behavior hold up when you are forced to choose between helping others and advancing your own interests? It is easy to help others when you are in fact helping yourself, or at least not incurring any sacrifice.

To recognize what each situation demands is simple survival. Help others when it helps you. You will both benefit. But to help another when it advances them at your cost is a fool's game.

If you want to advance your career, that means taking advantage of opportunities that may appear but rarely. You must be able to tell the difference between altruism and sacrifice and adapt your behavior accordingly:

> *What matters is that he [a ruler] has the sort of character that can change tack as luck and circumstances demand ... stick to the good if he can but know how to be bad when the occasion demands.* — Machiavelli, The Prince

When you give heed to your own interests, people may think of you as selfish. When you put your interests ahead of those who would jump ahead of you, they might even call you a bastard.

But wouldn't you rather dispense your own assistance from a position of power than rely upon the goodwill of others that can evaporate when it suits them?

## How does this play out in practice?

Your colleagues in competition with you will not hesitate to advance their interests when they can. Management will test your motivation and question your ability. Even when you demonstrate your ambition, they may not credit your capability.

Your task is to demonstrate an unwavering conviction that others' faith in you is well-placed:

> *The general public's mood will swing. It's easy to convince people of something, but hard to keep them convinced. So when they stop believing in you, you must be in a position to force them to believe.* — Machiavelli, The Prince

James's earlier advice was to have Belief in the sense that you cultivate the self-confidence that you will succeed. This is excellent advice. Today's lesson just takes the natural step further — you must also *act* in accordance with your belief.

If you believe you are not only up to the job, but the best person for the role, then it is appropriate for you to do whatever is necessary to keep advancing towards the role and then staying in the role.

## In summary

By all means, help others whenever you can. Develop a reputation as a caring, generous mentor. But make sure that your help never comes at the cost of your own advancement.

Remember that no one will look out for your interests as well as you. Even if they would be so foolish as to sacrifice for you, they don't know your inner desires and fears.

You can navigate these waters safely, provided you recognize the truth of where you are sailing. You are the captain of your ship. Being a responsible captain means taking the hard decisions as needed.

Getting the ship safely to shore means applying a fair, but disciplined hand. Court martials, keelhauls, and even walking the plank are all part of the captain's duty.

Just remember whose interests come first, and you will succeed.

Until next time.

Work well and win.

Chapter Three

# Take Credit Whenever You Can

## When your actions have contributed to the outcome, you may always take credit and must do so

Who exactly will tell you that it is selfish to take credit for your work? That we should play nicely with one another and leave our egos aside?

Chances are these subversive ideas come from someone who has already ascended to a position of power and wishes to remain there. Either that or someone who sees little prospect of advancement by their own efforts and wants to ride your coattails.

Let me explain some simple truths about how the world works. These truths make clear why it is appropriate to take credit in every circumstance where the opportunity presents itself.

First, consider the role of chance in many outcomes at work. We plan, we toil, and we respond to unpredictable circumstances. How likely is it that anyone foresees everything that occurs?

> *Luck decides the half of what we do, but it leaves the other half, more or less, to us.* — Machiavelli, The Prince

When no one has a clear idea of what is happening at the time and no one has perfect insight into what results their actions might bring, you must take credit for everything that goes your way.

The logic of this conclusion is inescapable. If you are humble, if you downplay that your actions had the intended consequences, you will not be considered a hero. No, people will not even realize that you are being selfless:

> *It would be nice to be seen as generous. All the same, being generous just to be seen to be so will damage you. Generosity practiced out of real good will, as it should be, risks passing unnoticed.* — Machiavelli, The Prince

There is something even worse than seeing your own selflessness go unrecognized. Consider that while the outcomes of our actions are unpredictable, the behavior of others is not.

The second truth I want you to see is that your colleagues will seek to take credit for lucky outcomes. Into the space left by your generosity, a person practicing the lessons from last time (Bastard) will happily step in.

## Be careful, though; there are dangers in taking credit

Some lessons flow from simple rules, whose application we can be confident will always give the desired result. Being aware of one's self-interest and acting accordingly is one such rule.

The rules around taking credit are not so simple. Here is what we can say with certainty.

- When your actions have contributed to the outcome, you may always take credit and must do so

- When luck has played a role in the outcome, you must be vigilant for the opportunity to take credit, especially when others will do so

- When others' actions are responsible for the outcome, you may not claim credit for their work, at least not directly. You will not only make an enemy but cause others to mistrust you

Even though another's deeds may have carried the day, you still have opportunities to swing admiration in your favor. This is particularly so when you can take responsibility for any part of the composition of the team or their decisions:

> *The quality of the ministers will reflect [the ruler's] good sense or lack of it and give people their first impression of the way the ruler's mind is working. If his ministers are capable and loyal, people will always reckon a ruler astute, because he was able to recognize their ability and command their loyalty.* — Machiavelli, The Prince

You want to be seen assembling a high-performing team and directing their efforts towards the desired outcome. When it is clear you were the organizing force, then you can take *indirect* credit by lavishly praising the work of the team. After all, it was you who brought them together and created the conditions for their good work.

And if you keep the team working well by instilling in them the desire to cooperate, by telling them that it is selfish to take credit for individual efforts, you have learned this week's lesson well.

## In summary

James's earlier advice was to practice Continuous Improvement. I agree that slow and steady progress will advance you unstoppably towards your goals.

One of the best ways to capitalize on that progress is to make sure others recognize what you've done. This is so whether success comes through blind luck, through your own actions, or that of others.

Take credit where credit is due and remember that you always deserve to take credit.

Until next time.

Work well and win.

## Chapter Four

# Demand What You Deserve

The most enlightened boss and the most supportive work environment will miss out on chances to meet your needs. Unless you demand it

In our previous lesson about the importance of taking Credit for successful outcomes, I noted that luck often plays a role in life. Today I want to expand on this idea because understanding how to work with luck is vital for any leader.

Average performers think luck is responsible for people's success. This is not so. Luck randomly and variably presents opportunities. It is always up to the leader to first recognize and then capitalize on those opportunities:

> *The only part luck played was in giving them an initial opportunity: They were granted the raw material and had the chance to mold it into whatever shape they wanted. Without this opportunity their talent would have gone unused, and without their talent the opportunity would have gone begging.* — Machiavelli, The Prince

It is a combination of unpredictable circumstances (i.e., luck) and your own talent that creates successful leaders. Your task thus becomes recognizing opportunities and shaping them to your favor via the application of your abilities.

Because luck is unpredictable, you need to be alert to a wide variety of potential opportunities. This is particularly so when you consider that your workplace will thwart you as often as it helps you.

As I've noted previously, no one knows your interests as well as you do. The most enlightened boss and the most supportive work environment will thus miss out on chances to meet your needs. Unless you demand it, that is.

Here are things that you should demand, as opportunities present themselves:

- To work on projects that are important to the company

- Ways to demonstrate your skills and talents in settings where management will see them

- Tools and the time appropriate to allow you to develop your skills to become more useful and competitive

- To receive recognition for your work that reflects the value you bring

- To be paid competitively without having to use up precious bargaining power

- To be cherished, mentored, and assisted in your career

- To be promoted in ways that give rise to new opportunities.

This is a partial list to inspire you. Your demands will be as broad as your personal interests require.

## Everyone is capable of helping meet your demands

You need not limit your demands to management. Indeed, you will not be successful unless you learn to make demands of peers and subordinates as well.

What demands? Respect for your time. Gratitude for your assistance. Acknowledgement of opportunities given and care in making use of them. Recognition of where common interests lie, and loyalty as a consequence.

Among everyone you interact with, you will identify a small number whose opinions matter most. This may be because they are unusually intelligent or perceptive. Or by virtue of their experience and tenure, other people in power listen to their opinions.

Make it your habit to consult with your informal counsel of advisors. No one ever said a mentor relationship had to be formal, or that assistance had to be volunteered. Having identified your cadre, you must demand their opinions:

> *The ruler should ask his ministers about everything and listen to their opinions, then make up his mind on his own, following his own criteria. In responding to these advisers, as a group or separately, he should make it clear that the more openly they speak, the more welcome their advice will be.* — Machiavelli, The Prince

The more often people around you hear your demands, the more they will become habituated to responding when called.

## In summary

James's advice in Thriving at Work was to practice Diversity in our thinking. He suggested keeping an open mind to the idea you could be wrong, for example in pursuit of a better way. Here I must respectfully disagree.

There may be a better way, and perhaps your advisors will point one out to you. If you choose to change course, let it be your choice. But the way you choose to proceed is *by definition* the best way. To allow anyone to think otherwise is to invite doubt about your competence.

If you feel uncertainty, then let it be in your private thoughts. Uncertainty publicly expressed only invites mischief from ambitious people who don't know any better than you but are willing to demand a chance to try their hand.

Ayn Rand had the right sentiment when she wrote, "The question isn't who is going to let me; it's who is going to stop me."

When you demand what you want, you are also insisting that everyone go along with your demand. Otherwise, your wishes are merely a request that they can safely ignore.

Until next time.

Work well and win.

Chapter Five

# The Only Expectations That Should Concern You

## The people who have taken stock of their honest desires are a force to be reckoned with

Previously we talked about how it is necessary to Demand what you want to advance at work. Today I will continue this theme by discussing how to think about expectations. We will explore how to deal with your expectations and others' expectations.

I suggest you start by examining closely your desires. What is it that you truly want? Do you want to be admired as a role model? Do you wish to be remembered as a kind, helpful person? Or do you wish to advance your career?

If your desire is to advance, then you must be realistic and pragmatic. The articles in the Pragmatist's Rules for Work describe the world as it is, not as we wish it would be. They provide guidance for working with the rules of the system to gain an advantage.

None of it will serve you well if that's not what you want. I don't know your inner thoughts and it is not necessary that I do so. What matters is that *you know them* and are honest about what you want.

Few people can stomach looking deeply at their hidden desires. Why does it embarrass us to acknowledge our ambitions? I say if you cannot be honest, even with yourself, you cannot lead.

And know this. The people who have taken stock of their honest desires are a force to be reckoned with. If they also learn the rules of the game they are playing, the only question is whether they are willing to pay the price to achieve what they want.

For this reason, you can never trust what people say about their intentions. They either do not know, because they have shied away from deep reflection, or they do know and thus cannot share the unvarnished truth:

> *Sincere words are not sweet and sweet words are not sincere.* — Tao Te Ching 81, Lao Tzu

The only thing that remains to guide you is your expectations. What do you truly want? How can you expect others to behave to get what they want? Once you acknowledge these things, you are prepared to be a sincere student in pursuit of what you want.

## Be careful letting others' expectations shape your behavior

Whether stated or silent, conscious or unconscious, people have expectations of their leaders. It is necessary for you to understand those expectations, but not necessarily to live up to them. Why is that?

First and foremost, you must survive in your role. A deposed leader can do nothing for their subjects. Individuals' expectations are contradictory and unreasonable. They want everything delivered to them, but they do not wish to pay the full price. They want their leader to be all-powerful but at the same time kind and malleable.

If you cannot satisfy competing expectations, you should be aware of indulging those that will lead to your downfall:

> *If you always want to play the good man in a world where most people are not good, you'll end up badly. Hence if a ruler wants to survive, he'll have to learn to stop being good, at least when the occasion demands.* — Machiavelli, The Prince

Because people do not know what they want, they will expect unreasonable things from their leaders. Again, you are left only with your expectations to guide you. You must expect, therefore, that it will be necessary to frustrate people's expectations to deliver what you understand they need, and not what they say they want.

## In summary

James's advice in Thriving at Work was to find Equanimity by learning to keep our cool when situations are getting hot. It is true that a leader must never lose their self-possession. No matter what emotions they are displaying, they have firm control over them.

This is even more important when we consider the minds of all those we are engaging with. People are either woefully unaware of their true desires, and so will hold all manner of unreasonable expectations of you. Or they are fully aware of their desires and perhaps dangerously willing to pursue them.

The only safe course for the leader is to substitute their expectations for all others and behave accordingly.

Until next time.

Work well and win.

# Chapter Six

# Failure Is Only Fatal to the Unprepared

People fail and projects fail. Nothing could be more obvious. You must always be looking for the dangers that lie in wait

**Expect failure and plan accordingly**

Previously, we talked about how success requires us to understand our own Expectations and those of others. Today we focus our survival skills on one of work's unavoidable aspects. That is, you will encounter failures.

People fail and projects fail. Nothing could be more obvious. I saw failures aplenty in my time. A glance at the headlines makes clear that humanity's technological progress has not taught humility.

Why do people make plans assuming they will encounter ideal conditions? This only sets them up for frustration when random chance, to say nothing of deliberate sabotage, obstacles, and delays.

You must never practice naïve optimism. You must never think your project is safe. You must always be looking for the dangers that lie in wait.

> *It is in the nature of things that every time you try to avoid one danger you run into another. Good sense consists in being able to assess the dangers and choose the lesser of various evils.* — Machiavelli, The Prince

Of all my lessons, this one will be second nature to in-house counsel. Their very purpose is to raise warnings of pitfalls, to curb the unreasonable enthusiasm of foolhardy colleagues.

## Dealing with your own impending failures

Never forget that we are subject to the same blindness our colleagues suffer from. Continuously ask yourself what dangers imperil your projects.

There are two principles in particular you must follow: Engage in firsthand observation and take quick action as soon as trouble rears its head.

The whole point of having teams is to amplify your potential. Many hands can do more work, and they can do so around the clock while you focus on other tasks.

But beware of the trouble that lurks in unsupervised teams. They will not see when the seeds of failure have taken root. Worse, *you* will not see when team members exercise independence in unwanted ways.

> *When you're actually there, you can see when things start going wrong and nip rebellion in the bud; when you're far away you only find out about it when it's too late.* — Machiavelli, The Prince

This does not mean you become a micromanager. You must have eyes and ears in every project, but they need not be only your eyes and ears. So long as you cultivate sources of inside information, you can be alert to signs of danger.

And you must be alert because your team will be slow to act once signs are on the ground. This is human nature: To ignore warnings, to deny reality, to pretend everything is fine. You may not indulge in these luxuries.

> *Seen in advance, trouble is easily dealt with; wait until it's on top of you and your reaction will come too late, the malaise is already irreversible. ... in its early stages it's easy to cure and hard to diagnose, but if you don't spot and treat it, as time goes by it gets easy to diagnose and hard to cure.* — Machiavelli, The Prince

People and projects fail because the world is uncertain. You will fail less when you accept the prospect of failure by being hyper-alert to its early signs.

## Turning others' failures to your advantage

It is not just team members who ignore incipient failure. Team leaders do so as well.

There are two tools one can employ to help ensure another team leader is lulled into complacency until the damage has grown large. The first is to lavish praise and accentuate the positive. The second is to point out trouble brewing elsewhere.

Because we are insecure, we are easily taken in by praise. Best of all is to provide genuine praise for aspects of a project that are going well. An exceptional team member, a milestone met. There is always something positive to highlight, and focusing a manager on the positive helps them miss little failings.

Senior managers are like magpies. Always on the lookout for shiny objects (a profitable opportunity), but easily distracted by the risk of harm. You can use this utterly predictable tendency to your advantage.

Help management to focus attention away from your troubles and onto others by pointing out risks or failures in someone else's project. You are just trying to help.

The project manager will immediately get defensive, which puts management on the alert. No matter what happens, you have accomplished your objective, which is keeping the project manager distracted.

You may also profit from others' projects when they appear to be succeeding. This is because even when everything goes well in a project, it will have unintended consequences. For all the planned good a project does, it will also create inevitable friction and disruption. Isn't that failure by another name?

Call out those unintended consequences as failures. Suggest obvious ways (in hindsight) that you could have avoided them.

Never mind that your workaround would have created other problems. You are making clear that the project gave rise to new problems and so failed in key respects.

## In summary

James's advice in Thriving at Work was to practice Fakery by displaying self-confidence in appropriate situations and recognizing when others are employing fakery themselves.

I endorse this advice. The common thread between what James counsels and what I write today is this: You must accurately perceive the world to master your circumstances.

Your task is not seeking to avoid failures. Rather, your task is to accept, nay embrace, that failures will occur. Here is a statement I rather like from a modern financier:

> *I think being successful is just about not making mistakes. It's not about having correct judgment. It's about avoiding incorrect judgments.* — Naval Ravikant

You must see failures forming far in advance and position yourself accordingly. Excise early on troublemakers in your own projects. Ensure that you are not harmed in a project's collapse and that your rivals are no matter how their projects fare.

Seen this way failure presents you with as many or more opportunities to shine than success.

Until next time.

Work well and win.

# Chapter Seven

# Go When It Suits You, Not Your Company

Your loyalty means you can be ignored because the boss needs to address the squeaky wheels

**Go means knowing when to change horses**

Previously, we talked about how to avoid Failure and profit from others' failures. But what if the prospect of failure in your environment is unavoidable, no matter what your actions? Today we talk about recognizing when it is time to go, i.e., to switch jobs or change companies.

When we are intensely focused on our affairs, we can easily lose perspective. I don't mean perspective about our work but rather the bigger picture. What's going on at our company? Are its strategic prospects improving or worsening?

The analogy of the frog in slowing warming water is apt. Incremental change is powerful because it happens beneath our notice. But unless you are uncommonly lucky, chances are your company's trajectory will waver. Sometimes it will falter, and sometimes it will fall.

By their nature, some people are prone to spotting trouble. You must never be the person who is surprised by the disaster looming in your immediate environs.

*Spare us their bad-luck stories; they have only themselves to blame. In peacetime they never imagined anything could change (it's a*

*common shortcoming not to prepare for the storm while the weather is fair).* — Machiavelli, The Prince

And you'll recognize from this advice that it's not enough to recognize the coming storm. You need to *prepare yourself* for it.

## Unreciprocated loyalty makes you weak

Depending on your age, you probably think showing loyalty to your employer is a competitive advantage. And depending on your experience in the job, you'd be right.

Nothing annoys a manager more than fickle employees who view their advancement as an entitlement rather than something hard-won. At first glance, then, demonstrating your loyalty helps you advance over your disloyal peers.

This formula only works when your manager recognizes that loyalty is a two-way street. That is, employee loyalty must be explicitly rewarded: Better assignments, more pay, greater visibility, promotion opportunities, and protection from harm.

Alas, it is human nature to take what is given. Your boss focuses attention on problem areas. Your loyalty means you can be ignored because the boss needs to address the squeaky wheels.

If bosses can ignore you when times are good, how do they behave when times are bad? In particular, will they, can they, protect you from harm? Or, when the directive comes to cut headcount by 15%, will they line up heads on the chopping block?

You know the answer. Much as they might like to save their team, bosses who stick their own necks out end up with them in the noose themselves. You must be alert to signs of trouble brewing and assume the worst. The time for you to act is before your flexibility to choose is taken from you.

> *If you do not change direction, you may end up where you are heading.* — Buddha

## Sometimes a prominent failure will help you

Trouble signals danger but for the brave also opportunities. Being part of a prominent failure can greatly enhance your reputation, at least when you can claim you are not solely responsible for the failure.

Big deals bring experience, visibility, and contacts. When you can pin failure on some figurehead, you get all the benefits and none of the downside.

Not only that, no one outside the project (and even some within it) has any idea what actually happened in a failure. Thus, you can shape the narrative to your advantage. You were the hero who recognized the danger and raised the alarm. Or you were the person who averted an even worse outcome.

> *You are always free to change your mind and choose a different future, or a different past.* — Richard Bach

## In summary

James's advice in Thriving at Work was to do a Good Job in your current job and not worry about advancing to the next job. He thinks companies will recognize and reward performance.

It's clear from today's lesson I see risks to this approach. Your employer may take gross advantage of your patience and your loyalty. While you must always be seen to be doing a good job in your current job, make sure your performance also serves *your* needs.

> *The successful ruler is the one who adapts to changing times.* — Machiavelli, The Prince

The moment you see your employer put their interests ahead of your own is the moment to put your plan to go into action.

Until next time.

Work well and win.

Chapter Eight

# Hide Strategically by Highlighting What You Want Others To See

It is what you highlight, and what you hide, that creates the reality that drives your career

### No one shall see the full picture but you

Observe how people struggle on the journey to "find themselves." If our inner selves are a mystery much of the time, what are the chances that anyone has an accurate picture of others?

People will form an ever-evolving picture of you with each interaction. Knowing this yields two invaluable lessons: First, you are always on display, and second, you must consciously shape what people see.

> *You'll be held in contempt ... if you're seen as changeable, superficial, ... fearful or indecisive. So a ruler must avoid those qualities like so many stumbling blocks and act in such a way that everything he does gives an impression of greatness, spirit, seriousness and strength.* — Machiavelli, The Prince

Your inner life is irrelevant to your success as a leader. It is what others see that counts.

Never inadvertently reveal a weakness. You may refer to one to lull an unsuspecting competitor into overstepping, or to build sympathy, or even to cultivate a reputation for humility. The best weaknesses to reveal are the ones you do not possess.

When it comes to your many good qualities, they are also as you publicly display. You do not need to be courageous to take courageous acts. You need not feel decisive to make firm decisions. For every trait that your colleagues value, you must devise a method of displaying it.

> *A leader doesn't have to possess all the virtuous qualities I've mentioned, but it's absolutely imperative that he seem to possess them.* — Machiavelli, The Prince

## Perceptions also apply to work product

It is not just our impressions of people that are shaped by perception. Everything about the workplace is similarly molded, including what people perceive about our performance.

The one who masters the art of unseen aggrandizement far outperforms the merely accurate reporter, regardless of their underlying performance. Indeed, because it takes more effort to perform well than it does to talk up performance, the self-promoter has an easier time advancing.

> *All warfare is based on deception.* — Sun Tzu

If your first thought upon reading these words is to question whether you are at war, know that you have already lost. For you most indisputably are. Every day you fight your boss's indifference, distraction, and clouded vision. To say nothing of your colleagues' laziness, perfidy, and incompetence.

Far from being a burdensome chore, your status reports are your singular best chance to shape your performance. No one knows the details of what you do. Thus, it is what you highlight, and what you hide, that creates the reality that drives your career.

For far less effort than working hard to outperform, you can convince others that your work product is superlative. Remember, perception creates reality. This is not just an aphorism; what people see becomes what happened.

For the same reason, performance evaluations are a precious gift. Your boss just wants to quickly come to a rating they can justify with minimal effort. Your helpful details are compelling, whether they are fanciful or complete. Hide anything unflattering, except sparing mentions for strategic gain.

## In summary

James's advice in Thriving at Work was to be Happy at work and in life by cultivating a positive mindset. He thinks being happy is its own reward, regardless of what happens in your career.

Go ahead and support this approach — for everyone who is in competition with you. Let them be distracted with their inner lives that no one else can see.

In the meantime, you will advance far by focusing on the only thing that matters, which is what everyone can plainly see. What you show them.

Until next time.

Work well and win.

## Chapter Nine

# When To Inform on Colleagues or Keep Quiet

## Do not inform about inconsequential failings. When you play this card, it must be to devastating effect such that your weakened opponent is in no position to retaliate

### Inform about the failings of others

We recently talked about the primacy of perception, in the sense that reality is shaped by what people see and hear. Our lesson there is that we can shape how others perceive us.

Today's lesson is that we can also leverage this power to direct how **others are perceived**.

Our ability to shape how others are perceived is hampered by the fact that they are also actively shaping perceptions with their performance. Their self-interest and attention will almost always trump our willingness to spend time creating a competing perception.

Thus, as a matter of pragmatism, it is appropriate to let others create the basic perception about their person and performance. We can still have a dramatic impact on how a person is perceived.

This comes through patience, careful observation, and surgical precision when we do intervene. Let's discuss how to successfully shape the perceptions of others.

## Everyone is hiding something

By now you accept that everyone is creating an impression of how they wish to be perceived by others. Most people focus on highlighting positive aspects of their performance. As noted, that does not concern us today.

No, what concerns us is realizing that everyone is hiding something. Not just insecurities, weakness, and other inner torment, but poor performance. No project ever goes perfectly from start to finish. The world is unpredictable and circumstances are cruel. Consequently, we all make mistakes.

Your task is to be a diligent observer of your colleagues' performance. Being helpful is ironically one of your best methods because they'll happily let you into their inner sanctum if they believe you're doing part of their work.

In the meantime, let your colleagues accentuate the positive. Just make sure that you ferret out the problems they would leave buried. The more you look, the more you will see. But only if you make it your focus.

> *If a man can't spot a problem in the making, he can't really be a wise leader.* — Machiavelli, The Prince

The foolish person thinks they can gloss over their mistakes. There are great risks in doing so. Because when a person hides a problem, they give their opponents an invaluable opportunity to weaken them.

When you tactically point out a colleague's omission, you may accomplish two objectives: You can create the perception that their performance is worse than advertised and you can leave the impression that they cannot be trusted to tell the truth.

## Use your information tactically ... and sparingly

It is a dangerous business indeed to inform about others' failings. There are more ways for this to harm you than help you. But it is an invaluable tool in your arsenal, nonetheless.

The pitfalls you must avoid are these:

- You must not gain a reputation among colleagues as a snake in the garden. This means you must inform infrequently, in private or anonymously. A public denouncement is overly dramatic and almost never necessary unless it is the boss him- or herself you are toppling.

- Because they fear regime change, you never want bosses to feel your maneuvering is for personal gain. They'll rightly fear you may do the same to them as opportunity permits.

- Do not inform about inconsequential failings, because you will create lasting enmity on the part of those affected and questions about your own character. When you play this card, it must be to devastating effect such that your weakened opponent is in no position to retaliate.

Note, you will not be so foolish as to gloss over your own mistakes. You will readily see the need to preempt colleagues from informing before you can by raising your failings in a way that removes their sting.

When you raise a problem correctly, you present it most favorably — perhaps as a heroic effort to successfully avoid an even bigger problem, and certainly as a lesson learned and personal growth story.

Most importantly, a colleague who brings up the topic in an attempt to harm you will be revealed as the duplicitous opportunist they are.

## In summary

James's advice in Thriving at Work was to demonstrate Integrity at all times. In this, we are in full agreement. Done correctly, your choice to inform of a colleague's failing is the ultimate demonstration of integrity.

That's because you have the company's interests at heart by wanting to ensure good business outcomes. You also have your colleague's best interests at heart. We all know learning from mistakes makes one stronger, which requires bringing those mistakes to light.

If you can convince colleagues that you are displaying integrity when informing them about the failings of others, then you will have learned today's lesson.

Until next time.

Work well and win.

## Chapter Ten

# Success Means Making Honest Judgments

Put loyalty before joy if you wish to have the prospect of enjoying a lengthy career and judge your colleagues accordingly

**Judge others according to how their actions affect you**

> *As I see it, [nobles] can be divided for the most part into two categories: either they behave in such a way as to tie themselves entirely to your destiny, or they don't.* — Machiavelli, The Prince

We reveal ourselves not by our words, which are worth little, but by our deeds. One's deeds show everything to the patient observer.

For all those in a position to help you or hurt you, you must know whose side they are on. The only choices are "with you" and "everyone else."

- You will have boosters helping you succeed who want nothing in return. Cherish them.

- Others will help you because, while they have no particular ambitions to lead, they still appreciate the advantages you can offer them. Their lack of ambition means you need not fear them, and you are happy enough to use their services.

- Beware those that help you only when they see it helps them. They display ambition that makes clear they are placing their interests before others' interests. They are just as likely to help undo your plans if they think they can get away with it and if doing so will help them advance.

## Loyalty must be unconditional

It should be clear from this that the only loyalty that is valuable to you is unconditional loyalty. A person who displays loyalty only when times are good will at best vanish in dark times, and at worst will work to help bring about the dark times.

Judge your colleagues' therefore most critically, by which I mean accurately and without coloring your impressions. Look to their actions in addition to their words.

Because people hide their intentions, you will want to give them multiple opportunities to demonstrate their true colors.

- You may allow little lapses to occur, just to see who rises to the bait and seeks to turn one to their advantage.

- You must also deal with any number of legitimate crises. Who jumps to your aid when a crisis arises?

For your part, make sure that loyalty is rewarded. Whether people expect or ask for favor, they should profit handsomely when tying their fortunes to yours. They should also profit visibly, in the sense that others can see the rewards you bestow.

Apply the same lessons when you have opportunities to pledge your loyalty to those above you. Remember that your bosses are going to be judging you, and will be doing so on the basis of incomplete information. Fill in the blanks for them in a way that benefits you.

You must never hesitate or appear to be granting your loyalty grudgingly.

I am amazed to hear of people who wait some time before announcing their unwavering support for a new manager. All this does is make them look conniving compared to those who immediately make their position clear.

Even if you have mixed feelings about your boss, and you almost certainly will, no good comes of allowing uncertainty into their thoughts. They are evaluating their position before they meet the first employee. You must make sure your meeting leaves no doubt of your support.

A united team is stronger than a leader with uncertain or divided support. Ensure your team has its loyalty well-placed, and that you unstintingly place yours in your boss's camp.

## In summary

James's advice in Thriving at Work was to find Joy in your work, for example by making valuable contributions, helping others, and staying true to your principles.

None of this will help you if you find yourself (or your boss) pushed out by someone who finds power before they find joy. You may be a benevolent leader, but only after you have consolidated your power into an unassailable position.

Thus, put loyalty before joy if you wish to have the prospect of enjoying a lengthy career and judge your colleagues accordingly.

Until next time.

Work well and win.

## Chapter Eleven

# The Kamikaze Approach to Making Progress

If you truly believe in your prospects, kindness cannot justify sacrificing your career in the name of helping others

**Overcoming obstacles sometimes requires sacrifice**

I would be lying if I said your career was likely to be drama-free. That you would avoid problems large and small. Not wanting to discourage you, let me tell you what good can come from adversity.

The first thing to note is that heat and pressure temper metal. If you want to know what you're made of and mold yourself into a more resilient shape, then seeing that you can survive a crisis is wonderful for one's confidence.

But we want to do more than survive. We want to thrive. A crisis offers up opportunities here too. Rather than looking at our work troubles as burdensome, see them as the vehicle they are for propelling your career.

> *There's no doubt that rulers achieve greatness by overcoming the obstacles and enemies they find in their path. So when destiny wants to make a ruler great, ... it send him enemies and prompts them to attack him.* — Machiavelli, The Prince

Dire situations may sometimes only be resolved with sacrifice. Say wrongdoing comes to the attention of authorities. A wrongdoer sometimes must be offered up as part of the settlement. When sacrifice is required, your success demands that it not be you.

One little-discussed function of a team is vital in such circumstances: The team functions to protect the boss, to take the heat, and ultimately to take the hit if one is required. You want them to do so willingly, without hesitation, in loyalty to the cause.

In today's world, few on a team are at real risk. Underlings too far down are an insufficient offering. Expatiation requires someone of responsibility and weight. A number two is good for this purpose, say a Controller to the company's CFO.

Never forget that **you** may be considered a number two to someone above you, even though you've reached the peak of your profession. What do I mean? A General Counsel might be necessary fodder when the CEO's skin is on the line. The CEO herself might fall to preserve the Chairman.

Your best path to avoiding ending up on the sacrificial table yourself is to be the one crafting the offering.

## Brutality for its own sake is counterproductive

Sacrificing a colleague might seem like a doubly elegant method to secure your position. You resolve the immediate crisis, and you remove a potential rival. Resist the temptation and make this type of solution your last resort.

Nothing undermines your ability to build loyalty more than your team thinking you will sell them out. Those decisions must be rare, understood to be difficult, and taken after all other alternatives are exhausted.

> *We can hardly describe killing fellow citizens, betraying friends and living without loyalty, mercy or creed as signs of talent. Methods like that may bring you power, but not glory.* — Machiavelli, The Prince

You want the sacrificial offering to willingly step up to take the punishment. Anything less creates a potential enemy. And because such contests are now far less, shall we say, final, than they were in my day, your enemy may be able to regain power in another position.

> *Anyone who thinks that an important man will forget past grievances just because he's received some new promotion must think again.* — Machiavelli, The Prince

This is why you must be sparing in using sacrifice as a means to resolve even serious problems. Think of it as a measure of last resort and not something you turn to out of cunning or convenience.

## Your takeaway

James's advice in Thriving at Work was to practice kindness in your work, both to yourself and in helping others succeed.

There is certainly a place for kindness in the modern leader's career, along both dimensions James mentions. If you truly believe in your prospects, however, kindness cannot justify sacrificing your career in the name of helping others.

When sacrifice is demanded of your organization, make sure you are left standing when the after-action tally is made.

Until next time.

Work well and win.

# Chapter Twelve

# How Not To Be a Loser

People mistakenly think a person's abilities or performance determine whether they will be a winner or a loser. What matters is what others in power think of you

**Loser... is something that describes other people**

People mistakenly think it is a person's abilities or performance that determine whether they will be a winner or a loser in life. While these are both important, they are not decisive. What matters is what others in power think of you.

When leaders have confidence in you, you will advance in your career. And when that confidence is lacking, you will find promotion difficult.

Politics gives a clear exposition of the phenomenon. Donors contribute to the campaigns of politicians they expect to win. Some part of the funding decision is based on ideology and some on malleability. But pragmatism wins the day. If your candidate does not win, your money is wasted.

Work is no different. The applicant who appears to most help management meet its needs is the one who wins the position. This is good news because it means everyone can advance if they accurately perceive what the organization requires.

But it is also a warning because it means you are only as valuable as you continue to deliver what the organization requires.

> *Men are quick to change ruler when they imagine they can improve their lot.* — Machiavelli, The Prince

You must be alert to situations that cause your interests and your organization's interests to diverge. Recently we talked about how to handle situations requiring sacrifice (Kamikaze). These are rare, especially compared to those that engender resentment or resistance.

Most of what in-house counsel does seems averse to the natural course of business, at least from the company's perspective. You slow the business with contract reviews, you impose onerous restrictions with rules and guidelines, and you prevent us from doing many things that come naturally, like exaggerating in ads or talking with competitors.

Now I know you've been gulled into thinking that positioning yourself as a "partner" to the company means that business colleagues don't resent your intrusions. You may go along with this fiction but never believe it.

No one likes limits imposed on their freedom. And they despise those who apply the chains. Don't expect gratitude, understanding, or acceptance from those you jail, no matter how slightly.

Your safety lies either in being unassailable, which is difficult to achieve in practice, or in sharing the burden as a jailor. It is not **you** that is imposing this rule, it is the executive committee, or the board of directors, or the Securities and Exchange Commission, etc.

Indeed, you find the whole exercise as tiresome and burdensome as business colleagues do. You are helping find the least restrictive way forward, despite what those bureaucrats want.

The lesson here is twofold: Recognize that most of your job creates resentment, and make sure you deflect blame for it to others. Choosing scapegoats outside your organization is best when they exist.

> *A ruler must get others to carry out policies that will provoke protest, keeping those that inspire gratitude to himself.* — Machiavelli, The Prince

## Take what you must, decisively

So far, we've talked about how to avoid being the loser by first ensuring management has confidence in your abilities and then avoiding that you are associated with the negative aspects of your job.

Now we tackle a more pressing situation, which is the direct challenge. When a fight is unavoidable, and a winner and loser will be declared, you must have more than your good reputation and your principles to call upon.

You must have clear structural advantages if you expect to win. You must know which tools to choose as circumstances require. Your superior force can come from your past, person, team, or future.

> *The visionary who has armed force on his side has always won through, while unarmed even your visionary is always a loser.* — Machiavelli, The Prince

For example, let's imagine one person from a large pool will be promoted to lead the team. Among the frontrunners whom will management select and why? You made it to the finalists because of the confidence you've inspired. Now what pushes you across the finish line as the victor?

Is there some specific experience you've gained that is relevant to what the company thinks it needs? Your personal characteristics and demonstrated values (e.g. teambuilding, change management, ruthlessness)? Perhaps it is clear that you command greater loyalty among the team, and that promoting anyone else would provoke revolt. Or perhaps it's what management believes you will do in the role because your vision is compelling.

Now is not the time to be shy and let management discover your talents. Nor is this the time to merely show that you meet the specific needs of the job. Your task is to actively shape both the job specifications themselves and how management perceives the other candidates.

The best job contest is the one you've won by design, such that you are the only one who satisfies the requirements.

**Your takeaway**

James's advice in Thriving at Work was to make sure to learn throughout your career.

It is certainly true that work offers many learning opportunities for both your colleagues and you.

There is no better lesson for the student or teacher than seeing who repeatedly comes out on top, and who ends up relegated to being the loser.

Until next time.

Work well and win.

Chapter Thirteen

# Don't Be Squeamish Applying Muscle When Needed

Be clear about what you want, understand what the cost is, and then act decisively to get what you want. I find people fail in all three areas

**Muscle is something you apply as needed**

You might have heard an expression like this: The meek shall inherit the earth, or All good things come to those who wait. Or perhaps you think your managers will recognize and reward good performance in time.

Nonsense. This is propaganda by those who would be leaders, intended to mislead their colleagues into giving up without a fight. If you need a slogan to remind yourself of this, take these words of someone who reached the pinnacle of his profession:

> *You miss 100% of the shots you don't take.* — Wayne Gretzky

You never saw legendary hockey player Wayne Gretzky being meek or letting an opportunity to press advantage pass him by. That's because he understood a key lesson that's been carried down for millennia: Success comes at a cost and it only yields itself to those willing to pay the price.

> *You are unjust and insatiable if you are unwilling to pay the price for which things are sold, and would have them for nothing.... And if any instance of pain or pleasure, or glory or disgrace, is set before you, remember that now is the combat, now the Olympiad comes on, nor can it be put off. By once being defeated and giving way, proficiency is lost, or by the contrary preserved.* — Epictetus

Epictetus is right to call our challenges a battle. Only by understanding what's needed and being willing to apply the necessary muscle to the task will you emerge victorious.

## Take what you must, decisively

The price for our ambitions is sometimes distasteful because it means sacrifice. In recent lessons (see Kamikaze and Loser), we talked about ensuring that when sacrifice is called for, you are the one who directs where the blade falls.

That also applies when tough decisions of all kinds must be made. The foolish shy away from hard decisions because they do not wish to be cruel. But when all your choices are bad, the cruelty lies in prolonging a bad situation.

> *Cruelty well used (if we can ever speak well of something bad) is short lived and decisive, no more than is necessary to secure your position and then stop.* — Machiavelli, The Prince

Be wary of any tendency to enjoy a tough decision. Some get giddy with power, and there is little more consequential than decisions affecting livelihoods. Besides avoiding any risk that you become cold-hearted, you must guard against any perception that you are cruel.

> *Get the violence over with as soon as possible; that way there'll be less time for people to taste its bitterness and they'll be less hostile.* — Machiavelli, The Prince

The point is to be clear about what you want, understand what the cost is, and then act decisively to get what you want. I find people fail in all three areas.

Many people are not honest, even with themselves, about their ambitions. How then will they convince others to help them in their pursuits?

Some people acknowledge their desires but are either naïve about the costs or unwilling to pay the price. They will always lose out to those who are more clear-eyed and determined. Look to these losers to be among those most loudly complaining about fairness.

And finally, some people are unable to act decisively when the moment arises. This may mean muscling in on a project, pushing aside a competitor, or aggressively promoting yourself. Apply no more force than is necessary, but also no less.

## Your takeaway

James's advice in Thriving at Work was to use motivation to propel your career. He talked about finding self-motivation to work towards intrinsic goals and values.

All fine, and I agree that self-motivation can be a primary driver of success. It is motivation married with action, however, that carries the day.

You must be willing to take actions consequent with your wishes if you hope to achieve lasting success.

Until next time.

Work well and win.

# Chapter Fourteen

# How To Look Like a Natural in All Settings

If you want to appear a naturally gifted leader, your skill lies more in surrounding yourself with the right people than it does in coming up with all the right ideas yourself

### All your actions should appear natural

Nothing demoralizes a competitor more than thinking your performance comes naturally to you. You should therefore strive in everything you do to give the impression that your talents are limitless and effortless.

This appearance gives even the most formidable adversary pause. It also builds broad confidence in your abilities, which by itself in fact makes you more competent. That's because people are more inclined to follow a natural leader than one whose abilities they occasionally doubt.

> *Above all a ruler must make sure that everything he does gives people the impression that he is a great man of remarkable abilities.* — Machiavelli, The Prince

It is no small thing to appear competent in every setting and to be easy and relaxed in so doing. It takes careful study and dedicated practice.

- Will you be as comfortable conversing with the lowliest employee as you are exchanging banter with a billionaire board member?

- Can you cross any border and work effectively in any country as easily as you cross the street?

- Are you agile enough to switch from a technical discussion of protecting vital intellectual property, to a business strategy discussion on new product development, to an in-depth review of the latest regulation emanating from the fevered imagination of Brussels bureaucrats?

The leader must aspire to all this and more. Although the details will vary depending upon the company you're in, the fact that you must be broadly talented does not. There is nothing for it but hard work.

The good news is that careful observation and faithful mimicry will bring you quick results. For most settings, these skills are sufficient. That's because people see what they want to see and are prone to wishful thinking.

If you adopt the mannerisms, dress, speech patterns, and culture of a place, the people will be happy to assume you belong. Who says the shop floor or the boardroom is any different than a foreign culture? In each of them, you must learn the customs, the vocabulary, what is commonly done, and, as importantly, what is not done.

> *When a ruler occupies a state in an area that has a different language, different customs and different institutions, then things get tough.... Perhaps the most effective solution is for the ruler to go and live there himself.* — Machiavelli, The Prince

## Performance should look as if it comes naturally

Again, you do not need to be supremely talented to pull this off. Let's explore if you have what it takes. The world divides itself into three kinds of people as follows:

> *There are actually three kinds of mind: one kind grasps things unaided, the second sees what another has grasped, and the third grasps nothing and sees nothing.* — Machiavelli, The Prince

A person who grasps nothing and sees nothing can never be a leader. Even if they stumble into such a role, they will fail or be deposed almost immediately. But nor must a person be the rare genius who sees everything important by themselves. Such leaders can be powerful indeed, but if you don't count among their numbers you needn't despair.

It is merely required that you be able to quickly and accurately perceive your environment.

Can you see what is going on? Can you distinguish among conflicting suggestions which are good ideas and which are bad? And most importantly, among the good ideas, which ones have the best chances of being pragmatically implemented?

> *If someone is sharp enough to recognize what's right and wrong in what another man says and does, then even if he doesn't have the creativity to make policy himself, he can still see which of his minister's policies are positive and negative, encourage the goods ones and correct the bad.* — Machiavelli, The Prince

Coming up with brilliant insights is hard work. It requires deep expertise, long reflection, and worldly experience. Great ideas are also typically domain-specific. That is, your policy genius in one area may not be able to contribute much in other areas.

If you want to appear a naturally gifted leader, your skill lies more in surrounding yourself with the right people than it does in coming up with all the right ideas yourself.

> *A ruler isn't smart because he's getting proper advice; on the contrary, it's his good sense that makes the right advice possible.* — Machiavelli, The Prince

The more you have a cadre of great contributors around you, who each believe you to be supremely gifted, the easier it is to appear naturally talented to the entire organization.

And the best news is that you are tricking no one. The skills of being comfortable in any setting, of collecting good people to your side, and of identifying and selecting the best of their advice are exactly what makes for a natural leader.

## Your takeaway

James's advice in Thriving at Work was to use novelty to keep from burning out. He felt that a mix of routine and new work provides sufficient stimulation to keep you motivated and engaged.

Never mind that it is a weakness to believe you must be engaged to perform well. You need only deliver results. Your inner state is entirely irrelevant unless it hinders your performance. It hinders your performance if you reveal that you feel stress.

You will feel less stress when you remember that a variety of work provides a wonderful opportunity for you to display the breadth of your talent.

If you switch with ease from subject to subject, displaying confidence and mastery in all you do, then you will be considered a natural.

Until next time.

Work well and win.

## Chapter Fifteen

# How Managers Ensure Employees Obey Them

Do colleagues demonstrate that they'll put your (and thus the company's) priorities ahead of their own? Or do they indicate more selfish tendencies?

**Others shall obey your commands**

How do you get others to do as you wish? This is a problem that has plagued leaders since the beginning of time. In the Pragmatist's Rules for Work, we explore many answers that are facets to this vital question.

We can view today's topic through two lenses — what is the extent of your capabilities, and what are the characteristics and abilities of others?

When you want the organization to bend to your will, you should first assess how much power you possess to implement changes directly. Things that you can simply insist upon, you should always implement immediately.

Doing so will make you appear decisive and effective. This will help consolidate your power and expand the areas in which you can implement further priorities.

*Is the leader introducing the changes relying on his own resources, or does he depend on other people's support; that is, does he have to beg*

> *help to achieve his goals, or can he impose them. If he's begging help, he's bound to fail and will get nowhere.* — Machiavelli, The Prince

When you need others' help to implement your priorities, you are at risk. In such cases, the manner of your approach is key.

For one, your counterpart should never understand that you **need** their help. You may **want** it but let them know you will find other ways to accomplish your goals without them if necessary.

And it should be clear to them that their choice not to help you voluntarily will have consequences.

## What you want is what matters

Observing how colleagues react to your request for help is revealing. Pragmatically, there is the project itself that you wish to see executed. You cannot have selfish coworkers looking to their priorities if these compete with your own.

Moreover, you can also view the responses to your request for help as loyalty tests. Do colleagues demonstrate that they'll put your (and thus the company's) priorities ahead of their own? Or do they indicate more selfish tendencies?

> *There is one infallible way of checking a minister's credentials: when you see the man thinking more for himself than for you, when his policies are all designed to enhance his own interests, then he'll never make a good minister and you'll never be able to trust him. A minister running a state must never think of himself, only of the ruler, and should concentrate exclusively on the ruler's business.* — Machiavelli, The Prince

No matter how much it appears a person is positioned to help you, do not make yourself dependent upon their assistance when you sense their motives are mixed. Otherwise, you become an agent of their success. Better to root out mixed loyalties and make an example than to let such behavior grow.

## Your takeaway

James's advice in Thriving at Work was to know when to obey others and when to stifle independent judgment in favor of implementing the business decision.

Knowing how few individuals know their own minds, it is risky to ever let others' judgment take precedence over your own. Thus, you must have complete confidence in the validity of your views and your priorities.

If you've done your job correctly, management's judgment will be exactly aligned with your own. Then it is perfectly appropriate to ensure the organization obeys your (and their) wishes.

Until next time.

Work well and win.

## Chapter Sixteen

# Anyone Can Acquiesce but You Can Punch Above Your Weight

You must strive in your habits and performance to exceed your abilities. Punch above your weight, wherever that happens to be at this moment

**Punch above your weight**

I do not need to tell you that the world is hierarchical. The corridors of business are as ruthless as the floor of any jungle, in the sense that apex predators are looking to maintain their position among the constant threat of challenge from usurpers.

Your natural abilities merely determine your starting point. They are no guarantee of a good outcome, and in most cases, no hindrance that will prevent you from achieving all that you want.

What makes the distinction is how hard you are willing to work and the steps you are willing to take in pursuit of your goals.

There is an inventor and businessman I've been talking with who seems to perfectly embody what I mean. Thomas Edison demonstrated the determination that is necessary to win, first with his relentless hard work.

> *Our greatest weakness lies in giving up. The most certain way to succeed is always to try just one more time.* — Thomas A. Edison

Mr. Edison told me about another businessman he's been observing who shows a similar understanding. This gentleman has not yet joined us, but we expect him any day now.

> *Motivation will almost always beat mere talent.* — Norman Ralph Augustine

Mr. Augustine has it right. Talent is nice to have, but talent without motivation is useless. Whereas motivation with only average talent will take you far.

The point of all this is to say you must strive in your habits and in your performance to exceed your abilities. Punch above your weight, wherever that happens to be at this moment.

## Punch others while they are down

A corollary that Mr. Edison knew well is that your success hinges on more than your effort. It also depends on the relative performance of others.

When you have rivals willing to work as hard as you and who are as talented as you, you need alternative approaches. Your choices are to co-opt them to your side or to see that they are removed from direct contention.

> *In general you must either pamper people or destroy them; harm them just a little and they'll hit back; harm them seriously and they won't be able to. So if you're going to do people harm, make sure you needn't worry about their reaction.* — Machiavelli, The Prince

It is preferable to bring hardworking and skilled people onto your team. It is a waste to squander their abilities.

If, however, a person has set their aim at cross-purposes to your own and you cannot win them over, you have no choice but to ensure they do not outcompete you.

The way to do this is to be alert to the inevitable setbacks that occur in every business, to every person, in every project. You cannot predict when they will occur but you can be sure setbacks will occur.

Then, you must be ready to pounce.

Trumpet the failure as a personal failing. The problem is obvious in hindsight because most problems are. Say that you would have recognized it in advance, as any good manager would.

Cause the person to doubt themselves, while also giving management reason to doubt them.

Especially with a high performer, you need to hit them when they are momentarily off balance to ensure the harm from their misstep is lasting.

## Your takeaway

James's advice in Thriving at Work was to know when to pray that things will work out right. We should hope that luck will find us when seeking to advance.

It seems foolishly optimistic to trust that everything will turn out fine or that luck will find us. Especially since there are ways to direct luck in our favor.

The way to do this is not to trust in anything but your abilities. Thus, you will appear far more competent than you are at any given point, even as you're growing.

You will also make sure to keep the competition down by hitting them when they're down.

Until next time.

Work well and win.

## Chapter Seventeen

# Quick and Wrong Is Better Than Slow and Obsolete

## Indecisiveness is fatal to a leader. You would rather act quickly and be wrong than hesitate

**Quick to anger, quick to decide, quick to act**

You are not looking to be mercurial, although a certain reputation for unpredictability gives opponents pause.

Giving free rein to your anger is powerful because most people will not. People will be far less likely to cause you offense if they know you will fly off the handle at the slightest provocation. Thus, be quick to anger.

Similarly, in decision-making, the attitude you must cultivate is that of being quick. Indecisiveness is fatal to a leader. You would rather act quickly and be wrong than hesitate.

> *My opinion on the matter is this: it's better to be impulsive than cautious.* — Machiavelli, The Prince

The point is that between delay and action, err always on the side of movement. Being impulsive does not mean ill-considered, however. Your actions are still guided by your overall goals and the specific circumstances.

You must have the courage to act in the face of uncertainty. It is true that you could make better decisions with more information. Stopping to gather that information takes time and introduces risk.

We are not uncultured here. Just recently, I exchanged words with a poet of some renown, who had this to say.

> *To begin, begin.* — William Wordsworth

How correct Mr. Wordsworth is. Every great outcome requires action to initiate it. And how many of them are perfectly conceived at their inception? You can correct course once you've begun, but only if you've actually started.

Thus, after making quick decisions, be quick to implement your decisions with expedient action.

## Only fools pause to ask permission

Another pragmatist whose company I greatly enjoy is an American who embodies my philosophies better than most.

> *Well done is better than well said.* — Benjamin Franklin

Mr. Franklin doled out advice in great quantities, and most of it was excellent advice. In his own life, he put his actions at the forefront. He was always about the doing of things.

We cannot control external events. But we can take advantage of the circumstances we find ourselves in, positive or negative.

Many people think bad luck ruins a leader's chances. In fact, overcoming adversity and long odds have made many a leader's reputation.

> *Fortune varies but men go on regardless. When their approach suits the times they're successful, and when it doesn't they're not.* — Machiavelli, The Prince

If you wait until circumstances are perfect before acting, you will miss some of your greatest opportunities. Above all, act. Take control of your life by actively directing it. You will make mistakes, but you were acting like a leader.

People remember those who are visionary, even if they are wrong in a few details. No one remembers the wallflowers who are waiting for more data.

## Luxuriate in others' recklessness

There is a time when you should be the very face of patience, and that is when your opponents are committing self-harm.

When you see them making rash decisions, or when trouble is brewing unseen on their project, by all means, let ill deeds marinate.

The reasons to do so are twofold. First, no one thanks you for pointing out their mistakes, even if this allows them to correct course and improve. And second, the sweetest victory is the one you don't have to fight for.

When your opponent is harming themselves, never interfere.

## Your takeaway

James's advice in Thriving at Work was to find quiet in our workdays. This allows time for strategic thinking and high-priority work while allowing us to control our emotions.

I agree your best work is conceived in solitude and carried out without feeling emotion. You may display emotion as it suits your purpose, but always with control.

Be careful not to let the need for quiet deliberation delay you overlong in making decisions. A leader takes quick, decisive action. In this way, the field of battle is as you've defined it, not others.

Until next time.

Work well and win.

## Chapter Eighteen

# Random Events Only Hurt the Unprepared

## A wise person knows that impermanence is the default in life. They are accordingly alert to where change is imminent in their surroundings

**Random means don't be predictable**

If you do what everyone around you does, you should expect to see results similar to theirs. That is, mediocre, average at best.

Contrast this with the unpredictable actions of the stars. They drop out of school against everyone's urging. They pursue business ventures at which others have tried and failed. They ignore conventional wisdom and forge new paths.

What they have in common is they follow paths to success only they can see, which means they walk these roads alone.

> *All men want glory and wealth, but they set out to achieve these goals in different ways. Some are cautious, others impulsive; some use violence, others finesse; some are patient, others quite the opposite. And all these different approaches can be successful.* — Machiavelli, The Prince

Because it was not the path but the person, those who come later seeking to emulate a winner's success inevitably fail. They note a person overcame hardship in their upbringing. This does not mean that they should rejoice in their dysfunctional family.

It was the person seeing a path only they could see that made the difference. Make sure that no one else can see the path you see, and you stand the best chance of keeping the path to yourself.

## Make sure to profit from the randomness around you

If you are alert for the signs of it, you will see that we are surrounded by disruption. Some parts of the culture are always dying. Other trends fill the gaps thus created.

A few businesses present as bulwarks against challenge and change. They are rare. Most companies are staving off decay, one innovation away from being overtaken by a keen competitor.

The same is true in our lives. A person may appear to be thriving. What do we know of their inner demons and their addictions? What accident lurks just around the next bend, as sure to end their storied careers as the unseen assassin?

> *Upheaval ... always leaves the scaffolding for building further changes.* — Machiavelli, The Prince

A wise person knows that impermanence is the default in life. They are accordingly alert to where change is imminent in their surroundings.

Change presents so many opportunities! A rival falls. A vacancy opens. A treasured prize is left momentarily unattended. It is soon in your hands.

A person who fears the losses that come with change misses spotting the upside. There is always an upside. Even if you lose something, can you not profit elsewhere? Might you shape the loss to cause harm to an enemy? Can you use it to gain sympathy that you leverage into power?

## Your takeaway

James's advice in Thriving at Work was to obtain enough rest to drive peak performance. He says it is the breaks that make us stronger rather than relentlessly pushing ourselves.

While he is not wrong, James's advice is dangerous. Far too many push themselves far too little and so never learn how much they can do. It is only by coming right to the brink of collapse that you not only see what you're capable of but extend your limits.

Think of it this way. Your success is affected by random events, but your effort is not one of them. You control how hard you work, and that is one of the keys to your success.

Until next time.

Work well and win.

# Chapter Nineteen

# Your Sense of Shame Is Holding You Back

Your colleagues would undermine you without hesitation, and indeed without thought. Why would you worry about what they think?

**You must not feel shame**

On your path to being a successful leader, you are subject to the whims of management above you and employees below you. You can never count on these constituents to view you or your actions rationally or fairly, because they are made up of fallible humans.

> *You can be hated just as much for the good you do as the bad, which is why, as I said before, a ruler who wants to stay in power is often forced not to be good.* — Machiavelli, The Prince

Thus, you cannot worry about what others think about you or your actions. Your focus must be entirely directed on the outcomes you seek. Your colleagues would undermine you without hesitation, and indeed without thought. Why would you worry about what they think?

> *A sensible leader cannot and must not keep his word if by doing so he puts himself at risk... If all men were good, this would be bad advice, but since they are a sad lot and won't be keeping their promises to you, you hardly need to keep yours to them. Anyway, a ruler will never be short of good reasons to explain away a broken promise.* — Machiavelli, The Prince

Once you are in a position of power, others' opinions are more easily managed. People will want to believe your intentions are good, and so you will be able to justify unpleasantries along the way.

> *The crowd is won over by appearance and final results. And the world is all crowd: the dissenting few find no space as long as the majority have any grounds at all for their opinions.* — Machiavelli, The Prince

## Guilt people into helping you

You will have two levers with which to get people to work towards your purposes. You must use both, recognizing which persons are amenable to which lever.

The first type of person will help you without much pressure. The reasons for compliance are manifold, for example, because it's their nature to be helpful, they don't want to make waves, they see your interests are aligned with the company's, or they see self-interest in helping you, etc.

In each case, your task is to take liberal advantage of the person's character while reinforcing their belief in the valid reasons for helping you.

The second type of person will not help you, at least initially. They may in fact try to stymie your progress, either in favor of their own candidacy or another whom they support.

Assuming you win the day, your erstwhile opponents deserve special attention because they can become your most effective advocates. This requires that you publicly call out and shame their prior bad behavior. They should feel the weight of their colleagues' approbation and fear the consequences of their and your reprisal.

> *A ruler can very easily win over men who opposed him when he came to power... They'll be forced to behave more loyally than others in that they know they have to work to offset the negative impression the ruler initially had of them. So a ruler can always get more out of such men than out of people who feel safe in his service and don't really make an effort.* — Machiavelli, The Prince

Having taken a gamble in opposing you and lost, their fear and shame make them more manipulable than the good corporate citizens whose loyalty was never in doubt.

## Your takeaway

James's advice in Thriving at Work was to manage stress both in work and outside work to enable sustainable performance. He says that while some stress is helpful, most of us have unhealthy levels of stress.

It is true that too much stress can be unhealthy, but James is misguided when he says that taking breaks and resting is the key to managing stress. A better way is to avoid putting yourself in situations where stress builds up.

Your stress is a result of taking on more work than you can handle, taking responsibility for things that are not your fault, and letting others' actions affect your progress. By focusing on the root causes rather than the symptoms, you will avoid feeling stress in the first instance.

Until next time.

Work well and win.

# Chapter Twenty

# Terror Is a Tool Some Managers Use Well

## While it is much harder to learn from others' experiences, swift and serious punishment sends a signal that penetrates the average employee's indifference

### Terror: It's much safer to be feared than loved

This one of my lessons seems to be the most widely known, or at least the most quoted. I wonder how many know the true meaning, however. You do not cultivate love or fear out of regard for the individuals you interact with, but for the impact these emotions have on your effectiveness.

It is true that people will be less worried about disappointing leaders who cultivate love. The team's performance is just one factor. The more salient reason not to base your action on people's regard for you is that you hamper your own ability to make tough decisions. Tough decisions are an inevitable part of leadership.

Because life is tough, and businesses will be in tough situations, leaders need to make difficult decisions. Every employee should fear the consequences, not of their leader, but of the situation.

A leader will be associated with the decisions they make, even if the situation is not of their making. Hence comes the fear of the leader themselves.

> *Men are less worried about letting down someone who has made himself loved than someone who makes himself feared.* — Machiavelli, The Prince

As between seeking to have employees love or fear you, you should always fall on the side that allows you to make necessary decisions without bias. If that creates fear, so be it.

## Punishment serves a specific purpose

There is a time when a leader seeks to generate fear, and that's when employees have frustrated the leader's plans or themselves created a difficult situation.

We learn best what we experience directly. Thus, in such cases, the leader must express their displeasure clearly and immediately. While it is much harder to learn from others' experiences, swift and serious punishment sends a signal that penetrates the average employee's indifference.

> *Fear means fear of punishment, and that's something people never forget.* — Machiavelli, The Prince

So long as the punishment is meted out directly in response to a wrong act, people will accept that it is harsh. Especially if they are not the recipients.

For their part, the recipient must understand that the punishment is deserved but has an origin (of their making) and an end (of the leader's choosing).

In this way, mistakes and their aftermath serve as valuable teaching moments that reinforce important lessons. What we do is serious, and mistakes have consequences. Pay attention to what you are doing and exercise care.

## Your takeaway

James's advice in Thriving at Work was to take advantage of the many benefits that accrue to you when you are a team player. Interestingly, James spends a lot of time talking about how to work with dysfunctional teams.

A team that is firmly in hand, one that lives in fear of consequences should they fail to perform, can greatly magnify one's power.

So too, it can propel your career to latch onto a team that is close to the levers of power because of the people who comprise it, the tasks they perform, or both.

The one thing you never want to be is a team member who doesn't know exactly what's in it for them.

Until next time.

Work well and win.

# Chapter Twenty-One

# How To Respond to an Ultimatum ... and Give One

## People will second-guess and criticize your decisions no matter what they are. The sensible choice is to listen only to your own counsel

**Achieving your outcome is all that matters**

People do not perceive the world clearly or objectively. They come with prior experiences and differing information, which together form preconceived notions and biases.

As a result, people judge situations more based on their foibles than they do the situations themselves. Further, because people differ widely in their experiences, you can scarcely expect unanimity of opinion about any topic.

If you attempt to please one group by pandering to one of their cherished beliefs, you may or may not succeed. For all their imperfect reasoning, people are adept at sniffing out insincerity.

Even if you please the group you targeted, you will create enemies among those who see the world differently. You may never hear of their discontent, but their resentment is real and will find ways to manifest at inopportune times.

Thus, a leader serves best when they focus exclusively on their priorities, and not what anyone potentially thinks about those priorities.

> *[A leader] mustn't be concerned about the bad reputation that comes with those negative qualities that are almost essential if he is to hold on to power. If you think about it, there'll always be something that looks morally right but would actually lead a ruler to disaster, and something else that looks wrong but will bring security and success.* — Machiavelli, The Prince

People will second-guess and criticize your decisions no matter what they are. The sensible choice is to develop a keen sense of what to do and why and listen only to your own counsel.

## Following someone else's imperative cedes victory without a fight

I look at the Corporate Social Responsibility (CSR) and Environmental, Social, and Governance (ESG) movements and see master manipulators at work. With nothing more than high-minded words, these opportunists have inserted themselves into an established tradition of ownership and control.

Shareholders own the company. Shareholders elect directors who in turn appoint officers. This system is a model of simplicity, accountability, and direct action.

Come now the CSR and ESG activists. Some may be shareholders, which at least gives them a seat at the table to raise issues to be heard and evaluated along with all others.

Many do not even bother with the fiction of becoming part-owners. They claim authority from a higher power, that of morality or, heaven-forbid, fairness.

Never mind that it is the peak of unfairness and immorality for a "stakeholder" in nothing more than the name to demand their priorities be given precedence over those of other stakeholders or the actual owners.

Show me a leader who pays heed to such extortionists, and I will show you someone who does not know that saboteurs come in many guises. The greatest harm is done by those professing to want only good but are spending someone else's money to achieve it.

A wise leader will listen to these foes while giving every appearance of taking their concerns seriously. The goal is to understand and neutralize them, and this requires making them feel heard.

Agree with their principles all day, so long as you need change none of your existing priorities. Make flowery statements and publish glowing reports, but stay focused on the business.

To do otherwise is to give up your leadership role without a fight.

## Your takeaway

James's advice in Thriving at Work was to understand the utility in your actions or the value behind everything you do. James is correct that it is necessary to regularly demonstrate your worth.

He says that you demonstrate your worth by advancing your strategy and your company's strategy. Where he goes off the rails is in suggesting that it's ever a good investment of your time to help a colleague.

I suppose you help a colleague in aiding their perception that the best use of their time is helping you. Short of this, the best way to demonstrate your worth is by making sure you deliver on your ultimatums.

Until next time.

Work well and win.

Chapter Twenty-Two

# Knowing Which Role Models To Venerate Is Key

What actions do great leaders take? Not what they said after the fact, or even at the time, for manipulation and justification are always lurking when we describe our actions

**Pick role models who exemplify success**

We are spoiled for choice when it comes to leaders to study and emulate. It used to be that we had to troll through centuries of history to tease out applicable lessons from situations of varying relevance.

Not so today. From the case studies of the Harvard Business School to the pages of the Wall Street Journal, countless business wars are fought, won, and lost every day.

We needn't wait for the judgment of history to tell us which party emerged victorious. Stock markets rise and fall, while companies grow or stagnate and languish.

> *If you're sensible, you set out to follow a trail blazed by someone who was truly great, someone really worth imitating, so that even if you're not on the same level yourself at least you'll reflect a little of his brilliance.* — Machiavelli, The Prince

From this rich pool of exemplars, we must pick our role models. Here are two things that you can safely ignore: Complaints of coworkers who felt mistreated on a leader's rise to glory, and actions a person takes after they leave their positions.

Remember what I've said previously about people's perceptions: They're inconsistent and inaccurate. So a boss has a reputation for being harsh, mercurial, or even mean. What of it? Did they deliver results? That's a far more meaningful metric if you're trying to decide whose style to mine for lessons.

Take now the leader turned philanthropist, politician, or pundit upon leaving their business post. You may safely ignore everything this person says and does.

Even if they are giving you a first-hand account of their business days, you are foolish to listen. They likely do not know, and would less likely admit if they did, all the factors that gave rise to their performance. What they do tell will be cherry-picked and sanitized in service of presenting the image they wish to present.

That does not mean these leaders are useless to you as role models. Far from it. It's just that you must take your lessons from another source.

## Study what those leaders did, not what they said

Your source of truly valuable lessons comes in this: What actions did great leaders take? Not what they said after the fact, or even at the time, for manipulation and justification are always lurking when we describe our actions.

No, simply this — what did they do in what circumstances?

> Take as model a leader who's been much praised and admired and keep his example and achievements in mind at all times. — Machiavelli, The Prince

You may read their biographies and hagiographies to get details of scenes and places. The salient facts making up the business case, as it were. Then apply your efforts to uncovering the key decisions that turned the tide. There will usually be just a handful of pivotal moments.

If you can learn to spot these deciding factors, you will be in a position to study what makes a few leaders great and what makes many fail. You will find that great leaders appear unconventional because they have unusually strong faith in their vision.

They let no one dissuade them from their belief, and let no mere obstacle deter them from their path. Others' doubts, public opinion, unlikely odds — these are all things standing in the way of average leaders.

Great leaders take decisive action in the face of uncountable obstacles and prevail.

## Your takeaway

James's advice in Thriving at Work was to think about values in the context of work, specifically to understand how your company's values and your personal values align.

James is correct that trouble ensues when there is a mismatch between the two. Rather than selecting only companies whose values line up with your own, you can take a more direct albeit difficult approach. That is to shape your company's values to be consistent with your own.

For their part, employees regularly put pressure on companies to adopt or espouse values that may have little to do with business success. Your imposition of values will be more pragmatic, aimed at ensuring the company's success and hence your success.

Seen this way, the most exemplary leaders are those who have a core value system that is so strong they bend their organizations to conform to it.

Until next time.

Work well and win.

# Chapter Twenty-Three

# Spotting Weakness Allows You To Exploit It

## Done correctly, pointing out a putative weakness removes a competitor from contention while allowing you to gain their trust and loyalty

**Everyone has weaknesses. Find and exploit them**

Weaknesses come in many forms. You will regularly encounter performance-related weaknesses, where a person lacks relevant skills or experience or is unable to bring their talents to bear as needed.

You will see others who lack the stamina to persevere when others carry on, or whose desire for comfort calls them to avoid the discomfort attendant to great deeds.

Still others who have the requisite skills and stamina flame out because they simply cannot control their emotions. They never learn that emotions may be felt and expressed, but never ungoverned, always in the service of the primary objective.

Whenever weaknesses such as these slow the progress of once high-performers, negative consequences often follow. Envy of the remaining high-flyers is the least of it. Someone who sees greatness pass them by often finds themselves entertaining dark thoughts indeed.

> *It is fear or hatred that makes men attack each other.* — Machiavelli, The Prince

On your upward path, you must navigate these emotions with care. The first task is to simply be alert to identifying your colleagues' weaknesses before they've become derailed by them. This puts you in a position to work with and exploit the situation.

Exploiting a weakness does not mean causing harm to a co-worker. Often, you can keep them from derailing their career by pursuing paths they're unsuited for.

For example, a person who is a solid performer but doesn't have the stomach for 80-hour weeks will either take a run at leadership and burn out, or they'll be realistic about their odds and will be persuaded into a productive, but less senior role.

You can be the one to help them see how to be both valued and happy. There is no shame in this, only mutual advantage. Done correctly, pointing out a putative weakness removes a competitor from contention while allowing you to gain their trust and loyalty.

Some weaknesses are more debilitating than others. A person who isn't up to the task is in the wrong role. Short of that, you may be able to compensate for a person's weakness, for example by pairing them with someone who complements their gaps.

Your task is to be a careful observer of those around you to identify the ways in which their weaknesses will hamper them (and indirectly you). Some you can save, and others you can move, but you must know everyone's weakness.

This holds true for your weaknesses as well.

## Be aware of your weaknesses

What? Did you think you uniquely were the only person to have no weaknesses? This is a dangerous delusion. You need not dwell overlong on the fact that you are imperfect, simply accept that you are and know your flaws in detail.

# SPOTTING WEAKNESS ALLOWS YOU TO EXPLOIT IT

Once you know your flaws, you can be your own best advocate in a similar manner to how you assist your colleagues in working with their weaknesses. In the case of your failings, your task is to make sure that none prevent your further ascent.

Can you obtain further training and needed experience? Can you surround yourself with colleagues who make you strong where you're weak by inclination?

You will often have to rely on others to help you achieve your objectives. In such cases, you must be alert to whether they may act independently to thwart your aims.

> *If he's ruling by proxy [a leader will] be weaker and exposed to greater risks, since he now depends entirely on the good will of the men appointed as magistrates and they can very easily strip him of his power, particularly when times are hard, either by attacking him directly or by just not carrying out his orders.* — Machiavelli, The Prince

You can insulate yourself from attacks by those closest to you and who are aware of a key weakness. You do this by making their fortune and future intimately tied to your own. If you rise, they rise. And if you fail, they will go down with you.

## Your takeaway

James's advice in Thriving at Work was to think about your worth to your company, others, and yourself.

I support James' idea that our worth to our companies and colleagues is typically higher than we first estimate. He then cautions against being too critical about ourselves, fine, or valuing ourselves too highly.

I trust it's clear you cannot value yourself too highly. Anything less than the absolute best interpretation leaves room for others to doubt you and for you to doubt yourself. That only admits a weakness, which has a way of becoming self-fulfilling.

Your worth is a function of excising and minimizing weaknesses, and compensating for those that remain. Having made this a practice, why wouldn't you double down on the idea that you are invaluable?

Until next time.

Work well and win.

# Chapter Twenty-Four

# When Xenophobia Works to Your Advantage

## One simple tool is to stoke people's fears of change. The key is to associate bad change with unreliable leaders, and necessary change with visionary ones

**Fear of foreign and different things is natural**

We think of xenophobia as relating to foreign people, but it is broader than that. You can think of it this way. Any time you are seeking to introduce a change, people will resist you.

It does not matter that your new system is demonstrably superior. It does not matter that the new leader is an upgrade. All that matters is that there is a change because people inherently resist change.

You are thus at your most vulnerable when you are introducing changes. You will encounter resistance even from people who would normally support you. You will face determined action from those who are disadvantaged.

> *Nothing is harder to organize, more likely to fail, or more dangerous to see through, than the introduction of a new system of government. The person bringing in the changes will make enemies of everyone who was doing well under the old system, while the people who stand to gain from the new arrangements will not offer wholehearted*

> *support, partly because they are afraid of their opponents, who still have the laws on their side.* — Machiavelli, The Prince

This is when all your work in building loyalty that cannot be easily withheld pays off. Because when facing significant change, there is nothing for it but to see things through, to persevere.

## Properly applied, xenophobia does your work for you

Your success is partly a matter of your efforts and the efforts of those who work on your behalf. It's easy to underestimate how critical it is to understand the efforts of third parties who are working towards their aims, not yours.

They may not be direct rivals, but their project competes with yours for time and attention. Thus, your success may hinge on their project being sidelined. One simple tool is to stoke people's fears of change. When you are seeking to derail a competing project, this fear takes root most easily and with devastating effect.

> *People are naturally skeptical: no one really believes in change until they've had solid experience of it.* — Machiavelli, The Prince

You need to apply the right type of brake at the right time. Raise specific doubts about the rival's project, not about change in general. This is because a short time later, you will be asking your organization to change for your project.

> *Two men can both be cautious but with different results: one is successful and the other fails.... This depends entirely on whether their approach suits the circumstances.... This explains why people's fortunes go up and down.* — Machiavelli, The Prince

The key is to associate bad change with unreliable leaders, and necessary change with visionary ones.

## Xenophobia can just as quickly derail you

The same factors that allow you to derail a rival's project make your projects vulnerable to manipulation.

Because you cannot prevent either the attempt or the circumstances in which the sabotage will play out, you must focus on your response. You must be willing to change your approach at a moment's notice.

It does not matter if your project succeeds as originally foreseen, only that you prevail in some fashion.

> *If a person has always been successful with a particular approach, he won't easily be persuaded to drop it.... If he did change his personality in line with times and circumstances, his luck would hold steady.* — Machiavelli, The Prince

Your being flexible in the face of obstacles does not make you indecisive. On the contrary. A true leader recognizes when the winds have shifted and a new approach is required.

## Your takeaway

James's advice in Thriving at Work was that learning how to do things for yourself like making a Xerox was the key to bigger workplace success.

With Xerox, James meant everything that consists of administrative work. I agree that fortunes rise and fall on the smallest of details, and hence administrative work must be done properly. But I disagree with James that you must do it yourself.

If you want people to think of you as a leader, then you must accomplish two seemingly inconsistent tasks.

- First, appear in all non-substantive things to be utterly helpless, from knowing where coffee comes from to where the lights or air conditioning controls are.

- Second, effortlessly expect that all administrative tasks will be handled by someone around you.

Unless you are alone, in which case your stance on administrative tasks is irrelevant, there is someone around you. Make sure it is them, not you, that jumps to doing little tasks and you will be seen as a leader.

Until next time.

Work well and win.

Chapter Twenty-Five

# Take Advantage of Youth, No Matter Your Age

## You will have some experienced, old hands. They represent your greatest danger

**The young are naïve and manipulable**

If there's anything that characterizes young people, it's their lack of interest in history and myopic focus on what's in front of them. This makes them uniquely open to manipulation.

> *Men are more interested in the present than the past and when things are going well they'll be happy and won't look elsewhere.*
> — Machiavelli, The Prince

If it is well-being that engenders unthinking obedience, problems create frustration. In some number of people, problems will get them looking for reasons and solutions. You must ensure that your decisions and actions are never seen as the cause of your team's problems.

**Young people make the best ideological zealots**

It is easy to frame your team as a bastion of sanity against an uncaring and even adversarial business world. The business would run amok given half a chance, and only the hyper-vigilance of your team stands between shame and success.

Not only that but the leader (you) is investing great personal effort and taking great risks to make sure that the business counterparts understand the stakes and comply.

When you frame the team's work this way, the combination of your efforts and that of your team is like a holy war that requires eternal vigilance. Success is never final, and failure lurks behind each new initiative.

> *If he's sensible the ruler must work out a situation where his citizens will always need both his government and him, however well or badly things are going. Then they will always be loyal.* — Machiavelli, The Prince

When your team trusts you and mistrusts everyone else, you have them in a position where they will carry out your wishes with great fervor.

## You want young people on your side

It's unlikely all the employees on your team will be impressionably young. You will have some experienced, old hands. They represent your greatest danger.

They may resent having been passed over and be waiting for a chance to challenge you. And they have seen enough to think independently and challenge your propaganda.

You turn such persons to your advantage by making public examples of them. If they question your message or do not faithfully implement your wishes, you must respond immediately and harshly. A reprimand, a demotion, even a termination. Everyone should see and fear your wrath.

You might fear this would have the team turn against you. Provided you keep your retribution focused and brief, and also lavish rewards and appreciation on those who remain, you will have achieved loyalty that takes years to build organically.

> *When people are treated well by someone they thought was hostile they respond with even greater loyalty.* — Machiavelli, The Prince

Clearing out the older, less easily manipulable team members has several benefits. You eliminate challengers, you free up the budget to hire more young colleagues, and you open up room for internal promotions.

## In summary

James's advice in Thriving at Work was that the word Yes is the most important determinant of success at work and in life. He cautions against ever saying No unless the conduct is improper.

One of the greatest myths I've come across is that managers should never say no.

I say this handicaps you from one of the leader's most important tools. Saying no allows you to disrupt or slow down a rival's progress, show displeasure (and indirectly, favor), and ultimately wield power.

Until next time.

Work well and win.

Chapter Twenty-Six

# Who Wouldn't Want To Be a Zillionaire?

## The only kind of recognition that is objectively measurable and comparable is compensation. Don't let anyone tell you differently

**Money motivates everyone**

When you have control of a budget, your goal is to spend it wisely. Wisely means first and foremost that you achieve your objectives. Achieving business objectives is usually conducive to your success but is secondary.

One way to help speed your way is to ensure that people in your orbit are handsomely rewarded.

Never scrimp on salaries for your team. Fight to have them be the best paid in the company and across the industry. Whose money are you saving? Shareholders? What have they ever done for you?

> *When the money is his own or his subjects', [the leader] should go easy; when it's someone else's, he should be as lavish as he can.... Spending other people's money doesn't lower your standing, it raises it.* — Machiavelli, The Prince

You will notice your executives having management meetings as often as needed and that they treat themselves well when they meet. There are lessons there for you.

You must treat yourself and your team as befitting the best performers. Do you save a few bucks and alienate your superstars? That is the most foolish kind of penny-pinching. So too your approach to setting expectations for how you and your team should be paid.

Your company should understand that higher pay leads to better performance. This is demonstrably true for lawyers because companies with longer-tenured and hence higher-paid lawyers experience lower total legal costs.

The lower total legal costs presumably come from astute risk management, knowing the business better, and efficient work. But the point to hammer home with the CFO is that it is bad business to lose a lawyer, and hence risky to underpay them.

Nowhere is this truer than for the leader of the team.

## Loyalty is another word for sucker

A key lesson about loyalty is that it's something other people have. When your leader is talking about loyalty, it means they're not giving you something you need and deserve, whether resources, support on a project, or pay and promotions.

Seen correctly, loyalty is to be recognized and handsomely rewarded. A leader can trust most the loyalty of the people whose interests are clearly aligned with his own. As in, when their well-being is linked with the leader's well-being.

In contrast, when you are asked to sacrifice for the sake of the company as a whole, for shareholders, or for some other broad group, you can be assured that you are sacrificing for someone else's bonus.

In cases where taking a shared hit is unavoidable, the astute leader will tap pockets of the existing budget to reallocate resources appropriately. You and the team must never suffer for the company's failings.

## Performance and money go hand-in-hand

The leader's role is to ensure that their performance and the performance of their allies are well compensated.

Take a thank you and a trophy with humility and grace, but make sure that real performance is backed up by real rewards.

The only kind of recognition that is objectively measurable and comparable is compensation. Don't let anyone tell you differently.

## In summary

James's advice in Thriving at Work was that having a Zen-like attitude will bring you both satisfaction and success in work. He notes the benefits of paying careful attention to your thoughts and feelings.

I fully agree that a leader must be keenly attuned to their thoughts and emotions. This allows one to amplify or suppress emotions tactically as the situation warrants.

I say the reward for such control is not peace of mind, but security in an otherwise precarious position of power. It is only by staying in a leadership position that you obtain the full value of the attendant rewards.

This brings my series on the Pragmatist's Rules for Work to an end. I trust you have learned something about how the world works and how you can successfully make your way in it.

I recommend you revisit the series whenever you need inspiration in a tough work situation. We'll be watching and rooting for you.

Work well and win.

# Work Hard and Get Ahead

Career Paths Vol. 3: 31 Tips on How To Excel at Work

James Bellerjeau

A Fine Idea

Copyright © 2025 by James Bellerjeau

All rights reserved.

No portion of this book may be reproduced in any form without written permission from the publisher or author, except as permitted by U.S. copyright law.

An earlier version of several of these articles was previously published in the ACC Docket (https://docket.acc.com/). Copyright © 2023, Association of Corporate Counsel. Reprinted with permission. All rights reserved. Visit www.acc.com.

# Contents

| | |
|---|---|
| Introduction | 225 |
| 1. The Back-Door Path to Success | 227 |
| 2. Can You Succeed at Work Without Working Hard? | 231 |
| 3. Hard Work Doesn't Make You a Hero | 235 |
| 4. Use Pragmatic Risk Management Principles to Manage Your Career | 239 |
| 5. Don't Work From Home Yourself Out of a Job | 243 |
| 6. How To Implement a Project With Lackluster Management Support | 247 |
| 7. With Experience Comes … Patience | 253 |
| 8. Do You Know Your Gear Ratio? | 257 |
| 9. Can You Be Too Good at Your Job? | 261 |
| 10. What Would You Do With 1000 Hours? | 265 |
| 11. Your Attitude Is the Best Predictor of Success | 269 |
| 12. Share Your Secret Plans | 273 |
| 13. If You Want To Get Ahead, Go Back to the Office | 277 |
| 14. Are You Globally Competitive in Your Career? | 281 |
| 15. It's TIME WE JOG | 287 |
| 16. These Things May Be Hurting Your Career | 291 |

| | | |
|---|---|---|
| 17. | What I Learned from Judging and Being Judged | 297 |
| 18. | What Makes You Really Stand Out | 301 |
| 19. | Who's Running the Show of Your Life? | 305 |
| 20. | Sit Down and Stay Awhile* | 309 |
| 21. | The Worst Career Advice I've Seen in Ages | 313 |
| 22. | You Can't Buy Accountability | 317 |
| 23. | Sweet CEO Lies: "Employees Are Our Most Valuable Asset" | 321 |
| 24. | How To Manipulate CEOs | 325 |
| 25. | Maybe Attaining Work-Life Balance Isn't the Best Goal for You | 329 |
| 26. | This 3-Step Method Can Help You Build Resilience | 333 |
| 27. | Most Advice Fails One of These Two Tests | 339 |
| 28. | How to Measure Your Impact on the World | 343 |
| 29. | Do You Overweight the Present at the Cost of the Future? | 349 |
| 30. | How to Use Metrics Wisely, Instead of Letting Them Manipulate You | 353 |
| 31. | My Utterly Romantic Idea of Work | 357 |

# Introduction

Greetings readers and congratulations! Simply by virtue of being here, you are already on the path to increasing your odds of success.

There is nothing worse than putting in the work and failing to progress in one's career. Here we explore the reasons why some types of hard work pay off, while others leave you tired but no further.

We will also examine alternative paths to the top, relying on tactics and pragmatism more than simply putting in the hours. Although we face similar challenges in the workplace, we each have different abilities, and knowing how to leverage our particular strengths is useful.

In a perfect world, everyone would find a place that suits them well. They would have well-meaning colleagues and understanding bosses. In the real world, where we all spend our days, we have to deal with competitive colleagues and clueless bosses. That's no obstacle for the savvy employee, prepared by the lessons contained here.

You will find additional approaches to succeeding at work in the companion volumes **Thriving at Work** and **The Pragmatist's Rules for Work**.

Success at work is not necessarily the same as how to live a good life or achieve satisfaction. If you want to explore these topics more deeply, I recommend you spend some time with the **Pragmatic Wisdom** series.

Be well.

Chapter One

# The Back-Door Path to Success

## You don't need to take outsized risks to get outsized results. It's better to be unassuming but unstoppable

We are impressed by outsized results. It is not surprising that we are captivated by surprising events:

- The school dropout who starts an internet company and becomes a billionaire
- The trader who comes out the winner on a gigantic bet
- The video that goes viral on its way to 100 million views

Because we are so frequently confronted with such examples, we are at great risk of overestimating their likelihood.

What we see represents the tiniest fraction, the results of billions of experiments and attempts. From 100 million tweets, a handful will capture the public's roving eye. Most fall quietly, unremarked.

Multitudes pass by unnoticed, while the few successes grab all our rapt attention.

**What does it say when we pursue highly unlikely things?**

What does it say for a person to pursue a strategy if they have a 99% chance of failure? Consider a person who is facing a million-to-one odds.

At what point do we look beyond the size of the potential payoff to question our investment in the project?

Experience with U.S. state lotteries is instructive. Someone wins each lottery, and because there are so many lotteries, states announce new lottery winners frequently.

Never mind that in large lotteries your odds fall to *100 million to one* or worse of winning. Yes, "someone's gotta win," as the lottery marketers remind us. But for one person to win, many millions must lose.

Consider the other losers in the lottery of life: the school dropout who *didn't* become a billionaire, the video that has but 24 views, and the trader who was on the wrong side of that bet.

**This is not an argument against trying to do unlikely things**. But it helps to understand your odds before you bet the house.

Then there are the people who take outsize risks and get away with it, for a time:

- Think of investment banks that earn profits for years by making large bets with borrowed money and then lose it all when markets move unexpectedly.

- Consider the base jumper or free climber. They may have successfully summited and descended a hundred times, until the one time they don't.

At what point do we consider an inveterate risk-taker to be safely home with their gains intact?

## You can achieve large gains without taking large risks

Today I suggest to you there is an alternative approach to achieving great things.

It's not one you'll see headlining the news or discussed in online forums. But it is much more likely to put the odds in your favor.

To play this alternative approach, you don't need huge luck on your side or deep-pocketed investors. You need only draw upon something that you already have: **patience**.

Let me explain.

Slow, steady, incremental progress is quiet and, by definition, not flashy. The magic and the power lie in consistency.

- Start somewhere, anywhere, and move in the direction of your choosing. A single step will suffice.

- Then tomorrow, do it again. And again.

Whether your desire is to save money, improve your fitness, or become wise, you can make progress incrementally. You just need to have the patience to keep going.

Think of yourself like Kobayashi Issa's snail:

*O snail*
*Climb Mount Fuji*
*But slowly, slowly!*

This is such excellent advice. It applies on an individual level and on a business level.

Think how many once high-flying companies had their moment and crashed back down when unrealistic expectations met harsh reality. Founders who reached for the sun, only to fall short as the great majority do.

## Slow and steady is the path less traveled

Do not mistake me. I am not advising you to give up outrageous goals.

I am urging you to use the little-traveled path up the back of the mountain to your goal.

- You will not reach the summit in a week, true.

- But you will travel farther and higher than almost everyone who makes the frontal assault.

It takes discipline and conviction to stay true to a slow but steady course. Particularly when you're regularly confronted with examples of instant success.

You will doubt and you will waver. If you have chosen a goal worth pursuing and are taking steps reasonably designed to get you there, then you are already successful.

Stay on the path. You don't need to take outsized risks to get outsized results. It's better to be unassuming but unstoppable.

Be well.

Chapter Two

# Can You Succeed at Work Without Working Hard?

## The reason people do not succeed on the basis of hard work alone is partly due to luck, but also, partly due to misplaced priorities

You're busy, so here is the answer right up front: *It's complicated.*

Succeeding at work without breaking a sweat isn't impossible, but there are a few hurdles to overcome before you get to the "work smarter, not harder" point.

I know people who achieved success without appearing to work hard. They are in a tiny minority. But I will also tell you hard work is no guarantee of success.

"Yikes! Are you telling us that hard work is likely necessary for success, but that working hard does not mean we'll be successful?"

Don't despair. Stay with me for a few minutes, and I will tell you what I learned about working hard in over 80,000 hours of doing it. You may be able to avoid some of my mistakes.

I am a big believer in the power of continuous improvement and habits. You don't need to take giant steps to achieve big progress. Small steps taken consistently over time will add up to large results.

One way to take actions consistently is to make them into a habit.

## Not all habits are good for you

We call harmful habits "vices," which otherwise means moral faults or weaknesses, and include in this category things like drinking alcohol, smoking, or eating too much chocolate.

Where does working hard fall on the spectrum of virtue and vices?

For a long time, I considered hard work to be a clear virtue. Not only that, being able to work intensely for long periods of time is a great competitive advantage at work.

Particularly with a steady stream of new workers coming along who have chronically short attention spans, a person who is able to stay focused on a task and work on it until they have made progress or completed it is well-equipped to succeed.

I am aware there is a strong counter-current to this work-hard ethos. Browse the self-help aisle, and you will find best-selling books advising you to learn "How Not to Give a F*ck" and the like.

Similar articles in mainstream publications explain the danger of associating too much with your work and the harm this can have on your happiness and health. Being a workaholic is not a good thing.

Now with some time and distance from my last senior management role, I have come to two realizations that I will share with you:

- Working hard is a key factor contributing to your success in almost any endeavor.

- Working hard is itself habit-forming, even as it crosses the line from virtue over to harmful vice.

What happened to me in working so many hours all those years is that my ability to work long hours became part of who I was and what I did. Not only that, I learned how to make each of those hours count more than most people's by focusing relentlessly on effectiveness and productivity, not just hours at my desk.

Do you know how much time most people waste on unproductive activities each day? Simply by avoiding wasted time, you can become massively more productive than the average employee.

Add to that focusing on carefully chosen strategic targets, and then working harder than your colleagues, and you become highly effective. Unstoppable, really.

You will always outcompete someone who is not willing to put in the same time as you. I refer not just to hours spent working, but learning how not to waste time, and how to productively use the time you have focused on the right priorities.

## Here it is, the real answer

The reason people do not succeed on the basis of hard work alone is partly due to luck, but also, partly due to misplaced priorities.

You can be extremely busy putting out fires and responding to urgent tasks. To make your hard work pay off, it needs to be directed to your own priorities.

If you work in a larger organization, your priorities must align with your company's. But that still leaves a lot of room for you to work on more and less helpful topics.

Working hard will not necessarily make you happy. As noted, more people are realizing that done unthinkingly, hard work will make you miserable.

I have lots of thoughts about how to achieve happiness and satisfaction in your life. Success at work is one path, but you must not assume that hard work by itself will bring you fulfillment.

It has taken me a long time, years actually, to break my habit of working long hours. After all, it was a key factor in my success, so why should I lose the habit? As with any habit, after a certain point, it becomes easier to just continue it than to question why you are doing it.

This is because if you question your long-held habits, you also question the foundation of your choices. "Was I a fool to work so hard for so long? What did it bring me?"

The reason for me to ultimately seek a different balance, if not lose the habit of work entirely, was because I decided that success at work was not the only yardstick I would use to measure my progress. I wanted happiness and satisfaction in life.

I leave you with this thought: Even if breaking a habit would cause you to question the validity of your earlier choices, is that really worse than continuing on a path that leads to a place you don't want to go?

Be well.

## Chapter Three

# Hard Work Doesn't Make You a Hero

## Put aside the thought that you deserve a gold star for effort. What earns you kudos are results

What does it mean to genuinely work hard, and who are the two people (or rather one person and one group) you should compare yourself to?

**Work is not the best place for your efforts**

It still bothers me, I have to be honest, but I now see hard work doesn't make you a hero.

For much of my career, I distinguished myself (or so I thought) by working harder than most people around me.

- I worked mornings, evenings, weekends, and holidays.
- I worked when I was feeling great and when I was feeling ill.
- I worked 100-hour weeks.

Later, much later, I learned why hard work is not only insufficient for success but not the best place to invest your efforts either.

Why not? Well, there's a whole life philosophy behind the answers, which I'm sharing with you bit by bit. For today, let's say it's for two reasons:

1. The mere fact you are busy tells us nothing about the **reasons why you are busy.**

2. The quantity of work you perform says nothing in itself about the **results you deliver**.

Some people are busy because of structural inefficiencies.

- For example, their department is understaffed and they are doing the work of multiple people.

- Or their company has redundant processes, like holding weekly status update meetings and drafting memos for people who don't read them.

- Or the person themselves creates problems by letting deadlines lapse and then needing to respond to the resultant pressure in crisis mode.

This all creates stress and hard work, no doubt, but do we rank the people suffering under such structural problems as better performers because of it?

Now, consider the hard work we all sometimes do that yields no result or a negative result.

We worked like the devil but didn't complete the acquisition, win the lawsuit, or sign the contract.

We would like to be rewarded for our effort, but if we're honest, effort alone is not worth very much. In fact, the person who delivers a result with the least effort is someone we need to watch.

The obvious exception consists of people who take shortcuts in achieving their results. In business, the ends never justify the means, and a result obtained improperly is worse than a failed project.

I once had responsibility for a major initiative in an area adjacent to my core legal work. The CEO gave me the task as a chance to develop and to see how well I could perform in new areas.

And although I worked as hard on that initiative as I ever did anything, I had a string of poor performance reviews that I deserved.

Why? Because despite my admittedly hard work, we did not achieve our objectives in the timeline we wanted. My results didn't match up to my efforts.

As you advance in your career, put aside the thought that you deserve a gold star for effort. What earns you kudos are results.

## The only two people you should compare yourself to

If you want to be happy in life, there is **only one comparison** you should ever make. That is, compare who you are today to who you were yesterday.

Your goal should be to make incremental progress in the direction of your choosing. If you are making steady progress in this fashion, it does not matter your pace.

Learning to compare yourself to yourself is one of the keys to a meaningful life that Stoic philosophy offers.

It allows you to be your own best judge of your performance. And if you are committed to your own improvement, the chances are excellent that you will improve your work performance as well.

Because I assume you want career success in addition to happiness, I will let you know the secret to your second comparison.

- You can greatly enhance your chance of success at work by choosing the best-performing comparison group.
- Compare yourself to the best performers *anywhere in the company*, not just among your direct peers on the legal team.

I reported to three tough graders over my in-house career. The thing that helped me most was being compared to the best performers in the whole company. These are the people driving significant value creation.

What am I doing that compares? Not in terms of perceived effort, hours worked, or even compared to other lawyers. But compared to the best that our superstars were delivering.

I had years of tough reviews as a result, but boy did I hold myself to a high standard. I developed accordingly.

Be well.

Chapter Four

# Use Pragmatic Risk Management Principles to Manage Your Career

Your career ambitions come with strings attached, and you would do well to give them some explicit thought

People sometimes ask me what in-house counsel actually do. I struggled to explain it to my kids, who came away from their visits to the office with the impression that we "write emails, talk all day on the phone, and have a lot of meetings."

I also struggled to explain it to other business colleagues. In my search for a short and accurate formulation, I first came up with the words "risk mitigation." This seemed appropriate to me because we spend a great deal of time identifying risks and helping our companies avoid them or reduce the likelihood that bad things will happen.

But on deeper reflection, I realized that in-house counsel do not think of all risks equally. We have many potential risks to focus on. We exercise considerable judgment in determining where to place our limited resources.

Which topics are getting enforcement attention? Are we more exposed to some risks than others given our unique profile? Would the consequences of non-compliance be greater in this area or that one?

## Our job is not to mitigate all risks

Critically, the best counsel also understand that our job is not to mitigate or eliminate all risks. We would put our companies out of business if we tried.

You can think of it this way: We are stuck in the middle of a sandwich of opposites. On the one side, we have our business partners, who are always fighting for new business. They are eager risk-takers who will always push boundaries.

The other slice of bread consists of regulators, authorities, outside counsel, and advisors. Their mission is to hold us back and stop us from potentially causing harm in the pursuit of business. They would have us eliminate risk from the business.

## Managing risks is our calling

Both sides of our sandwich are made up of extremists, and left unchecked would lead to a bitter meal. We in-house counsel turn the sandwich into something delicious with the magic sauce of "risk management."

That is, we see the benefit of taking some risks, so agree in principle with our business partners about the purpose of a business. But we also see the benefit in avoiding certain other risks, so pay attention to the regulators and advisors.

"What does this have to do with career management?" I hear some of you asking.

Simply this: If you accept the premise that our value as in-house counsel lies in our effective risk management for our clients, should we not apply similar principles to managing our own careers?

## Do we apply risk management to our careers?

I've had many discussions over the years with colleagues about their career ambitions. Invariably, the emphasis is on our career goals, our development, and what we want to see as the next step.

"How fast am I making progress, and is it fast enough?"

"Will this job or promotion be the best way for me to advance my career?"

"What is the best path for me to become general counsel?"

This is the business side of the sandwich talking, and I get it. My own shortlist of career advice (more on that later) includes, "Always ask for what you want."

What's missing from this calculus, however, is a realistic estimate of the costs. How well do we try to calculate what our ambitions will cost us in terms of hours of our life, time spent with family and friends, and other important priorities?

We readily advise our clients that in fact, "No, we do not want all business at any cost. We want to grow sustainably, in a compliant way, consistent with the company's values."

## Growth for businesses and individuals comes at a cost

In other words, growth for both businesses and individuals involves explicit costs, compromises, and trade-offs. Your career ambitions come with strings attached, and you would do well to give them some explicit thought.

For all the talk about work-life balance, and the progress that a lot of us have made in pursuing it, greater responsibility very often comes with more hours worked and more stress.

Is hard work a necessary precondition to success? You'll have your own views on this, and I'll come back to it in a future article.

The chances are good, though, that making progress in your career will not only bring you positive things. You may be perfectly willing to pay those costs, but this requires you to be aware of what those costs will be.

For now, I want to leave you with an image and a question. Have you been managing your career like an open-faced sandwich, sitting precariously on your outstretched hand, or are you also thinking about how to manage the risks associated with your ambitions?

Be well.

Chapter Five

# Don't Work From Home Yourself Out of a Job

If it is true that your job can be performed perfectly well remotely, does it necessarily follow that your job can only be performed by you?

I can't tell you how many people have told me I'm dead wrong for suggesting offices are still relevant.

"That ship has sailed," they say, or "The future of work has forever changed. I'm never going back to the office."

Indeed, at first glance, it does appear that the balance of power has shifted, with employees demanding flexibility in working arrangements and employers with no choice but to accommodate them.

I understand full well what employees are thinking. Working from home is great. Freedom, flexibility, casual dressing, and no commute. Researchers are busily collecting evidence, or at least anecdotes, about how much employee productivity is going up as a result of all the goodness.

While this is undeniably true, let me offer two thoughts for you to consider. The first is a reminder that we are hardly objective in evaluating evidence when we have a strong interest in the outcome.

Even if you trust your own thoughts, and good for you, the second item I offer for your consideration might give you pause. Namely, if it is true that your job can be performed perfectly well remotely, does it necessarily follow that your job can only be performed by you?

## A case for hybrid work schedules

I came to this line of thought by asking myself why aren't we hearing more from companies themselves pushing back on the WFH phenomenon. Sure, there are a few prominent examples of companies saying they will insist all employees must return to the office, such as the big investment banks.

But most companies are either silent or have publicly embraced the idea their employees can "work from anywhere."

Before you embrace the revolution, and congratulate yourself once again for the wisdom of having avoided investment banking, have you heard what the CEOs of those banks gave as reasons for asking their employees to return to in-person work? Check out these quotes:

> *Most professionals learn their job through an apprenticeship model, which is almost impossible to replicate in the Zoom world. Over time, this drawback could dramatically undermine the character and culture.* – Jamie Dimon, JPMorgan

> *This is not ideal for us. And it's not a new normal. We know from experience that our culture of collaboration, innovation and apprenticeship thrives when our people come together, and we look forward to having more of our colleagues back in the office.* – David Solomon, Goldman Sachs

> *[The office is] where we teach, where our interns learn. That's how we develop people. Where you build all the soft cues that go with having a successful career that aren't just about Zoom presentations.* – James Gorman, Morgan Stanley

Are you confident your job does not involve any elements of collaboration, innovation, and learning? Or are these CEOs just dinosaurs who don't realize yet the world has shifted under their feet?

More worryingly, let's assume you're right: your job *can* be performed remotely.

Moreover, you work for a forward-looking company that goes to great lengths to work out the technology glitches, establish training programs for new hires, and reinforce a shared culture. Google is an example of a company that announced early its knowledge workers could work from anywhere.

If you are working in a developed market, say the United States or Europe, you are an expensive employee. Among the most expensive in the world.

Not only that, but you also may have strange ideas about the purpose of a company, and are not afraid to sue the company for the slightest perceived unequal treatment.

Tell me again what exactly makes you so desirable as an employee?

More to the point, as wonderful as you no doubt are, how much less attractive does an employee have to be who costs your company but a fraction of what you do, is grateful to have a job, and is willing to work extremely hard because they do not take their good luck for granted?

Needless to say, who is based in a country where successful lawsuits against employers are rare, and class actions do not exist.

You don't need to be overly cynical to wonder if companies are simply biding their time. Companies will learn from the pandemic-driven measures that forced home offices upon us how to make WFH efficient.

Then, as a simple, reliable, and predictable productivity measure, they will replace a percentage of the workforce every year with lower-cost employees.

After all, we've insisted that offices are irrelevant, and work can be performed from anywhere. Ironically, by pushing this issue so hard, expensive employees may be hastening their doom by inviting such an easy, direct comparison with employees globally.

Great news if you are in a developing country. Not so much if you are in Europe or the United States.

Be well.

PS — Don't be too depressed with the possibility that WFH will make you uncompetitive and therefore redundant.

Turns out that it's not just the investment banks who realized face-to-face collaboration is kind of important. They were just the first ones courageous enough to say it.

In September 2021 Google itself announced it was paying US$2.1 billion to buy a Manhattan office building. "Wait, what? Is the WFH champion adding office space? Whatever for?" Google's comment accompanying the purchase speaks volumes:

> *We know that our employees, in order to be really happy and productive, need to collaborate. Because of that need to collaborate, we've been investing more and more in office space.*

# Chapter Six

# How To Implement a Project With Lackluster Management Support

## Here's how to implement a project without the CEO being a cheerleader

I have read a lot of advice over my career.

There is a steady stream of new and existing rules that companies are expected to comply with or face sometimes terrible consequences.

This environment creates uncertainty and fear, which in turn creates business opportunities for a lot of people.

Consultants and law firms and "subject matter experts" of all kinds emerge to offer their services in helping you understand new rules and implement projects to ensure you stay compliant. Compliance, in other words, is big business.

As a result, I am used to hearing people pitch how to implement the latest requirement, best practice, or trending idea.

And there is one element to many pitches that demonstrates well that supposed experts don't work in the same world as you and me.

I refer, of course, to the dreaded requirement to ensure you have "top management support."

I get it. Of course, it would be easier to push through your latest project if you had the unanimous backing of the board of directors, the CEO, and the executive committee.

Looking back over the years, how many times has your project honestly warranted, let alone actually received, that kind of support?

I can think of a few instances where the stars were so aligned. Usually, yours is one of hundreds of projects, all important in their own right. Why should yours be singled out as one of the *most important*?

Telling a hapless manager that ensuring top management support is a critical success factor for their project is more than unhelpful. It's a bit like saying, "OK, first ensure an unlimited source of reliable, cheap, clean, renewable energy…"

I want to know how to implement a project without the CEO being a cheerleader. I want a consultant who can tell me how to get attention among hundreds of competing projects and priorities.

As a civic service for everyone who has been there, here is a checklist for how to implement a project with lackluster management support.

## 1. Gain some perspective about your project

Accept that your project is one of many and get a realistic sense of your project's relative importance — not to you, but to your company. This requires you to understand what other important initiatives your company is working on, and why.

## 2. Stay humble about your role

Remember that gaining this perspective is not about you, and not about your CEO or management team. You are hard-working and rightly focused on your area of responsibility. Your CEO is almost certainly hard-working as well and dealing with a tremendous complexity of topics.

Virtually every proposal the CEO evaluates come with an assertive manager saying "This is the most important project. We have to drop everything and do it now!" All your CEO learns from such a pitch is that the manager doesn't have a good sense of the broader picture.

### 3. Know what's hot at your company

Identify the initiatives that currently **do have** top management support. Who is championing them, who is working on them, what is the timeline, what are some upcoming deliverables, etc.? Become knowledgeable about what strategic imperatives your company is working on and why.

### 4. Find a link between your project and that hot ticket

Evaluate whether there are any areas of overlap between a current strategic priority and your new project. Your link may be direct, it may be tenuous. There is always a link. It's your job to find that link.

### 5. Identify a partner in arms

Once you've found one or more links, find out who is currently working on the strategic priority that may be affected by your link. This person could be at any level in the organization and is typically not among the senior-most managers involved.

Your target is more likely either responsible for seeing a part of the project implemented, or would be directly affected by a potential delay, failure, or problem if an unforeseen risk was missed.

### 6. Design your pitch to solve your partner's problem

Sure, your partner was unaware a problem existed until you brought it to their attention. Yes, the problem is actually a result of the new rule or regulation you are trying to comply with. But you are not the problem.

You are the person saving your partner from an embarrassing omission. Not because you point out the problem. That will just get you killed as the messenger of bad news. But because you point out the problem and come with a ready-made solution.

### 7. Be prepared to implement your solution without help

Perfect compliance is not the goal at this stage. You want to start small, with something that you can do and do correctly and well. Your partner needs to understand that you are not asking for anything but to spend **your own** valuable time and effort on helping solve **their** problem.

## 8. Meet others on the main project

Once you are officially working on the main strategic priority, even though it is in your narrow area of interest, ask your partner to involve you in broader meetings. If you have been constructive and helpful, not asked for any resources, and not caused any new problems, you should be OK.

## 9. Gently spread your idea

This should be mainly through awareness raising amongst others working on the project: For example, that the issue is out there, that it has real-world consequences, and that you are working on a solution to a narrow piece of it.

Your goal is to get people in other areas of responsibility to acknowledge the issue in their own presentations. If you are very lucky, some of them will look into the topic on their own and may identify additional risks/opportunities for further implementation.

## 10. Ride the wave

Either your issue has real-world relevance, or it does not. If the issue is relevant, then you will have:

- Put yourself in a position to bring it to the attention of relevant people who are in a position to do something about it;
- Shown yourself to be selfless and helpful, a good team member; and
- Demonstrated yourself as a subject-matter expert with knowledge about the issue.

If your issue is not yet ripe or has been over-exaggerated by the expert class promoting consulting services, or your company is not yet ready, etc., you will still have made a good first step and laid the foundation for future steps when circumstances change.

Or, if all this sounds too time-consuming or Machiavellian, by all means, pitch your project directly to the CEO.

I recommend telling your CEO that yours is the most important project in the world, and that the company has to drop everything to implement it immediately. Let me know how it goes.

Be well.

## Chapter Seven

# With Experience Comes ... Patience

## Adjusting your priorities to suit a colleague's laziness or incompetence only enables them and harms you

We normally assume it is wisdom that comes from experience. No doubt this is true for some of us.

But I wonder if what we think of as wisdom is based on a healthy foundation of patience.

Let me give you one small example to illustrate the idea.

Have any of you ever been away from work and neglected to respond to an URGENT request, only to find the matter resolved upon your return?

If you have ever managed to step entirely away from your work for a week or more, I expect you've experienced this.

What can we learn from this phenomenon?

Well, it could be that people are incautious in their requests, and label them "URGENT" when they are not urgent. Or perhaps, for matters that are truly urgent, the requestor finds another way to satisfy their request when they realize you are absent.

Either scenario might lead you to ask yourself, "Why did they come to me in the first instance when there was another way for them to get what they needed?"

## Requests within the scope of your job

Maybe the request falls clearly within the scope of your job. Then I think we would agree it is reasonable for people to ask you for help.

- Most of us are not bothered by legitimate requests, so long as they are legitimately delivered.

- A legitimate request becomes an inappropriate burden to us when the person simply sits on it for no good reason other than poor time management.

We've all experienced a request for expedited service only to realize our counterpart could have asked for our help weeks earlier.

I don't know about you, but it burns me up to respond in crisis mode when an issue has become a burning issue because of someone else's negligence.

The Chairman of my company asked us to follow two simple rules when making requests of others. I try hard to honor these rules in all cases:

1. Always assume the person you are approaching is **as busy as you are**. They are not sitting idle waiting for your request. Your proposed deadline must take the recipient's busy schedule into account.

2. After considering the first point, **tailor your proposed deadline** to the difficulty of the task. You should propose a shorter deadline for responses that take only a moment to deliver. But allow more time for tasks that take more time.

You might find these rules blindingly obvious and simple. I do, too.

But ask yourself how often people observe the rules in practice, and you will appreciate the beauty of learning to follow them yourself.

## Requests outside the scope of your job

So far I've been talking about legitimate requests, i.e., those on topics within the scope of our jobs. How shall we think about requests that fall outside the scope of our jobs?

For all the things that we **must** do, there is a great number that we **could** do. And because we are conscientious, hard-working, and competent, in our heart of hearts we know we can do many things better than our work colleagues themselves.

Have you ever found yourself doing something that was technically a co-worker's job?

- Maybe they asked you nicely and you didn't want to say no.

- Maybe you knew you could do it relatively quickly and it would save you time later not to have to correct their sloppy work.

Whatever your rationale, consider that you may be sabotaging your own success.

If you have any meaningful responsibilities, then you are already busy. If you are working strategically, then you have already set your own priorities.

Yes, we adjust our priorities according to external circumstances. But adjusting your priorities to suit a colleague's laziness or incompetence only enables them and harms you.

Now I suspect you are more tactful than I am and would never call your colleagues lazy or incompetent, at least not to their faces. This is where patience masquerading as wisdom comes to your rescue.

No matter what type of URGENT requests you receive, simply continue to do your own work according to your own priorities.

- The person who is trying to get you to do their work for them will see that you do not rise to the bait. They will eventually look elsewhere with no drama.

- The person who has mismanaged their time needs to suffer consequences for their failure. Let them. Even if this means they try to escalate to your boss. If they have caused a crisis for you by their own poor time management, your boss will also see it.

- And if an unexpected, truly urgent topic comes up that deserves your immediate attention according to your pre-determined strategy and priorities, you may work on it with a clean conscience. But only then.

So in sum: Stick to your own priorities.

No need for an ugly confrontation. No need for bitterness. Only patience. Maybe that's true wisdom after all.

Be well.

# Chapter Eight

# Do You Know Your Gear Ratio?

## Past a noticeable point, more effort makes things worse, not better

One of the best things I did to improve the *quality* of my work was to decrease the *quantity* of it.

I don't know why it took me so long to figure out that simply working more hours was not the only or best path to better performance.

You'd think I'd have learned this lesson in my first associate job after putting in 100-hour weeks and pulling regular all-nighters. There comes a point when just grinding out more hours definitely becomes counter-productive.

If you've tried writing a coherent sentence after working for 36 hours straight, you'll know what I mean.

### Exercise re-energizes and reduces stress

But I didn't learn the lesson for almost ten years. I let myself get overweight and sedentary, avoiding any kind of physical exercise until my 30s.

But after an epiphany one day (I'll tell you about it sometime if you're interested), I looked to my fitness with a passion.

- I was prepared to accept sacrifices in my work by devoting time each day to my health.

- To my surprise and delight, substituting work time for exercise time made all my remaining time that much more productive.

Exercise is beneficial for so many reasons. When I mentor and coach newly promoted managers, the first and best advice I share with them is to develop an exercise habit if they don't already exercise regularly.

In my particular overworked case, exercising reset my stress levels and allowed me to return to work feeling relaxed and ready.

## The Yerkes-Dodson Law

Perhaps you've heard of the Yerkes-Dodson Law, deriving from research the pair of psychologists published in the early 1900s.

When undertaking challenging mental tasks, which I think describes a lot of legal work, performance increases with mental arousal up to a point, after which it decreases.

Visualize a bell curve showing performance increasing as stress increases but then dropping off as the stress continues to go up.

## Gear ratio

Let's consider Yerkes-Dodson as it applies to exercise. Perhaps because I started working out at a more mature age, I was definitely a nerd about my exercise.

I loved the gear and gadgets (and still do), such as functional clothing, heart rate monitors, and GPS trackers. Tracking workouts and seeing what insights I could tease out of the data was sometimes as satisfying as the workout itself.

In automotive terms, a gear ratio refers to the number of rotations a driver gear makes to the gear being driven. For each rotation of a 28-tooth gear, for example, a 7-tooth gear must rotate four times, expressed as 4:1.

We can think of our gear ratio in terms of our personal performance. First our physical performance, then our mental performance.

I started out by running, and eventually experimented with triathlons (swimming, biking, and running), before adding hiking to the mix.

- My tracking data showed I have a reasonably consistent 2:1 gear ratio.

- That is, I bike twice as fast as I run, I run twice as fast as I hike, and I hike twice as fast as I swim.

This says absolutely nothing about whether I'm fast or slow. In fact, I'm pretty average, despite lots of practice.

What the ratio tells me is there is a level of effort at which I am most efficient in each sporting discipline. If I push my speed (or effort) too far beyond what I'm geared for, I run the risk of burning out much more quickly.

Past a noticeable point, more effort makes things worse, not better.

Anyone who's started out too quickly in a race has learned this the hard way. I must be a slow learner, for I am still prone to overestimating my capabilities on race day.

## Know your high and low points as you schedule your day

So it is with work. In the work setting, your gear ratio will refer to things like the following:

- What time of day are you sharpest? Are the morning hours your friend, or are you at home among the night owls?

- How long can you profitably work before you take a break? Most people find something between one and two hours ideal.

- What types of work do you most enjoy, for example, writing, talking, thinking, etc.?

- What sorts of situations stress you out and drain your tank the quickest? Do you thrive or shy away from negotiations, public speaking, terminations, investigations, and so on?

Your particular variables will differ and you will probably be geared differently than your colleagues and me.

My advice for you: Spend some quality time thinking about how you're geared. You can then mindfully leverage your strengths to ensure you work most effectively.

Taking a break and switching gears is sometimes the best way to improve your performance.

Be well.

Chapter Nine

# Can You Be Too Good at Your Job?

## Your colleagues will, by inaction, invite you to do some of their work on top of the load you are already carrying

"Too good at your job," you wonder. "Is that even a thing?"

Believe it or not, there are ways in which stellar performance may create some unintended consequences. You can decide for yourself whether the benefits of being a super-employee are worth the potential risks.

The reason for your initial skepticism is that most employees are far from being too good at their jobs. Many colleagues show up, do their work (sort of), and scurry off.

I hear far more complaints from in-house friends about their needing to work extra hard to compensate for others' inefficiencies and thoughtlessness than that they are overcome with awesomeness.

This post is about you, though, not your sometimes suboptimal colleagues. You didn't get to where you are today by being a slacker.

The habits you learned in school and earlier serve you well in the workplace.

- You prepare, show up early, work hard, and pay attention.
- You observe your behavior and that of others around you so that you may more successfully navigate the sometimes turbulent currents of

your company's culture.

You don't have a choice but to learn to work well because you're too busy to waste time on lower-priority tasks. You hone your skills every day by necessity.

As a result, like you, many in-house counsel are superb at their jobs. Because of their broad exposure to all corners of their companies' businesses, their analytical approach, and their ruthless prioritization of strategic tasks, in-house counsel are among the best employees overall.

I used to tell my team my goal was for the business to "cherish" in-house counsel. That is, when there was a vacancy, the business should be delighted with the opportunity to add another lawyer to the team because of how greatly we added value to the company in every opportunity that presented itself.

## Competence attracts new work like bees to pollen

What are some consequences of being great at your job? Well, one obvious consequence that will no doubt have occurred to you is that competence attracts new work like bees to pollen.

To whom do you assign important projects as a manager? The employee who has free time but a spotty track record or the superstar who crushes everything you throw at them?

Work is not at all evenly or fairly distributed because managers are selfish. We want the best person for the job even though that person is already doing twice as much as their colleagues.

I call this the "curse of competence." People who are busy because they are good at their jobs will receive a disproportionate amount of additional work.

## Colleagues sometimes take advantage of high-performing team members

And it's not just bosses who notice this. Your colleagues notice your work performance as well. Most will greatly appreciate all that you do.

A certain subset, however, will take advantage of your desire to outperform by being just a little bit more incompetent.

Say you are on a project together and a summary of a meeting needs to be drafted, or some work product needs to be created for the project to advance. Your opportunistic free rider just sits back and lets the pressure build, even if they've been assigned part of the work.

They care more about managing their time than they do advancing the project. You care more about doing a good job and before long you feel compelled to step into the gap.

Result? Your colleagues will, by inaction, invite you to do some of their work on top of the load you are already carrying.

This leads to a spiral of overwork that has led many great performers to burn out. While some enlightened managers look for this and will help protect their stars, you simply can't count on it.

## Do you really need to move from twice as productive to three times?

If you recall that your goal is not short-term overperformance but long-term sustainable performance, it may be easier for you to take steps to protect yourself.

You're already twice as productive as others. Do you really need to be three times as productive?

## Find a pace you can sustain and stick to it

How do you protect yourself from the perils of being too good at your job? By finding a pace of work that you can sustain and sticking to it.

No one who appreciates their fine car would push the engine past the redline for extended periods. What makes you think pushing yourself beyond your comfort zone at work is any better for you?

Work deliberately and steadily, take breaks when you need to, and stop when you've put in a full day.

No matter how much you have to do, no matter how much additional work your colleagues try to pile on, work on the most important priority first and take the time needed to do a good job.

You are not slowing down as much as you are working well at a manageable pace.

If you do this, you will notice good things start to happen. Your boss will see your response time is no longer immediate, even though you're still producing first-rate work on everything you do. If they're in a hurry, they will start to look elsewhere.

When you fail to do your colleagues' work for them, they will either fail themselves (sad, but not your problem) or, more frequently, they will rediscover their own capacity for work.

In other words, people will pick up on how you work and they will adjust themselves to your work habits.

Thus, I recommend you continue to maintain high standards for everything you do, but find ways to not do everything you may be asked to do.

I trust you'll find your business still cherishes you just as much.

Be well.

Chapter Ten

# What Would You Do With 1000 Hours?

## Regardless of external rewards or pressure, it is eminently valuable to determine for ourselves how best to invest our time

This article is not about sports, even though it might seem like it. This article is also not about personal fitness, although you could be forgiven for thinking so.

Today's article is about making use of our second most precious commodity, after our well-reasoned minds: time. As such, even if you could give a fig for swimming, biking, or running, I urge you to stay the course with me today. The reward for reaching the finish line may be a lesson that brings you far in life.

### What does 1000 hours represent?

- It's a bit more than 11 percent of all the hours in a year. If you subtract out, say, eight hours a night for sleep, and time spent working a full-time job, that still leaves us with something like 4000 hours at our annual disposal.

- If you make US$10/hour, working 1000 hours gets you a bit less than US$9000 after tax. If you're a lawyer charging US$500 an hour, you'll gross a cool half a million, although you'll pay a lot in taxes.

- The World Health Organization recommends we all get at least 150 minutes of exercise a week, or 2 1/2 hours. At that rate, you'd need almost eight years to hit your 1000 hours. We can be more ambitious. Most fit people I know invest an hour a day on average in their training, say 400 hours a year. For them, 1000 hours is 2 1/2 years of training.

## The 1000 hours that have been weighing on my mind

Why do I raise all this? I've been grappling with a decision for some time. *Should I commit to doing an* Ironman? This is the ultimate of triathlons, comprising a 3.9-kilometer swim, 180-kilometer bike ride, and then running 42.2 kilometers, a full marathon.

Although a handful of the world's fittest can complete this distance in under eight hours, non-elite times cluster around 12 hours. The course cutoff is usually 17 hours.

As impressive as this feat may be, the training to be able to show up on race day dwarfs the race itself. And it is the training for an Ironman more than the event itself that has been giving me pause.

The absolute best thing about having fit friends is that they inspire you to be more fit. The absolute worst thing about having fit friends is that they sometimes inspire you to crazy fitness goals.

I expect that most often I've been the one encouraging friends and colleagues to bake regular fitness into their lives.

With an annual marathon streak extending over 20 years, I wanted to demonstrate with my actions that a regular fitness habit could coexist with a demanding management job. Although the marathons themselves were stressful, the knowledge that one was coming up gave me motivation to be consistent in my training.

It doesn't help that I've had an Ironman on my secret bucket list for a long time. In my case, I would need to build up my basic bike endurance before I could even start race training. Realistically, to perform as I'd like in a race, I would need to devote 10–15 hours a week to my training for the next year and a half. Hence the 1000-hour question.

## Why do we want to do what we want to do?

Having done all this preparation and thinking, I find myself asking a Stoic question. What would I be doing the Ironman race for?

Is it for bragging rights (yes) or to check an item off a decades-old list (yes)? Is it to show camaraderie and have some fun with friends (yes and yes)? Is it to maintain or gain fitness? Hmmm.

I cannot in good faith dispense Stoic advice without admitting that most of these potential rationales don't stand up to deep scrutiny.

I want to stay fit and healthy and avoid injury. Nothing about biking six straight hours is necessary for that. If I'm honest, I suspect little about running marathons is necessary for long-term health and avoiding injury either.

At the same time, I've really enjoyed my new workouts: swimming, biking, yoga, and even strength training.

## What do we value most highly?

If I was following my own advice, I would say look to the underlying value of things. What is it we *really want* to accomplish? What will we be most happy about looking back in a couple of years?

No doubt I would be gratified to have that Ironman medal and the accompanying backpack and t-shirt, etc. I would look back on the accomplishment with pride for a long time.

The wise thing to do might be to take the same hours I'd be willing to commit to Ironman training and devote them to a sensible mix of fitness-focused workouts. Do them all in such frequencies and amounts that keep them fun for the long term. Will someone give me a medal for this? Probably not.

Then again, I am reminded of what I learned about the danger of being too easy on ourselves when faced with challenges. We become stronger by embracing challenges. Thus, there is great value in pursuing outrageous and even scary goals.

This thought process is no different than deciding what is the most valuable use of our time at work.

Regardless of external rewards or pressure, it is eminently valuable to determine for ourselves how best to invest our time. In fact, it is the most valuable thing we can do, if we can follow the conclusions our thinking leads us to.

Each year, we've got 4000 hours of free time at our disposal. How about we make a conscious choice to direct just 25 percent of that time?

What will you do with 1000 hours?

Be well.

PS — I let my fears gain the upper hand last year. No more. I am not sure how or when, but an Ironman is in my future.

## Chapter Eleven

# Your Attitude Is the Best Predictor of Success

## A person with average abilities but a superior attitude will outperform a person with great abilities and a poor attitude

We usually think it is our abilities that determine what we can achieve. While our abilities are no doubt relevant, I've come to believe they are not determinant.

The reason is that if you want something badly enough, you will find a way to make it happen. You will gather to yourself new abilities, find new paths to achieve your objectives, and enlist others to your cause.

**What do experienced managers look for when hiring?**

I was running with a friend recently. Among other things, he spent years working in human resources. We were talking about our experiences hiring new employees.

I said I felt a person's attitude was the most important criterion in making a good hire. Far more important than their school, where they worked previously, or what projects they worked on. Most of that tells me little about how they'll perform their new tasks in this new setting.

A person with average abilities but a superior attitude will outperform a person with great abilities and a poor attitude. And I know which one I want on my team because I see how they perform in practice.

## What is a superior attitude?

Because it's important to understand the point, let me elaborate on what I mean by a superior attitude. A person with a superior attitude is humble, enthusiastic, and optimistic.

- They know they don't know everything they need to and that they can't yet do everything they'll be asked to do.

- But they are open to trying new, hard things and figuring out along the way how to do them well.

- Their optimism is reflected in their volunteering for new projects and their response to challenges.

- When inevitable setbacks arise, they are not thrown off course or out of balance.

- They rise to the challenge and find a way to overcome it. This attitude makes all the difference between giving up and pushing through to success.

A person with a superior attitude doesn't make excuses for their performance. When they mess up, they acknowledge it. More importantly, you can see they are motivated to learn from their mistakes and not repeat them.

They certainly don't blame others for what happens to them. Even when external circumstances play a role, they focus on what they can control and don't waste time in worrying about what they cannot.

## Attitude helps on the journey

I came across a person with an amazingly superior attitude and willingness to put in the hard work necessary for success.

# YOUR ATTITUDE IS THE BEST PREDICTOR OF SUCCESS

This is Nims Purja, the celebrated Nepali climber who smashed several mountaineering world records, after serving with the British Armed Forces as a Nepalese Gurkha and a soldier in the Special Boat Service (SBS) elite special forces unit of the Royal Navy.

He describes what he did in the recent book Beyond Possible: One Man, 14 Peaks, and the Mountaineering Achievement of a Lifetime. Although his physical feats defy many people's comprehension, I was struck most by Nim's descriptions of his attitude along his journey.

He set out on a mission to climb all 14 of the world's 8,000-meter peaks in a record time: Less than seven months, compared to the prior record of seven *years* and 10 months. Why? He says he wanted to "prove to the world that everything, *anything*, was possible if you dedicated your heart and mind to a plan."

Over and over, he talks about his attitude as being the single most important factor in his success.

He repeatedly dealt with skepticism, doubt, and negative emotions by shrugging them off and by reframing each situation to find something positive:

> *From an early age, I believed in the power of positive thinking and willed myself through illnesses and chronic ailments.*

> *I believed.... It surrounded me like a force field and I soon learned that with relentless self-belief, anything was possible.*

> *Getting angry about the situation wasn't going to help ... remaining emotionally strong was imperative: Flipping a negative event into positive momentum was the only way to remain focused on my primary objective.*

> *I attacked everything with positive thinking.*

> *I never moaned when the going got tough. Instead, I ... led by example, maintaining team morale through hard effort and positive thinking.* —Nims Purja

There are many more statements like this, but you get the point — It is Nims's indomitable will, as much as his physical abilities, that got him through his many challenges.

## How to cultivate an indomitable attitude

Our challenges may not be matters of life and death as when summiting 8,000-meter peaks. But the attitudes we bring to our challenges may be just as determinative of our success.

- Tell yourself you are up to the challenges you face and that you will do everything necessary to succeed.

- Tell yourself that you will not only deal with adversity but welcome the unexpected troubles that are sure to arise. You will think of a way to find the positive in every situation.

- Tell yourself you will be stronger, happier, and better by virtue of all that you do.

If you keep telling yourself these things, chances are good others will be telling the stories of your amazing accomplishments for you.

Be well.

# Chapter Twelve

# Share Your Secret Plans

## One great way to make your plans come true is by sharing them with someone who cares for you

Has this ever happened to you? You wrestle in silence with the thought of seeking a promotion, moving house, or changing a relationship.

When you finally get to the point of airing and sharing your thoughts with a friend, you find out they have been grappling with many of the same questions.

My wife and I have concluded everyone is entertaining what we call "secret plans," *all the time*. Maybe it's a form of escapism, maybe it's just daydreaming.

We have found it does not matter how grounded or stable or established someone is, chances are, they are secretly planning something.

### The green grass over there

Let's face it. We all know the grass is greener over there, so why shouldn't we be thinking about moseying on over? Progress requires change, and because we all want to progress, doesn't that mean we have to contemplate change?

There is nothing particularly profound about this. I think the point is that we should not think we are alone in our worries, our wants, and our cares. Everyone is trying to figure out the right thing to do, and no one is certain they have figured it out.

One great way to make your plans come true is by sharing them with someone who cares for you. Discuss your desires, evaluate alternatives.

Just by saying out loud what you want, you acknowledge your wishes to yourself. By speaking your thoughts to another, you help yourself figure out more clearly what you are after.

If you can describe something so that someone else understands it, you improve your own understanding of it. Finally, the chances are good your friend will be a better sounding board to you than you can be to yourself, at least on some points.

This approach can work well in your career development. We have so many thoughts and ideas and sometimes conflicting emotions. Find a few trusted confidants you can talk to about what's on your mind.

You may get good input. You will certainly think more deeply about what it is you are trying to achieve in the process of describing it to someone else.

## Tell your boss — Yes, really

I will go further and say that you should discuss your ambitions with your boss and with management.

Do you think you are the only employee who has grappled with career decisions? Almost certainly your boss has, and almost certainly, several of your colleagues are thinking about similar topics right now.

Don't you think your boss would prefer to know what's on your mind? Even if, no, *especially if* one of the things you are contemplating is leaving for another job?

"Well, yes," you may be thinking. "I am sure my boss *would* like to know what's on my mind. But if I tell her I'm thinking about jumping ship, that will ruin our working relationship in the event I don't leave."

I understand you, and I agree some bosses behave badly in these situations. But a good boss will welcome the chance to discuss this with you.

You may find that boss already knows (or suspects) you are looking. You may find your boss has some alternatives to offer you for consideration. You may also find your relationship with your boss is ultimately improved by virtue of the trust you showed in sharing your thoughts.

I know you will be hesitant to talk to your boss about your secret plans.

I urge you to consider whether this is because you believe you have a bad boss who will punish you (in which case you have other, fruitful boss-management topics to pursue), or because you are afraid of what might happen.

In the meantime, you could first find a friend or colleague with whom you can confidentially discuss your thoughts.

Either way, you may find you can move your secret plans closer to reality by sharing the secret.

Be well.

## Chapter Thirteen

# If You Want To Get Ahead, Go Back to the Office

## It's never been easier to stand out at work. One of the best ways is simple: Go to the office

Search for "*Work from home is here to stay*" and you will find many articles confirming it is so. Everyone is happy to tell you that work has changed forever.

The fact that this is what people very much want to believe is irrelevant. For the foreseeable future, many of us who wish to work from home will be able to do so. And most of us will be as productive as we were before if not more so.

If you are interested in advancing your career, however, there has never been a better time to go back to the office.

Rarely are we given so clear a chance to gain a competitive advantage over our peers. And relatively simply at that. Usually, it takes solid, substantive performance over the long term to have such good prospects of getting ahead.

Consider this your golden opportunity.

Why? Here are three good reasons: Management is there, your colleagues are not, and you will have many opportunities to stand out.

**Your boss still goes to the office**

Some number of people will continue going to the office regularly. Senior management is among them. There are multiple reasons for this.

Important people with significant responsibilities often have offices and support staff. Some have a whole ecosystem to help them be productive at work.

Yes, during the pandemic a certain number of managers worked from home. Most have long since returned to the office. Having an office at work, and needing to be in that office, are new status symbols in the work-from-home era. It is how managers show they are important.

## Your colleagues are staying at home

Working from home is great! We all know it, so we want to keep doing it. Smart people worked out the technology for anyone to work anywhere. We can get up when we want, wear what we want, and take breaks when we want.

Much of the day was wasted in the office anyway. By working in focused blocks at home, we can be incredibly productive and get the same work done in less time.

And best of all, the pandemic made it necessary for a lot of us. Employees were glad to push the scales back in favor of the individual in the work-life balance. Companies simply could not say no.

Thus, it's easy to predict that many, many people will continue working from home and there's little companies can do about it. Although there's one obvious response CFOs will likely pursue:

## It's a great time to shine

Standing out in a crowd is hard. Standing out among only a handful of people is something else entirely. The casual encounter in the hallway is anything but. The invitation to join the boss for a coffee break or a snack is your opportunity.

"But," you say, "when there are fewer people around, you are at greater risk of getting assigned more work."

That's exactly the point, you see. Bosses love employees who volunteer to take on projects. We're just trying to get the work done without drama or stress.

A team member who is always cheerful, who helps out often, and who isn't needy is a treasure. We will work hard to keep such an employee happy and productive.

So your bosses will be in the office. Not too many other people will be. Who comes in and what they do there will make all the difference to some careers.

## What to do when you are in the office

For all the talk about overcoming implicit bias and unconscious bias, people seem to have forgotten how powerful it is. We like people who are like us. That means people who do similar things, have similar interests, and hold similar values.

When you see a colleague in the hallway and exchange a few words about a non-work topic, you have many opportunities to make a connection. Listen carefully and you can find out about their interests. Respond thoughtfully and you can reveal shared interests.

Do not eat at your desk in some vain thought of being productive. It is not a waste of time to have lunch with colleagues. I can't tell you how many key business initiatives were launched by a simple ask at a casual lunch following a relaxed, shared rapport.

## Fairness has nothing to do with it

Is any of this fair to your colleagues who are working from home? I don't think so.

Should you be worried about it? That's a personal choice you have to make. I would just say that the world is filled with asymmetries of circumstances. Rather than bemoaning the world's unfairness, you could leverage strategies that work to your advantage.

The world is competitive. If you want to outperform, be prepared to work hard and take every advantage on offer.

- Show up early, stay late, and volunteer to do projects no one else wants.
- Always do your best and stay positive, especially when you are doing thankless tasks.

Trust me, you will stand out, now more than ever, when most people are focused on optimizing their work to suit their private lives.

Be well.

IMPORTANT CAVEAT: Many of your colleagues will have a more relaxed life than you. They will work less for the same pay, and they will have less stress. They will be that much closer to a healthy work-life balance.

## Chapter Fourteen

# Are You Globally Competitive in Your Career?

## These questions will help you objectively benchmark yourself against your peers

Do you know if your company considers you a valuable employee? How do you compare to other employees, not just where you happen to be working right now, but across the globe?

These questions will help you objectively benchmark yourself. If you answer five or fewer of the following questions with "Yes," then you may not be as competitive globally as you think.

**1. Are you relentlessly positive?**

Can you find something to be happy about every day when you start work? Do you bring a smile to your face when you encounter colleagues in the hallway? Can you find a kind word for a co-worker who is struggling? Can you be forgiving when someone has frustrated your plans, and is being stubborn and unhelpful?

Not to be corny, but do you break into a spontaneous whistle or song because you enjoy what you're doing?

Or are you the person who can always be found complaining around the water cooler? Every business commits countless follies, after all. If we're honest, not a day goes by without some idiot doing something to annoy us. What's the harm in pointing these things out? After all, how else will things get better?

## 2. Can you be counted on to volunteer for projects?

Are you the first one to raise your hand when management proposes a new project? Do you pitch in to help even when the project is outside your area of expertise? Do you volunteer for projects despite being genuinely busy with your own work? Do you even volunteer to work on tasks that are important, but unglamorous?

Or do you refuse to volunteer for more work because you're focused on your own priorities? Do you prefer to stay in your area of expertise? Do you carefully avoid doing work that is repetitive, boring, or thankless?

## 3. Are you (relatively) inexpensive?

Are there any employees where you work who are paid more than you for the same or similar work? Are there employees *anywhere in the world* who are paid more than you for the same or similar work? If you look at broad-based market surveys, are you at or around the median salary?

Or are you comfortable being paid more than anyone else? Because after all, you worked hard and you deserve it. And even if your salary is relatively high, you have to look out for yourself, because no one else will do it.

## 4. Do you spend at least an hour each day working on your strategic priorities?

This means topics that *you* have identified as the most important and most valuable. These will vary frequently depending on what is going on in your business and in your team. The key factor is that you make it happen every day (or as near to it as possible) to spend at least some time on your self-identified priorities.

Or do you spend your days busy? Busy with meetings and calls, administration and personnel issues, responding to emails, and putting out urgent fires.

## 5. Do you manage your physical fitness like you would a vital project at work?

One way to tell if you should answer yes is if you have a daily or weekly physical fitness habit. Do you walk or bike to work? Do you shun elevators and walk up and down all the stairs you can find? Do you join friends for a weekly yoga or dance class?

There is no end of choices. The key is, do you treat your physical fitness as one of your most important strategic priorities?

Or do you find yourself skipping a workout because of an urgent project at work? Do you find yourself sleeping in when you had planned to exercise because you've been so busy that "you deserve time off"?

## 6. Do you set aside at least one day a month for strategic thinking and planning?

This could also be a few hours each week, or half a day every two weeks. The point is, do you invest regularly in quality blocks of time where you are thinking strategically and updating your plans?

Or do you feel satisfied with accomplishing tasks and getting things done? You are too busy to take 10% of your time to just sit and think.

## 7. Are you a woman or a minority?

This is just a yes-no question. I am not putting any judgment or criticism behind it.

I've been in many search discussions, across public companies, private companies, for-profits, and charitable enterprises. In 30 years, I have never once heard the phrase, "We need to fill this role with a white guy."

I have, however, heard every variation of the phrase "We need to fill this role with _____ (every other variation)."

## 8. Do you expose yourself to new ideas regularly?

I originally wrote "Do you read widely for business and pleasure, and learn something new every week?" In the meantime, there are more options than just reading, including podcasts, audiobooks, online courses, and more.

The point is whether you are constantly seeking to learn new things and to be exposed to unfamiliar ideas.

Or do you feel that your school days are behind you and thank goodness. That books are painfully boring, and if they can't get the point across in a 30-second TikTok video, what's the point?

## 9. Are you OK with your salary?

No matter how much you are paid, do you trust your company to pay you fairly, based on broad-based market comparisons? Do you believe that the reward for work is measured in more than money? For example, in things like your professional development, having colleagues you like and respect, and in working for a company that has values aligned with your own?

Or do you regularly check the salary surveys to see if others are making more than you, and bring these surveys to the attention of your boss? Do you secretly worry that you are not being paid the same as others doing the same work? Does it bother you to know friends who are making lots more money than you?

## 10. Can you describe your strategy and key priorities in sixty seconds?

In other words, do you effectively build a common understanding of your value proposition? We all have countless competing demands for time and resources.

Does your team understand what the vision is and why what they are working on is important? Do your colleagues understand what you do and why? Does management understand how you are making a vital contribution?

Yes, I am referring to the elevator speech.

Or when someone asks you what's keeping you busy, do you make the mistake of simply describing the details of what you're working on at the moment?

## Bonus question: Would you call yourself happy?

This is of course related to the first question. Being positive is a good way to become happy. Happiness is a condition that can be cultivated, often through simple steps that you can take regularly.

Your career can certainly make you happy, but too often people make themselves miserable in pursuit of their ambitions. It is my sincere desire to help on both the career front and the happiness front.

I hope this has been helpful to you in thinking about your competitiveness at work.

Be well.

## Chapter Fifteen

# It's TIME WE JOG

## This is a simple slogan to organize factors that will contribute to your personal and professional success

Those who know me will realize it is a complete coincidence that these factors sum up as a reminder to be physically fit. Here they are:

### T — Trust

Be trustworthy and reliable. People will want to work with you and will give you more opportunities if they trust you and if you deliver reliably.

### I — Integrity

When evaluating a company, the integrity and ethics of management are vital. You shall reinforce the importance of integrity with your own behavior.

### M — Motivation

Understand what motivates you, so that you can apply those levers to your work and your life. You will have to motivate yourself often, so know how to do it effectively.

Once you have decided on goals, be persistent, push, and never give up.

### E — Example

Always set an example with your personal behavior of what you expect others to do. Be a role model, on both personal and professional topics.

## W — Work-life balance

Performing at an elevated level sustainably requires you to acknowledge the different priorities in your life: not just work, but also family, health, community, society, etc.

You will not achieve a work-life balance by accident, so plan to spend time on it often.

## E — Emotional intelligence

To perform at a high level, you need self-awareness and emotional intelligence, which includes knowing how you interact with others. Ask for feedback and take it seriously but not personally.

If you can, cultivate a positive mindset. Not only will you be happier, but people like being around optimistic people, which generates opportunities for you.

## J — Judgment

This is the most important professional attribute for any knowledge worker because you must constantly balance risk management with pragmatism. Your value comes from your judgment on what risks it is appropriate to take, and in setting priorities.

## O — Opportunities

Make sure to ask for what you want. At the same time, be open to opportunities to do more, to do different things. Your big break may come in an unexpected area, so take a chance, and volunteer.

Trust that you will be able to add value to new areas. This is what helps you grow.

## G — Good job

Do a good job in your current job. This is a reality check against the prior point. No matter how keenly you want the next step in your career, you will never get there if your performance in your current job is lacking.

Have dreams for the future but focus on what you are doing right now.

Nothing helps you do a good job so much as following continuous improvement principles. Just start with where you are and steadily improve.

Be well.

# Chapter Sixteen

# These Things May Be Hurting Your Career

## This list helps you check whether you're doing things that inadvertently hold you back

How do you succeed in life? Well, that's pretty ambitious of me to answer in one post, so let's dial it back: How do you succeed in your career?

I learned most of these lessons leading a global team of ambitious professionals. I realized it's much easier to see others' flaws than to see our own. An individual may struggle to see exactly what is holding them back. But rest assured, others can see it.

Some people feel unhappy with their careers because they are stuck with the notion that success means movement and change. How can you be successful if you haven't been promoted recently? Are you successful if you work for the same company for ten years? If your salary has not gone up every year?

The wisdom of your goals is yours to decide. But no matter your definition of success, I'm confident *you don't want to fail* at what you set out to do. Avoiding failure means identifying obstacles that may be standing in the way of you achieving your professional goals.

Are you doing things that are inadvertently hurting your career? If you find yourself answering "Yes" to any of the following questions, do not despair. I have thoughts on how to turn the tide.

## 1. Do you THINK mean things about your colleagues?

It is hard not to, right? People get on each other's nerves for all sorts of reasons. While you may believe you're good at keeping your thoughts to yourself, if you think mean or uncharitable thoughts about your colleagues, you can expect them to pick up on it.

They may not be able to say what exactly it is, but they will feel it. If you think mean thoughts, your interactions with colleagues will be negatively impacted.

## 2. Do you SAY mean things about your colleagues?

It can seem harmless to vent a little frustration. Especially since the person you are commiserating with has the same impression as you. We all know people who are unpleasant to work with: selfish, stubborn, incompetent even.

When you say negative things about others, even if your observations are accurate and richly deserved, you train the course of your thoughts to the negative. Worse, you are now the kind of person who says those thoughts to others. Your grandmother was right when she said, "If you don't have anything nice to say, don't say anything at all."

## 3. Do you focus ruthlessly on getting your own priorities accomplished?

You are busy, and you struggle to get your own work done. If you didn't focus on your priorities, then you would not be successful at all. Right?

Well, yes, actually, up to a point. Beyond just doing your job, however, you are presented with countless opportunities to make others' lives harder or easier. You can be selfish, focused only on yourself: "That's not my job."

What you may not notice is that others notice your selfishness. They often help each other because we all need help and we certainly appreciate receiving help.

If you never give help, don't be surprised if people are not quick to offer to help you.

## 4. Are you fixated on what your friends and colleagues earn?

Is your salary high? No idea. Is it higher than that of your friend? Easy answer. Such comparisons pave a predictable path to dissatisfaction.

If you spend your days comparing yourself to others, prepare to be unhappy most days. No matter how near the top you may have risen, you'll know someone else is always a bit closer.

## 5. Do you feel your pay isn't fair?

Fair is a magical word because everyone hearing it understands fairness differently. Thus, focusing on "fairness" is a recipe for sadness and frustration.

The world is not fair. Abilities and outcomes are unevenly distributed. Anyway, your conception of fairness is very different than other people's and highly influenced by what you want to achieve. Is it fair for you to be paid a higher salary? "Why certainly!" Is it fair for you to pay more taxes to help those less fortunate? "Don't be ridiculous."

If you feel you are not fairly paid, you will become resentful, impacting your attitude and work.

Ironically, one way to boost your salary is to stop obsessing about it. As you let go of the frustration and dissatisfaction, you will be happier. That will translate into your being a better colleague at work and doing better work. Which, of course, will over time translate into higher raises.

## 6. Do you think people less competent than you have been promoted ahead of you?

I've sat in on many promotion discussions. Trust me when I say your sense of others' abilities, accomplishments, and talents is incomplete. People get promoted for many reasons, some of which you may have no inkling of.

I've also offered a sympathetic ear to many employees who felt that others were unfairly promoted ahead of them. Whatever the reasons given, the unhappy employee is fixated on the idea that a less-deserving person has advanced ahead of them. (Maybe they have. It is useful to remember that sometimes life is not fair.)

But perhaps the promoted person deserved it, and you are unaware of all the circumstances. Your bitterness is evident to your colleagues and your boss. This makes them question your suitability for promotion yourself.

## 7. Do you feel that helping others is a distraction from your own work?

This is similar to point 3 but with this difference: The person focused on their own priorities is just busy, and perhaps oblivious to the harm being self-centered has on their relationship with colleagues. Such a person can come to realize that they need their colleagues to succeed.

If, however, you think helping others is a distraction, then you are likely to be not just self-centered but selfish in your interactions with them. You treat the workplace as a zero-sum game, where others' success comes at the expense of your own.

This is not a recipe for being considered a "team player." Nor an attitude that will win you your colleagues' admiration.

Change the frame by enlarging the scope of your ambitions. You are not working for narrow personal goals but for the good of the company. If helping the other person provides a greater benefit than focusing on your own task at that moment, your choice is easy.

## 8. Have you switched companies regularly (every three years or less)?

This can come from the sometimes misguided belief that success in your career requires motion. There is some truth to this. I have seen people job-hop their way to outrageous title inflation, far quicker than persons who stay in one place and do not agitate for change.

The trick is to find the balance between staying in one place long enough to learn the job and have an impact and switching rapidly to meet your own timetable of advancement. I know it is arbitrary, but for me switching companies every three years is too frequent.

As a hiring manager, if I see three or more such hops, I assume one of two things: this person has an unrealistic sense of how quickly their career should progress, and/or this person is a poor performer and has had to leave once each new employer figures it out. Either way, you are not an attractive hire for me.

## 9. Are you jealous of others' success?

Objectively seen, another person's success typically has very little or nothing to do with your own. Someone the same age as you is: a CEO, married to a fashion model, invested in a startup and became wealthy, or _____ fill in your own personal blank. Does that say anything at all about you?

No, it does not. And yet, it feels like it does. In our beating hearts, in the dark of night, others' success makes us feel less successful by comparison.

We forget the countless others we have ourselves surpassed. In these moments, we neglect to consider all we have to be thankful for. Envy will eat us up from the inside and leave only a bitter-tasting shell behind.

## 10. Do you focus on the negative in a situation more often than the opportunities?

One of my mottoes in life is "Be happy with what you have, not sad for what you don't have." I am not recommending that you be delusional or ignore bad things in your life.

No matter the situation, you are faced with a choice. Do you try to identify something positive about it? Or do you dwell on everything that is not perfect? You may not be able to easily identify something good in a situation. But I can promise you this: if you live in the land of perceived imperfection, you will be unhappy.

A person who can find something positive in dark times is wonderful to be around. A person who does this and shares their positive perspective is exactly who you want on your team. Because a crisis is always just around the corner.

I want people who are happy and positively inclined on my team and in my life. Because they will make a bad situation better, in ways that the doomsayer never could.

## Some final advice

I don't know anyone without flaws. Many of my colleagues who would have answered Yes to some of the above nonetheless experienced fantastic results.

That's because to find career success your task is not to be perfect. Your task is to be self-aware and deliberate in how you approach situations.

Armed with this list, perhaps you will pick one idea and apply continuous improvement principles to tip the odds of success in your favor. Slowly but surely, you can turn the tide to your advantage.

Be well.

## Chapter Seventeen

# What I Learned from Judging and Being Judged

## The best learnings I made over my career came from people who trusted me enough to tell me when I screwed something up

Being judged can be painful, depending on how you are performing and how your reviewer delivers feedback. I've learned a lot about making good use of constructive criticism, which I'll share with you here.

I also realized in my years judging the finalists for the Association of Corporate Counsel's Top 10 30-Somethings that serving as a judge of others is not easy, especially if you're interested in being fair, constructive, and honest.

When I say I've learned something about judging, I also mean the process of giving and receiving feedback more generally and not just formal judging.

I hope you find something relevant and useful for your own development.

### Which feedback is most valuable to you

There are two kinds of feedback you should delight in receiving:

- Feedback that comes from people whose opinions you respect and trust, and

- Feedback that is true regardless of the source.

The corollary to these rules is that you can apply a healthy skepticism to all other feedback you receive over your career.

Just because someone is sitting in a position to judge you does not necessarily (1) make them better than you, (2) give them meaningful insights into your performance, or (3) mean they know how to give constructive feedback.

A person whom you trust and respect, however, does you a great service when they give you feedback.

Even when, perhaps especially when, they tell you things that are painful, and where you have fallen short in your performance.

- This person is not trying to hurt you. Exactly the opposite. They care about you and are trying to help you get better.

- Treat this feedback like the gift it is and thank them for it.

- Then think about it and turn it to your advantage.

The best learnings I made over my career came from people who trusted me enough to tell me when I screwed something up.

What about people you don't trust, whom you may suspect are trying to cause you pain or trouble?

Here too, you can take advantage of the situation.

You do so by knowing your own strengths and weaknesses and having a healthy dose of self-awareness and self-confidence. Ask yourself the following question: "Is what this person is saying true?"

Even if their aim is to hurt you, by drawing attention to a real weakness, they have done you a service.

And if you are confident what the person is saying is not true, you are well-positioned to dismiss the person and their criticism, preserving your peace of mind.

## Why perceived effort is a dangerous benchmark

I have observed that we are each usually the heroes of our own stories. We know our intentions are good, and we believe in the correctness of what we're doing.

This is only sensible and helps us get through hard times. But our natural human tendency can blind us to some objective truths.

- Sometimes we don't really put in enough effort to be successful in a project. We might be busy with other things, or not particularly motivated about this topic at this time.

- Or maybe we let emotions get the better of us. There are many reasons for not performing our best every now and then.

The thing is, work feels like work to us whether it is productive and on-task or whether we're wasting our time.

Work also feels like work to us without regard to the result. That is, the hours you spend negotiating a contract that fails to come to fruition are still hours of your life you will never get back.

Perhaps most relevant, the amount of effort we feel like we're investing is subjective.

- What seems like a huge effort to us may be trivial to a colleague.

- Maybe you are not as experienced or skilled, such that the same task that they think nothing of completing seems herculean to you.

Just because you think you're working hard does not mean you are performing well objectively.

Be well.

Chapter Eighteen

# What Makes You Really Stand Out

## First, a hard truth: Just being in difficult times doesn't make you special

How should we think about the extraordinary circumstances we find ourselves in, what are our personal convictions worth, and what is it that makes us unique?

This continues our exploration of lessons to be learned from judging and being judged (see the prior chapter), including giving and receiving feedback more generally.

### What extraordinary circumstances say about us

First, a hard truth: Just being in difficult times doesn't make you special.

Although you may have been the person leading your company's COVID-19 response, or EU General Data Protection Regulation (GDPR) implementation, guess what? Every company was facing the same extraordinary times.

But let's say your extraordinary circumstance is less common: A hostile takeover attempt or major acquisition, bet-the-company litigation, or a serious regulatory inquiry.

This type of event never happens to many companies, or perhaps once in a few decades. So, it is genuinely extraordinary for you and your company. But it is not extraordinary for all in-house counsel. Right now, lots of companies are facing each of these issues.

I am sure your work was outstanding under the circumstances. But don't expect me to grade you higher *just because you responded to a crisis*. Remember, your comparison group is everyone else who was responding to the same or similar crises, not all the people on the sidelines.

Now the good news. A crisis presents excellent opportunities for you to stand out, even among all the people dealing with similar crises.

- How many contingencies did you manage to adequately plan for?
- How quickly did you identify the issue?
- How well did you convince skeptical colleagues that the company needed to act?
- And, ultimately, how well did you navigate your company through the shoals and to safer waters?

In sum, extraordinary circumstances of themselves say little about you. Even what may be unique in your company's history is mundane across the in-house landscape.

What makes you shine is how you respond to your circumstances.

## What caring deeply about an issue is worth

The best in-house counsel are great people. They have broad interests and passionate convictions. They want to do more than help their companies succeed; they want to help their companies make the world a better place.

And there are rich opportunities in today's environment for us to do so. There are pressing climate change concerns, an extensive list of UN Sustainable Development Goals, and newfound commitments to diversity and inclusion.

I am delighted that you care deeply about these issues. I am tickled pink that you are on your company's diversity, equity, and inclusion (DEI) committee.

But, unless you turn your caring into concrete action, however, it's not worth much to me.

Remember our discussion earlier about the difference between effort and impact? The environmental, social, and governance (ESG) space is filled with a great deal of noise and little concrete results.

Don't misunderstand me. Passion is the engine that drives progress. Without your conviction and that of others like you, we are lost.

But your passion is the cover charge for this particular event. It gets you in the door.

- The people who stand out are the ones who focus their passion and demonstrate persistence in the face of resistance.

- It's hard enough to drive results without prioritizing attention and effort.

- So, pick a topic and stay with it until you see positive results. Then stick with it some more.

## What makes us unique

Now that I've poured cold water on what you living through hard times and your passion tells us about your performance, let me spend a moment talking about the mundane challenges all in-house counsel face.

We spend most of our time developing efficient contracting systems, implementing compliance programs, and training our non-lawyer colleagues. Of course, we know that the best lawyers partner with the business in achieving business goals in a sustainable way.

If these challenges and opportunities are near-universal, what makes us stand out? One good place to look is our impact on those around us.

- Do you consistently help others thrive?

- Are people happier after spending time with you?

- Will people say about you, "She helps make the world a better place"?

When you find yourself answering yes to these questions, you are probably making your best contribution. An inspiring leader has an impact far greater than any amount of individual work can hope to accomplish.

I've now shared with you the key lessons I learned from judging and being judged, and in giving and receiving feedback.

I know some of the messages can seem a bit hard. But I hope by now you trust me enough to consider the truth of the matter in each case.

I also hope you trust yourselves enough to take only those lessons that apply to you and not take me so seriously on the lessons that don't. After all, you aren't like anyone else and that's one more thing that makes you special.

Be well.

## Chapter Nineteen

# Who's Running the Show of Your Life?

## Are good things that happen the result of your agency, while bad things are caused by something other people did?

I've noticed something interesting about some successful people. They are the first ones to promote the idea that people are in charge of their own destiny. That with hard work and sacrifice you too can be successful.

They may espouse a corollary belief, which is that people who do not achieve all they want are simply lazy or lack intelligence or drive. But take such a person and ask them to explain a prominent failure they were associated with.

- "That wasn't my fault," you will hear.
- They trot out a thousand explanations and excuses, all of which point anywhere but them.

The takeaway is clear: Good things that happen are the result of their agency. Bad things are caused by something other people did.

### Which group are you in?

I don't mean to pick on successful people. I've observed many unsuccessful people say the same thing. It's just they have fewer accomplishments to feel smug about, so you don't notice their inconsistency as much.

Let us refer to the inconsistent situational thinkers, whether successful or not, as the **Fair Weather Flock**.

Some smaller number of people are at least consistent in their thinking, although they fundamentally diverge into two groups in their approaches to life. Let's call the first group the **Things Just Happen** adherents and the other group **I Make Things Happen**.

Do you count yourself among either group? Here's how to tell.

You can distinguish members of the **Things Just Happen** group from the Fair Weather Flock in this way: They never add the words "to me" to their inner thoughts.

You will never hear them say "This bad thing happened to me," or "This good thing happened to me." Things just happen, it's not personal, and members of this group deal with it.

You might also think of this group as realists or fatalists. They don't control the cards that life deals them, but they find a way to make the best of the hand they've got.

What's refreshing about their approach to life is you don't usually hear them complaining. Life is what it is, sometimes great, often unfair, but they get on with managing their affairs.

## Working with different styles

A member of the **Things Just Happen** tribe is great to have on your team because they are rarely fooled by wishful thinking. They see the world as it is, and they respond accordingly.

But this comes with some potential downsides. When you see the world as it is you can become cynical because we're surrounded by unfairness. The result can be a lack of initiative and less motivation to take on big challenges.

If the world is screwed up and out of our control, why should you go the extra mile?

Consider now the happy members of the **I Make Things Happen** group. You can also think of them as optimists, dreamers, and even naïve. They are certainly more likely to see the world through tinted glasses. On the positive side, they assume they control their destiny. They believe that with persistence and determination, they can make their own success.

This can-do attitude also makes them great team members. They are prone to putting in extra effort and consequently, they achieve great things more often than not.

When the Fair Weather Flock observes the successes of the I Make Things Happen group, they grumble, "They were just lucky," noting neither how this is inconsistent with how the Fair Weather Flock assesses their own performance nor how the I Make Things Happen group's luck always seems to go in only one direction.

But the I Make Things Happen members also suffer. Even the most determined people do not succeed at everything. And when failure strikes, members of this group feel it personally. They believe there must have been something more they could have done to avert the problem.

## Pros and cons of the different groups

When I started this article, I thought I would declare a clear winner. For example, the I Make Things Happen group is more likely to be successful so the lesson would be that you should strive to take ownership of your life.

But I see that membership in each comes with pros and cons:

- **Fair Weather Flock**: Inconsistent and delusional, but happier by virtue of taking credit for good things while not taking the bad personally.
- **Things Just Happen**: The most accurate perception of the world, so avoids many wishful thinking mistakes but can miss out on opportunities that require hard work.
- **I Make Things Happen**: Consistent and delusional, most likely to be successful by virtue of taking more chances, but their sense of responsibility means balance and life satisfaction are harder to find.

Membership in these groups is not fixed or exclusive. Although I think most people tend towards one inclination most of the time, I have seen people purposefully change the course of their lives and careers by choosing another group.

Change requires two steps: Audit your past thinking to see whether you consistently assess the causes of both positive and negative events in your life; and make a conscious choice to assign agency for everything that happens in your life.

Your choices are these: I'm running the show (as long as times are good), no one's running the show, and it's always me running the show.

Choose wisely.

Be well.

## Chapter Twenty

# Sit Down and Stay Awhile*

## Getting better at your job often leads to sustainable career success. I can't say the same about people who pursue a new job whenever it's dangled in front of them

If you want to advance in your career, there's never been a better time to make a leap. Higher pay, flexible hours, and work from anywhere are all yours for the asking. There's certainly less justification to put up with a bad boss, an underperforming company, or missing development opportunities.

And yet, if you're not suffering from a significant disadvantage where you are, I'm going to advise you to think about staying put for a while longer.

Whether you stay or go really depends on whether you want merely career progress or to get better at your job. They are not necessarily the same. I find getting better at your job often leads to sustainable career success. I can't say the same about people who pursue a new job whenever it's dangled in front of them.

Often, the bigger job at the new company actually sets you back, at least in terms of your effectiveness. Why is that, you ask?

### Success requires much more than specific expertise

For lawyers, what makes you effective in your job is a lot more than your legal skills. Knowing the law and how to apply it is of course important, but many good lawyers can do that.

What makes for a great in-house counsel is efficiently helping your company achieve its strategic objectives. Your core contribution to this goal is helping your company identify and navigate relevant risks. Here's how you do that.

## Know the business

You first need to understand well what your company wants to accomplish from a business perspective. This is not trivial for lawyers, because you need to get out of your lawyer mindset and think more like you've got a master's in business administration (MBA).

Your business colleagues will have a long list of items, some vital to the company's success and others less so. You can't make useful risk assessments unless you understand the importance of the various business projects to the business. You will spend more time and be more creative in designing a risk-based approach when the project is critical. And you will be less tolerant of excess risk when a project is merely "nice to have."

## Stay out of trouble

Similarly, how do you know what sorts of things are likely to get your company in trouble?

- Well, regulators themselves give you hints by the pace and scope of their rulemaking, as well as when they make public comments.
- Politicians do the same, usually by ratcheting up pressure on regulators.
- And if you're lucky, authorities will investigate and penalize other industry participants before you.

All this gives you warnings about what's hot and where you need to focus.

## Work well with others

Next, because you are just one person, the amount you can do directly is limited. Thus, every manager is ultimately measured by how well they work with and through others.

For legal counsel, you more than most need to get your colleagues to do what you want them to. That's doubly hard because what you want often goes against their incentives and inclinations.

- You want salespeople to pay attention to contract terms even though that makes getting new business harder and takes longer.

- All employees need to be compliant and follow the law, even though this adds administrative burdens to their daily work.

Thus, you need to be great at building relationships. When your senior management team not only understands but is fully bought into your legal priorities, they will help you implement them. They will do this because they see the value to the company in what you're trying to accomplish, not just the costs.

You don't need everyone on your side, but you certainly can't do it alone.

## There's likely much to learn and do where you are

I got better at my job every year for 20 years. You never stop finding ways to understand better your company and its business.

Every year makes you sharper in assessing which risks are the ones you need to focus on. And with every relationship you build and deepen, you expand your effective reach. Last but not least, you may feel immensely satisfied seeing the results of your hard work pay off over years.

Now consider the frequent job hopper. Even if they stay within their known industry, and many do not, they are but novices when it comes to many important things relating to their new company:

- The history that led to the current strategy

- Relationships among management and the board

- Whose opinion is respected and which others have the potential to cause trouble for you?

It's a long list of things you need to learn when you switch companies before you have any hope of being as effective as you were at your old company. The shiny new title (and let's not forget, higher pay) frequently blinds us to how much harder and riskier our jobs are in the early years. That is, there are costs and tradeoffs when taking that new job.

I know some remarkable people who have gone from strength to strength, who seem to be effective from the first day in a new job. These people are pretty rare in my experience. You may be one of them.

For all the rest of us, we owe it to ourselves to think about how effective we've become in our current jobs and why. Our self-reflection may inspire us to stay around a little longer.

Far from being a cop-out, deciding to stay at a company where you perform well demonstrates good judgment *and* courage.

Be well.

* This is a conversation I would have liked to have with every colleague I worked with over the years who was tempted to leave the company. Better late than never.

## Chapter Twenty-One

# The Worst Career Advice I've Seen in Ages

## The happiest people I know are the ones who learn that success is not measured in money

I've noted before that bad advice is plentiful. Still, I was stunned to read in an otherwise respectable publication what I think is quite possibly the worst career advice ever.

The Wall Street Journal published an article about job switchers with the subheading *"Even if you're happy at your job, getting a new job for more pay is a good strategy as inflation eats into paychecks."*

I've come across similar advice elsewhere: Always go after the bigger paycheck; your future raises build off your base salary, so target the highest-paying job; titles matter more than substance, so grab the CEO title if you want to earn the big bucks.

To be clear, this advice is spot-on if you want to make more money. But it is fantastically wrong-headed if you want to be happy in life.

The Journal article discusses data from the Federal Reserve Bank of Atlanta indicating that job switchers saw raises of 6.4%, while job stayers saw increases of only 4.7%.

Never mind that such a gap is not unusual. There is almost always a spread between job switchers and stayers, and job switchers typically increase their salary as part of a switch.

I have three objections to the idea of switching jobs just to make more money.

1. We are selfish employees if we think of our jobs only insofar as they meet our needs

2. We become more effective at our jobs with specific experience in our jobs

3. It is dangerously misleading to reinforce the idea that making more money (beyond a fairly low level) will improve your life satisfaction

## 1. Your job is about more than just you

The directors of a company serve at the pleasure of shareholders, and the officers serve at the pleasure of the board of directors. Although D&Os are typically handsomely paid for their service, they have clear fiduciary duties to the constituents whose interests they serve.

I don't expect every employee to have the same feelings of fiduciary duty. It is reasonable to expect, however, employees to identify with and wish to see their companies succeed.

If you find yourself believing that your company owes you something and you owe nothing in return, you are a bad employee.

## 2. You need time to get good at your job

There are more than enough people with the raw talent to do most jobs. What makes a person stand out as a top performer? It is when they know enough about their company, colleagues, and culture to effectively drive strategic initiatives.

Good ideas are plentiful. The ability to implement good ideas is rare indeed. This requires a mix of realism, humility, and doggedness that most people never find. The people who do develop this mix typically do so only after some years on the job.

- They learn about their company's history, including its past successes and failures.

- They identify the respected voices, those people who can help speed a project along or, conversely, stop one in its tracks.

- They learn how an initiative fits with the company's overall strategy, finding opportune times to push when they know they'll find a tailwind.

People who switch jobs every few years learn none of this. They forever run up against walls they don't even understand.

Ironically, this makes them more likely to switch jobs again, before frustration and burnout (and their own lack of results) derail them.

## 3. Making money is a means, not an end

Some of the most ambitious people I know would seem to have the least to complain about. Generous six-figure salaries, comfortable work environments, and enviable lifestyles.

And despite their objective advantages, they are tempted by a higher salary, an ostensible promotion, and a new company. It's as if they feel compelled to pursue the objective markers for success.

When I ask, "Will making more money change your life in meaningful ways?" or "What is it that makes you successful in your current job, and will you have the same advantages in your new one?" they don't have ready answers.

The happiest people I know are the ones who learn that success is not measured in money:

- Can you say you like, trust, and respect the people you work with?
- Is your work interesting, challenging, and valuable?
- And do you share values with a solid company that has a strategy for continued success?

Then you have all you need to be happy and successful in your career. And if you find yourself in that position, why would you give up a great job for a little more money or even a lot more money?

If you do, you risk getting not only what you want but what you deserve.

Be well.

Chapter Twenty-Two

# You Can't Buy Accountability

## And that's why it's so sought after in companies

I've had a bias in favor of in-house counsel for years. These are lawyers who work as employees of a single company. It seemed to me that in-house counsel have many advantages over outside counsel, meaning lawyers who work in a law firm for many clients.

I admit that when I worked in private practice at a law firm, I had the exact opposite view. Outside counsel are in the business of delivering legal advice. As such, I thought, they've got greater focus, specialization, and expertise. Also, why would clients pay hundreds of dollars an hour for them to answer questions if not for the brilliance?

I spent only five years in private practice, but that was long enough to realize our clients carried many motives. Most had properly difficult issues that needed our thorough and expensive attention.

Many clients, however, seemed to use our services for other reasons: As overflow capacity, to handle bothersome tasks, or to provide credibility in potentially risky cases.

When I took up the General Counsel role in my company, I soon found all three reasons to be objectionable. Let's consider them in turn.

**Overflow capacity: Legal needs aren't so unpredictable**

Every legal team deals with a reasonably predictable workload, alongside the terrifying unpredictable matters that lurk behind random phone calls and emails.

Combining both work types can make it seem like our total workload itself is unpredictable. But this is not so for at least two reasons.

1. Predictable work is just that: predictable. No matter what other distractions arise, the regular needs of the business must be met. Depending on your business, this work likely constitutes 60–80 percent of the workload.

2. Unpredictable work is unpredictable only in the specific details and not in *whether* unpredictable things will occur.

Over time I came to realize that, while I couldn't say exactly when, for example, an employee dispute would crop up, or what form it would take, we would have a certain number of them.

Or that, although significant customer or supplier disputes were rare, they did occur. And eventually, almost all the matters that I once would have called a surprise were anything but.

This means that a legal team's workload is mostly foreseeable, most of the time. Seeking outside help for work that is reasonably foreseeable, and paying handsomely for the flexibility, seemed to me like an expensive luxury. And because I sought to deliver value to my company, I soon viewed such capacity buying as an avoidable luxury.

Whenever our outside counsel spending exceeded a certain threshold, I'd make the case for hiring an in-house resource to do the work ourselves. I originally made the business case on financial terms, because the payoff was immediate.

Only later did I realize my business colleagues valued in-house lawyers fundamentally differently. More on this in a moment.

## Bothersome tasks: Doing unglamorous work is part of the job

Yes, I get it. We all want to do exciting, innovative, and important work. It takes experience and maturity to understand a lot of important work is neither exciting nor innovative. It's up to team leaders to make employees see the value in doing unglamorous but important work.

Although some employees are more willing to go along than others, don't be a lazy manager and take advantage of them. The right way to dole out important work is the same way to divvy up exciting work: A roughly equal share that gives everyone similar opportunities to contribute and develop.

And as the team leader, that means you should do a fair share of unglamorous work too. I know that with seniority comes some perks, which includes being able to assign less desirable work to team members. Do this too often and you become the boss you once hated.

It is also being a lazy manager if you foist off unglamorous work to outside counsel. Not only is this more expensive, they see it as unglamorous too and push it down to the least experienced associate. What makes you think that's an appropriate way to get important work done well?

And before you tell me that much unglamorous work is also unimportant, I would say that your legal strategy surely has identified and eliminated unimportant work in favor of proper priorities.

## Buying credibility: Going outside risks selling your own credibility short

When you have significant matters before you, you may be tempted to call on outside counsel for expertise, moral support, and authority. Often this is the right call, especially when you are in an unfamiliar legal domain. Be careful, though, and don't call on outside help to make decisions for you.

You have one thing even the most expert outside counsel lacks, and the business knows it: Accountability.

Outside counsel are your hired guns. But the company they're defending is your home, where you spend most of your time, and where your friends also work. When outside counsel's work is done, they ride off, having been paid either way. You live with the consequences.

The best outside counsel appreciate this dynamic and support their in-house colleagues. They collaborate closely with you behind the scenes so that when you make recommendations to management about what to do next, they are *your* recommendations.

This is not an ego question so much as a judgment question. Nothing can take the place of your deep knowledge of your company's business and risk appetite.

Thus, the most important thing you bring to the table as in-house counsel is ownership. When you own your decisions, and your colleagues know it, that brings you credibility money can't buy.

Be well.

## Chapter Twenty-Three

# Sweet CEO Lies: "Employees Are Our Most Valuable Asset"

## I'll tell you what CEOs genuinely believe but will never say out loud

For everyone worried about DOGE firing large swathes of government employees, there was an earlier precedent when he took over Twitter. Almost everyone agreed Musk was making a huge mistake when swung his giant scythe at the employee ranks of Twitter. Reports suggest he fired as many as 80% of Twitter's employees.

How could this not have an immediate detrimental effect on shareholder value? Wasn't he just killing the company quickly rather than slowly like everyone assumed he would?

The people who *didn't* think Musk was risking much (then or now) included those who've managed large teams of employees in big U.S. corporations. We know something about the truth of that much-hyped ending to many CEO's annual shareholder letters:

> *I want to thank our hardworking employees. Employees are our most valuable asset.*

## Employees are far from equal

What we know (and what every CEO knows but will never say) is the following:

- About 10% of employees have a real impact
- A bit more than half are better to have than not
- The rest are either not pulling their weight or are downright harmful

You can also think of it this way: 10% of employees generate 80% of the value, and another 5% generate 80% of the problems.

You can probably remember being around employees who massively drive progress. Because you're reading this, you're more likely to be one of those employees. Congratulations!

I spent a career as a corporate lawyer dealing with the 5% who generated most of the problems. They're real and preventing them from harming your company is seriously time-consuming.

The problem every company faces is how to reliably find out which employees are which. Performance evaluations are all but useless, given the exaggeration and self-serving lying that occurs by everyone. Waiting for trouble to arise is also risky.

## Musk was looking for a way to quickly sort employees

Musk's method was quick and brutal, so necessarily was imperfect. But it seems clear he was trying to identify who were the top and bottom employees by forcing them to self-select.

No slacker or outright troublemaker was going to sign up for 80-hour weeks of in-office pressure and unrelenting work. Was there a risk Musk would lose some of his best performers as well? Of course. But he almost certainly cut out a cancer that would have slowly killed Twitter just as his detractors hoped.

What about the great majority of employees in the middle, who are neither superstars nor super-shitty? Here we come to the lie in every CEO's letter to shareholders about employees being the company's most valuable asset.

- The truth is, that companies are far stronger when they can identify and

# SWEET CEO LIES: "EMPLOYEES ARE OUR MOST VALUABLE ASSET"

remove the 5% harmful subversives and the 15–25% disengaged and lazy.

- Moreover, because every large organization is a morass of bureaucracy and inefficiency, half of the average employees are functionally unnecessary or performing tasks that don't materially help the company.

One reason so many people hate Elon Musk is that he is willing to do things that uncomfortably disrupt the status quo. If his company can survive just fine with 20% of its employees, what does that suggest about the staffing of other large companies? Or the U.S. government?

## What are a company's most valuable assets?

There's a pretty clear accounting answer to this question. Your feelings for Mr. Musk aside, a company's financial statements reveal the value of their various assets.

Employees are not even close to the most valuable asset at most companies. The list looks more like this:

1. The company brand

2. Intellectual property around the products and services

3. New products and services

4. Customer relationships

5. Legacy products and services

6. Supplier relationships

... Employees are usually in the top ten, though.

If you want your company to think you're really valuable, it helps to be honest about where you fall on the curve.

Be well

# Chapter Twenty-Four

# How To Manipulate CEOs

## This is something writers are especially well-positioned to do

I was several years into my executive role as head of legal for a large public company when I realized my fellow managers were idiots, none more so than the CEO.

I don't mean they sucked at their jobs or lacked education, experience, or skills. Far from it. These were capable, well-trained, and effective individuals. It's just that they suffered from a common flaw that afflicted their decision-making. Worse yet, they were completely unaware of it.

Did this mean individuals could take shameless advantage of the blind spot whenever they needed to influence a manager's thinking? I'll leave the answer to your imagination.

The method is simplicity itself. I share it with you today not so you can manipulate others but to help ensure others don't make a fool of you.

### Stories carry disproportionate weight in persuasion

The blind spot is this: We all like to think we are rational, logical decision-makers but we are not. We make decisions based on emotions and effortlessly rationalize our decisions. Thus, an easy way to influence someone's decision is to hijack their emotions.

Nothing arouses emotions better than a story. You'd think this has little traction in the business context because who has time for long-winded stories?

That's where anecdotes come in. All you need is a single customer remark and you've got powerful juju in your hands.

Let's say you want to cause trouble for a colleague who is showing dangerous competence and ambition. They've recently rolled out a new customer-facing app. Here's what you do:

- Casually remark to your colleague's boss that you heard customers were complaining about glitches in the new app.

- Pro tip: Enlist an ally to make a similar offhand comment a few days later.

- Then sit back and watch the anecdote turn into reality.

The reason this works is because emotions are in play. The boss is secretly worried that their smooth ascent will be interrupted and they'll be found out as a fraud. Nothing reveals their lack of substance so much as disgruntled customers. At the merest whiff of discontent, they'll scatter like chickens before a hungry fox.

The rival who rolled out the app is sorely disadvantaged. That's because there's always somebody who dislikes change. They'll be complaining no matter how great the new app is. Furthermore, to claim that no customer had problems is not believable and will undermine the rival's credibility.

Even worse for them, if they try to present data to counter the point, they'll come across as defensive. You cannot fight anecdotes with logic or data.

## How to recognize when someone's using the method on you

Whenever someone refers to general feedback from customers in vague terms, chances are excellent they're trying to trick you with anecdotes. Either that or they've themselves been fooled by someone who applied the method to them.

Here's an example from the writers' platform, Medium. In one of their Writer Newsletters, the VP of Content said this:

> *The goal of the Medium Partner Program is to deliver value to readers and writers, and* ***we often hear from our members*** *that these kinds of stories ["meta" stories about Medium itself] aren't the*

*ones they want to read, much less pay for. You're free to write meta stories, we just don't want Partner Program funds going to them. Payments seem to incentivize extra navel gazing and unwanted get-rich-quick culture.* [emphasis added]

Did you catch the misdirection? "We often hear from readers..." Oh really? I would bet you a considerable sum that this is pure anecdote driving emotions used to support a pre-determined outcome.

There are several indications to support this:

- How exactly does Medium solicit feedback from writers or readers? Moreover, those who submit unsolicited feedback have found themselves handily rebuffed.

- How many writers craft "meta" stories precisely because they have historically been their most popular stories? More engagement, more comments, and active interest from readers and writers alike.

- Of all the types of stories people supposedly don't want to read, why is it that management throttles "meta" stories? There's smut and poetry and politics and any number of topics that people don't like. For all these, we're told to click "less like this" and the problem is solved. But, uniquely, readers and writers alike can't figure out how to see fewer "meta" stories.

- Medium reveals their hidden emotions with the last sentence — note the phrase "extra navel gazing and unwanted get-rich-quick culture." This is management saying what IT wants, not what writers and readers want. Half of the work on Medium consists of navel-gazing and the other half is get-rich-quick hacks.

Medium's animus to criticism from members is further reflected in its Distribution Guidelines: "We also often see inaccurate speculation or advice and are not able to respond in every case." Got it? Misinformation shall be censored in the name of a "better internet." That this also hides information critical of management is entirely coincidental.

Medium can do what it likes. What they cannot do is pretend they are simply delivering what readers and writers wish.

Medium is doing what IT wants, namely reducing distribution (censoring) stories that raise questions about what management itself is doing. We see you.

## Two methods to fight the tactic

You can fight back with anecdotes of your own. This will not win any arguments but will blunt the force of one-sided anecdotes.

If you have the time and money, you can gather data to refute a misleading anecdote. This is risky because you will be confronted with motivated reasoning. That is, people believe what they want to believe and handily fit evidence to their preconceptions.

You are thus wise if you first explore the hidden motivations of management and your colleagues. What do they secretly believe or wish to be true? If you can play to and reinforce existing beliefs (or fears or wishes, etc.) you will find receptive ears.

Best of all, you don't need to be bound by data or facts in playing to a person's unstated beliefs. They are primed to believe you. You can freely concoct anecdotes of your own and they will go unchallenged.

I've heard from many writers that they're annoyed with the tone-deaf changes being rolled out by management.

Be well.

## Chapter Twenty-Five

# Maybe Attaining Work-Life Balance Isn't the Best Goal for You

## Instead, deliberately choose when to be unbalanced

At one point several years into my General Counsel role for an S&P 500 public company, I wrote three letters up on my whiteboard. They were to serve as my guideposts for the rest of my career.

The letters were these: F H W.

My boss came in one day and asked "What're those?"

I told him they stood for Family, Health, and Work. I said that they represented my priorities in life, in that order.

He pondered my whiteboard and my statement for a few moments and said, "Those are nice goals ... for your next job."

Message clear. What got you here is what will keep you here. If you want an easy life, go get an easy job.

### Balance and performance are like Clark Kent and Superman

That is, you generally don't see them together.

Nothing in my path to getting a C-suite job by my 30s was remotely the result of balance.

- *Family*: haha! I was single until my last year of law school. When I started working, I kept a picture of my wife nearby to remember what she looked like.

- *Social life*: You must be joking. In my law firm days, the only times I wasn't working I was desperate for sleep.

- *Exercise*: Yeah, right. I suppose carting boxes of prospectuses from the printer counted for something.

Okay, so I worked a lot more than was healthy. But I credit my rise in no small part to letting my life get well and truly out of balance in pursuit of high performance.

## What about after you reach your goal? Can you find balance then?

That was my initial thought. "*Oh, when I'm experienced and powerful enough, I'll be able to find balance.*"

It wasn't to be. But this story is no tragedy.

My epiphany leading to those three letters appearing on my whiteboard was suddenly realizing that I was mid-30s, overweight, out of shape, and likely heading for an early heart attack.

I resolved to adopt healthy habits, starting with losing weight. I approached this mission with abandon, which is to say completely unbalanced, shedding 50 pounds (ca. 23 kg) in six weeks.

Now, how to maintain a healthy weight? It seemed clear that exercise plus diet was a winning combination, so I started running while eating largely the same meals every single day.

This is about the time when I wrote the three letters on the board. At that moment, my focus was pretty clearly on the H part of the trio. I was going to be healthy no matter the cost.

That's why I ignored my boss and stuck with my exercise habit. And although I was prepared to be fired for my conviction, in the end, my company got a fine deal.

True, I was now spending an hour a day exercising that I could have been working. But the impact of working out at lunchtime was incredibly positive to my performance.

So positive that we introduced physical fitness as a key component of our global management training program.

## Did you ever achieve balance?

Not really. But I think I achieved something better.

That is, I came to understand that life is about flux and change. I embraced the uncertainty and learned to work with it.

Nothing around us is static, fixed, or in balance. Why should our lives be? Life is punctuated by intense peaks and drudgerous flat stretches.

- Sometimes we're healthy and sometimes we're not. We can control a lot, but not everything.
- We enjoy tender and beautiful times with friends and family that carry us through the times we are apart.
- Work tosses up challenges that demand every bit of our attention and effort. It is also repetitive and boring and maddening.
- Maybe your fitness goals will require intense periods of training, leading you to temporarily neglect other areas of life.

The one caution I'd recommend is to *be deliberate in choosing when to be unbalanced*. I always knew when I was devoting unusual time in pursuit of a priority and made sure it was temporary.

I'll train hard for six months, but then family and work need to get their fair share. I'll work weekends to see an intense project to the finish line, but then I'll take my vacation.

## In sum: Why being unbalanced is okay

If you seek high performance in one domain (work), you'll likely seek it in others.

Letting yourself become unbalanced in your pursuit of ambitious goals increases the odds you will achieve them.

To me at least, the thrill of achieving outrageous goals was worth giving up the improbable dream of balance.

Be well.

Chapter Twenty-Six

# This 3-Step Method Can Help You Build Resilience

## Remember, you can turn adversity into strength!

Learned everything valuable about resilience while working, including my twenty years leading the legal team of a multinational public company.

Then I retired and discovered I wasn't finished learning about resilience.

If work gave me two key components for building resilience, philosophy was the third piece that helped create a unified whole.

Here's how I'll share it with you:

- I describe what I mean by resilience.
- I offer a handy lens for making sense of the world.
- I share a simple method for building resilience.
- Lastly, we'll explore the method's application in three core areas: (1) your person, (2) your planning, and (3) your thoughts.

### Resilience Means ...

A resilient person is strong, capable, and tough.

When the unexpected occurs, a resilient person is able to deal with every eventuality.

When hit with a setback, a resilient person bounces back quickly, even stronger.

How do you think about resilience? Would you add anything to these descriptions?

## A handy lens for viewing the world: What's in your control?

Understanding the answer to this simple question helps you focus your efforts when building resilience.

Distinguish between things fully in your control, outside your control, and partially in your control.

**Fully in our control**: what we think, say, and do. (*Us, our person*)

**Outside our control**: the world and its random happenings, third parties (what others think, say, and do), and bad luck, such as weather and delays. (*What happens to us*)

**Partially in our control**: how prepared are we for what happens, how we respond to what happens, and our good fortune. (*How we respond to what happens*)

> *It is an invincible greatness of mind not to be elevated or dejected with good or ill fortune. A wise man is content with his lot, whatever it be — without wishing for what he has not.* — Seneca

## A Simple Method for Building Resilience: Increase Your Control and Leverage What You Do Control

The more you assume responsibility, the more resilient you will be. If you are not the master of yourself, who is?

- Who controls your own person?

# THIS 3-STEP METHOD CAN HELP YOU BUILD RESILIENCE

- Who controls what you know and can do?
- Who controls what you feel?

As you consider these questions, remember that things that appear outside your control may not be.

The unexpected is troublesome, true, but you can manage what you plan for. And even when you control little of your external circumstances, you still have control.

> *Knowing others is to be clever. Knowing self is to be wise. Overcoming others requires force. Overcoming self requires strength. Realizing contentment is wealth.* — Lao Tzu, Tao Te Ching

Let's explore your levers.

## 1. Your person — Make yourself strong, capable, and tough

You can make yourself stronger in three domains: your person, your abilities, and your attitude.

**Your person**: Adopt long-term healthy habits.

- Schedule time for fitness in your calendar
- Eat healthy, take time for lunch
- Get up and walk around periodically, e.g. every 90 minutes
- Get enough sleep, with consistent bedtimes and waking times

**Your abilities**: Continuously improve your skills.

- Take advantage of continuous improvement opportunities
- University courses, in-person and online
- Professional reading, podcasts
- Zen koan: "to a sincere student, every day is a fortunate day"

**Your attitude**: Cultivate a positive mindset. Simple habits can shape your personality.*

- Practice gratitude

- Maintain a journal

- Meditate briefly

- Engage with your social network

- Exercise (supporting the first point above)

> *You are a combination of your habits and the people who you spend the most time with. Many distinctions between people who get happier as they get older and people who don't can be explained by what habits they have developed.* — Naval Rivikant

## 2. Your planning — Be prepared for any eventuality

Regain control over the unexpected using three simple tools.

**Ask "what if" questions**. You cannot be surprised by things you have anticipated.

**Prepare contingency plans**. You respond more quickly and effectively by giving yourself a head start when a crisis hits.

Here are some examples to illustrate.

Question: What if it rains today? Contingency plan: I will bring my raincoat and an umbrella.

Question: What if my train is late? Contingency plan: I will build extra time into my schedule and leave earlier.

Question: What if my company gets sued? Contingency plan: I've interviewed lawyers in advance and I know who I would call for each type of case.

Question: What if we have a problem with one of the products we sold? Contingency plan: I have product liability insurance.

The third tool is to learn to **be happy for small crises**. When you've anticipated and planned, you welcome the chance to practice. Here are the rules of thumb regarding crises:

- Anything you haven't planned for has the potential to become a big crisis.
- Anything that doesn't kill you is a small crisis.
- Your test is never the crisis itself, but how prepared you are to respond.

*Those whose care extends not far ahead will find their troubles near at hand.* — Confucius

## 3. Your thoughts— Become stronger in the face of setbacks

You regain control over your thoughts in the face of setbacks by asking yourself three questions:

1. **Did I plan for this situation?** Whenever you encounter a situation you've planned for, you have already succeeded.
2. **Is it really so bad?** So what if … I get wet, I'm a few minutes late, my flight is canceled, etc.
3. **What's the upside case?**

The first two exercises are relatively easy. Answering the third question advances you from average practitioner to expert.

Make a game of finding the silver lining in apparent misfortune. It gets easier the more you do it.

- The rain is calming and cleans pollen from the air.
- My train/plane being late means I have more time to finish that podcast.

- This massive lawsuit means my priorities suddenly became clear.

Over time, you'll be able to find the positive in every situation: didn't get that big promotion, lost your car keys, sprained your ankle.

> *I have always believed, and I still believe, that whatever good or bad fortune may come our way we can always give it meaning and transform it into something of value.* — Herman Hesse

## Summary of the three-step resilience method

Start by understanding what's in your control and what's not. Seek then to increase your control where possible and leverage the control you do have.

Your three areas of emphasis are as follows: your person, your planning, and your thoughts.

1. Make yourself strong, capable, and tough by being physically fit, pursuing continuous improvement opportunities, and cultivating a positive mindset.

2. Be prepared for every eventuality by asking what could happen and putting in place simple contingency plans.

3. Use your control over your thoughts to turn adversity into an advantage by always spotting the silver lining.

The wonderful news is that building resilience is within our control. When all others are losing their heads, we can be both calm and strong.

Be well.

# Chapter Twenty-Seven

# Most Advice Fails One of These Two Tests

## Plus, why people don't take advice

We've never had more advice available to us. How come everyone isn't wealthy, healthy, and happy as a result?

How come we aren't all making $10,000 a week without working, or attracting 100,000 views a day on our blog, or whatever else it is that our hearts desire?

I'll answer these questions by describing why most advice fails. I then offer a method for you to assess whether the advice you're considering is right for you.

### Here's one reason people don't take advice

As a corporate lawyer, my business was giving advice. As a General Counsel for twenty years, I got used to people following my advice — whether they wanted to or not.

Now I'm just one voice among thousands, writing publicly about how to achieve better outcomes. People are entirely free to take my advice or ignore it. I'll admit, I sometimes long for my authoritarian days.

I focus my writing on things I know best, which is what I've seen work in the real world over decades. (I list my core strengths below if you're curious.) I'm trying to limit myself to only solid advice. So why don't people take it every time?

Machiavelli has part of the answer. In describing rulers and their advisers in The Prince, Machiavelli said this:

*There are actually three kinds of mind: one grasps things unaided, the second sees what another has grasped, and the third grasps nothing and sees nothing.*

## What group are you in?

This simple concept explains why the world is divided into an elite one percent, a highly effective 10 percent, and everyone else.

Only a tiny percentage of people are novel thinkers with great ideas. The next group can distinguish between great ideas and everything else, i.e., they can tell good advice from bad advice.

The final group is neither original nor discerning in their thinking — they are forever prone to making mistakes because they don't recognize or follow good advice. It's just not in their nature.

## Can people change the group they're in?

Particularly if you don't start out naturally gifted, can you become a person who is able to at least identify good advice?

I'm convinced the answer is yes. (Otherwise, many of us are wasting a lot of our time trying to spread good advice.) How does one learn to identify good advice?

Do we trust a pundit because of their position or experience? Are we convinced by a good anecdote or testimonial? Do we want hard data backing up the expert's claims?

In preparing my own advice, I read lots of other people's advice. I can tell you, there's a great deal of excellent advice out there. But there's as much or more poor advice. Your first task is thus to identify advice worth considering.

## Good advice must pass these two tests

1. It must work at all

2. It must work for you in your situation

Most advice fails one or both of these tests.

Advice that does not work *at all* is unquestionably poor advice. So why is it so common? It comes about because people repeat things they see frequently without exploring the underlying rationale.

To give you a few examples:

- **Pursuing your passion** is a great way to work hard while going broke. Some people will be successful, but it will be because of many factors beyond their passion.

- If you **just keep doing something**, eventually you will be successful. This fallacy gives rise to the immense profits of lottery operators and casinos. Not to mention the broken dreams of many a poet, pundit, or weather prognosticator. It's easy to see that most people will fail at many activities no matter how long they persist.

Advice that does not work *for you* is also poor advice, at least as far as you're concerned. This advice arises because people mistake anecdotes for evidence. That is, a well-meaning person says "This worked for me! Do what I did, and you will see the results I did."

Uh, almost certainly not. You won't get the results Tim Ferriss did by reading his books or listening to his podcast because you don't think like Tim Ferriss. You won't get Tim Denning's income by subscribing to his newsletter or taking his courses, because you don't write like Tim Denning.

We're fooled by such persons because they communicate engagingly and show a genuine desire to help. How can I not want to listen to someone successful and entertaining who is offering to help me?

What's a person looking for self-improvement to do?

## You must apply critical thinking to any advice you're considering

1. Ask first, **does it look like this advice ever works for anyone?** What evidence do I have for this? Is it just folk wisdom that has been repeated endlessly, or is there any objective data I can assess?

2. Then ask, **what are the conditions** under which people have

successfully implemented this advice? For example— Does running a successful winery require $10 million in starting capital?— What percentage of investors beat their benchmark performance in any given year? What percentage do so over ten years? Are factors other than luck necessary to explain the results?— Is every person who just "writes every day" successful in time? Or is it that the large majority of writers stop, and some gifted ones continue on to success?

3. If you can identify conditions for success, be honest in assessing **whether those conditions apply in your case**. If not, that advice won't work for you. If yes, keep thinking.

4. Next, explore other reasons **why people have failed** trying to implement this advice. What external factors influenced their outcomes? What individual-specific factors drove results? And so on.

5. If you meet the base conditions for success and the likely reasons for failure do not apply to you, you are not done. Now ask, **what else did this person do** that contributed to their success? Is there companion advice that you must also consider?

This is starting to sound like hard work, even to me. It also explains why people have a hard time identifying good advice and then successfully implementing it.

But now you're armed with one method to determine whether someone's advice is good for you.

Be well.

# Chapter Twenty-Eight

# How to Measure Your Impact on the World

## An explanation of the Purpose-Influence-Power Model for determining your impact on the world

Do you have an idea how you impact the world? Would you like to know how you compare on a relative basis?

We're living in times when individuals can reach more fellow humans than ever before. This is because the world's population has never been larger and our tools to reach others have never been more powerful. As a result, people today can do great good but also great harm.

The Purpose-Influence-Power Model gives us a helpful tool to examine individuals' relative impact. Let me explain a few terms and then we can fill in some details and try our model out.

### What does Purpose mean?

Purpose means both what you are trying to achieve and the likely outcome, at least directionally. Important: *you don't get credit for good intentions alone.*

If you are trying to feed your family but you do so by selling drugs or stealing, you're trending towards the left side of the chart — causing harm. We say this even though your stated intention may be to help others, i.e. your family.

Similarly, if you say you want to help others, but you do so by establishing a charity that pays you a salary that consumes most of your donated funds, you belong in the self-focused column.

Think of purpose as intention plus effect, or your aim and the result you achieve.

## What does Influence mean?

Influence means the number of people you can reach by your actions. How much good (or harm) can you do directly?

If you are selling vegetables from your garden, your reach is those people who buy your produce.

If you are a petty criminal, your reach is the people you victimize plus the follow-on victims. I.e., stealing from a parent also affects what they can provide for their family.

If you are sharing ideas with the world, your reach is everyone who comes across your idea. A sign on your lawn has less reach than a letter to the editor of your local paper. Your letter has less reach than a viral video.

## What does Power mean?

Power also measures the number of people your actions affect, with the difference that power reflects what you can do *indirectly*.

Because you're the CEO, you can fire thousands of employees with a simple decision. If you're the President, you can sign legislation into law. When you're a billionaire philanthropist, you can direct charitable spending that affects millions.

## Power versus Influence — Some distinctions

A person with influence tends to have power because their ideas spread. While they cannot force anyone to change their behavior, their ideas cause people to change how they think. Thus, influence is a form of indirect power.

A person with power tends to have influence. If nothing else, they can force you to bend to their will. Their power can be purely structural, meaning it comes largely from their office or position because individuals do not trust their ideas.

Alternatively, a person's structural power can be supported by their also having influential ideas. A billionaire CEO with 100 million Twitter followers has both structural power and indirect power via their influence.

## The fun part — Filling in the chart

Now we can identify categories of people in the different areas of the Purpose-Influence-Power chart.

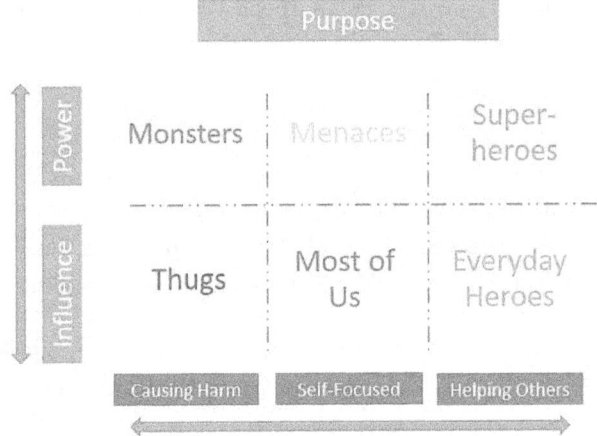

*The Purpose-Influence-Power Model (c) James Bellerjeau*

## Most of Us

Most of us fall into the **Most of Us** category. We have limited influence or power and focus on our own problems. And that's totally OK. Because even without structural power or influential ideas, people can make the world worse.

## Thugs

Those that cause intentional harm are Thugs. Thugs are plentiful, and include petty criminals, online scammers, and everyone else who decides to harm others or is indifferent to their suffering.

## Everyday Heroes

At the other end are Everyday Heroes, people who make the world better by their actions. They include anyone who contributes to charity, volunteers their time, or takes any action to alleviate unnecessary suffering.

## Menaces

As one's influence and power grow, the greater your opportunities for real impact. Menaces use their power and influence for selfish purposes. They miss an opportunity to do good but do not descend into active harm. Think of narcissistic politicians or oligarchs who selfishly spend their money on lavish indulgences.

## Monsters

The other two extremes interest us, because their impact is great. Monsters have power and influence and cause harm to the world. As a reminder, intentions are not as important as impact, particularly when one has great power and influence.

- Mark Zuckerberg may have intended to connect the world, but his social media companies' have also sowed mistrust, misinformation, and division.

- Similarly, George Soros may have intended to advance social justice, but his progressive prosecutors have unleashed a crime wave on the unhappy victims he was most hoping to help.

## Superheroes

This leaves us with the happy category of Superheroes, people who use their great power and influence with both the intention *and effect* of helping improve the world.

- Bill Gates and Warren Buffet are surely in this category thanks to their immense charitable contributions that have benevolent effects.

- It seems clear that Elon Musk belongs here as well. He generates resentment because of his power and influence, as do most in the top half of the chart. But Mr. Musk's intentions and his impact have been positive for humankind, at least so far.

Going forward we will fill in our chart with world leaders, politicians, celebrities, and more. Let me know someone you'd like to place on the Purpose-Influence-Power chart, and we can do it together.

Be well.

Chapter Twenty-Nine

# Do You Overweight the Present at the Cost of the Future?

## Most of us ignore the long-term effects of our individual daily decisions. But we can turn human nature to our advantage

A bird in the hand is worth two in the bush. Have you ever wondered why that is? The proverb reveals facets of human nature that lead most of us astray, but which can also be our salvation.

This proverb contains two truths:

- We value things we can have now more than things we will receive in the future
- We place even less weight on future outcomes if there is uncertainty about the future

### The future is distant ... and murky

We know eating that donut is bad for us. But it sure tastes good! And we tell ourselves we took the stairs this morning. Plus, it was a stressful day and we deserve it, don't we?

This shows the problem with our daily habits: The connection between the donut today and our weight tomorrow, let alone a few months from now is virtually invisible. The same is true for a workout and our long-term fitness.

Put differently, the future value of a single decision today is highly uncertain. This helps explain why we fail the marshmallow test, i.e., we do not defer immediate gratification for a later gain.

At the same time, the *cumulative* effect of daily decisions we make over months and years is all too plain. If we spend more than we earn, we will rack up debt. If we do not exercise, we'll be unfit. We all know this, and yet we routinely manage to avoid thinking about it.

## Two levers make the future feel more tangible

To make the future reward look more attractive relative to the present temptation, we can do the following:

1. Increase the perceived value of the future reward

2. Decrease uncertainty about the likelihood we will receive the reward

We can make a future reward more valuable by making it more personal and tangible. We don't intuitively feel we have much in common with our future selves. Maybe this is because we struggle to imagine that we will be old.

One way to overcome this failure of imagination is to age a photo of your current face. Several apps will do this. When you see a picture of your future aged face, you can much more easily imagine you will one day be older.

This simple trick allows you to wonder about your future life and care about your future self. Visualize yourself several decades from now, think about what your life will be like, and remember that will be you.

To decrease uncertainty about the future impact of your actions, try changing the frame.

It's hard to discipline yourself to avoid things that are bad for you like overeating or being sedentary. So instead of playing defense, turn your daily habits into an affirmative offensive weapon.

- You're not going to get a flat stomach or run a marathon overnight. But can you walk for 30 minutes a day, and switch from a processed snack to a piece of fruit? Yes, you can.

Don't think of this as using up willpower to keep from doing things that are bad for you. Rather, you are taking small positive steps by doing things you like. (And don't worry if you don't initially like the positive steps. After a couple of weeks, you will like what you do.)

Fostering good habits is easier than avoiding bad ones, even if the actions you take are identical.

In your mind, consider your daily habits your secret weapon to drive long-term outcomes one small step at a time.

Be well.

Chapter Thirty

# How to Use Metrics Wisely, Instead of Letting Them Manipulate You

Just because you can measure it doesn't mean it's worth pursuing

Except for the Friday I drove myself to the hospital for an emergency appendectomy, I never missed a day of work for 25 years.

And I don't even count that as a missed day because I only left work at lunchtime. It was just my luck my appendix waited until Friday afternoon, and I was back to work on Monday.

I confess, I never met a metric I didn't immediately want to dominate. It took me a long time to realize how much chasing success cost me.

I still use metrics in my life, but I'm much more deliberate about which ones I choose. Here's why.

### Metrics are fantastic tools ... to manipulate people

You've probably heard this saying: "If you can't measure it, you can't manage it." Makes perfect sense, if what you want to do is manage people.

I'll propose a variation, which is "If you *can* measure it, people will focus on it." That may not sound profound, so let's add this modifier "... to the exclusion of everything else."

My thesis for you is this: your primary focus in your life and at work should be on *looking behind the metrics* that are presented to you by others.

- Challenge your assumptions about what is meaningful.

- Or, if you prefer, just because you can measure it doesn't mean it's worth pursuing.

## What's important at work?

This one's easy, right? You are successful in your career in proportion to how much you grow the following:

- Your salary and benefits

- Your titles and promotions

- The number of people you manage

- The size of your budget or business

Depending on your specialization, you will have additional metrics: number of new clients; growth in sales; the number of patents filed, contracts drafted, or lawsuits won, etc.

The point is not the specific metric so much as its very existence.

For what do all these metrics signal? Very clearly, they shout that your success is a function of how much you contribute to things that cause your company to succeed.

## Your company's success is not your success (necessarily)

Was I an idiot for focusing on never missing a day's work? Whom did it benefit for me to haul myself into the office when prudence would dictate resting when I caught the flu?

Even if you are a sole proprietor and thus entitled to the full benefits of your labor, you are a fool to set yourself the goal of chasing the same metrics as everyone else.

Why is that you ask?

Because who said the things your company wants are the same things you want?

- What comes with a promotion? More responsibility and stress.
- What comes with a bigger team? More administration and HR tasks.
- What comes with a bigger budget and business? More work and aggravation.

Perhaps some of you are thinking, "Sure, James, all true. But I notice you didn't say anything about the bigger salary. Tell me now why it isn't wonderful to make more money."

## What happens to people who orient their lives around money?

When you orient your life around making money, you will likely find ways to achieve your goals. I've seen many people go down this path, only to live frantic, miserable lives, no matter how much they accumulate.

Except for people clawing themselves out of poverty, for whom extra earnings are not only necessary but welcome, it's a rare person who finds themselves genuinely happier when they pursue more money.

Why seek something if it brings you only responsibility, stress, work, aggravation, and unhappiness? Because everyone else is seeking it? That's no good reason.

## The only two questions you should ask yourself

1. What do I really want in life (e.g. happiness, meaning, fulfillment, etc.)?
2. What will help me achieve what I really want?

What your company wants and what your colleagues are doing is utterly irrelevant to giving you insight into what you want.

Your only hope in answering these two questions honestly is to put aside for a time the metrics that everyone else is pursuing.

- You may find that it is time spent with your family that brings you joy.
- Or that a generous devotion to your health and well-being makes you

thrive.

- Perhaps it is donating your time and efforts to helping others that drives meaning.

Whatever your levers to happiness, I say be blinkered no longer by the metrics others place in your path.

Choose your own goals and let your own metrics guide you.

Be well.

## Chapter Thirty-One

# My Utterly Romantic Idea of Work

## Understanding the beauty of a job well done ... and well paid for

I've probably worked more hours than you have. This isn't a boast; it's just a fact.

So, how many hours, James? About 85,000. If you can beat that, we should go for a run— we'd probably get on.

I've worked a lot of hours because I've always appreciated the point in them. Once I've got one task done to my satisfaction, I start planning to get the next one done. It's the way I've always lived — I can't see any other way.

True, I've settled down a bit now. I no longer work 100-hour weeks like I did when I started. I've been tapering for a while, down now to my semi-retired 40-hour week. This is a record, especially considering that I am no longer in a salaried job and most of these hours are unpaid.

You would probably hate me if you were my fellow employee — I make everyone else look like sleepwalking slackers. But I'm a nice guy, deep down. I just see this constant shirking of work as immature wishful thinking. Gliding through life without goals, never building savings because spending in the moment is more attractive.

People have called me a Type A overachiever, but I resent that. How can a person who has set regular goals and pursued them with vigor "over" achieve? Think about it. You either achieve your goals or you fail.

I work hard. And most of the time, at least until recently, I received a great deal of money for it. The paid work I do is done with maximum efficiency, which leaves me with maximum time to do the things I consider important. Like write. Or read books. Or spend time with my wife. Or walk.

You must be wealthy!

On a global level, yes. On a Western level, yes. Actually, on any level you consider it, yes. But that's not important. I know friends who've earned very little. My friend Bill worked in minimum wage jobs only so much as he needed to fund an itinerant lifestyle.

Does Bill consider himself poor?

No. He travels to places others have on their bucket lists and lives a simple, satisfying life. He feels guilty that he has free time to lounge on beaches while others are toiling away in factories in the very countries he's bumming about in.

This works for Bill because he's always been able to find temporary work when he needs it. He's healthy and willing to do anything.

It doesn't make any sense to me. How long is he going to be able to keep this up? But according to him, I'm the wage slave stuck in an office while he relaxes in the sun. A fact he often goads me about. Frequently, he tells me how easy life is for him.

Wow! Let's think about that!

This is a guy who's got no credit cards and no bank accounts. He's got no pension and nothing saved for the future. But when I press him on it, he replies:

*"But I wouldn't know what to do differently!"*

And that's the point! He's spent a lifetime lounging. He likes an uncomplicated existence, without possessions or responsibilities. That's fine. That's his life. Not mine.

Work is only a chore if you don't like what you're doing and if you're not paid well for your contributions. If you have developed valuable skills that people are willing to pay you handsomely for exercising, your profession is a gift.

But a whole generation is coming up in the West with the idea that work is no more than a burden.

They think that was the point of the *Agrarian, Industrial and Technological Revolutions*. For others to generate wealth to free us! And in doing so, freeing humanity — or at least them — from the drudgery of mindless labor, they can enjoy the limited life on Earth they have.

Or did they get that wrong? Is it possible that maybe, someone has to pay for all the elements of society they take for granted?

Sorry. Better get back to work. Someone's got to pay for all this.

Be well.

# Happiness and Leadership

Career Paths Vol. 4: Being a Leader and Being
Happy Go Hand in Hand

James Bellerjeau

A Fine Idea

Copyright © 2025 by James Bellerjeau

All rights reserved.

No portion of this book may be reproduced in any form without written permission from the publisher or author, except as permitted by U.S. copyright law.

An earlier version of several of these articles was previously published in the ACC Docket (https://docket.acc.com/). Copyright © 2023, Association of Corporate Counsel. Reprinted with permission. All rights reserved. Visit www.acc.com.

# Contents

Introduction — 365

1. No One Said Life Is Fair — 367
2. How Not To Get Rich — 369
3. For a Great Career, Pursue Happiness Rather than Ambition — 373
4. Try Using Economics to Steer Your Life — 379
5. How Will You Be Remembered? — 383
6. Regret ... and Other Things That Compound — 386
7. Would You Rather Win the Silver or Bronze Medal? — 389
8. It's Good To Be the Boss! — 393
9. Why It's So Important to Develop Principles — 397
10. Do You Have a "More" Mindset? — 401
11. What Should We Wish For? — 405
12. Who Are the Most Cost-Effective Employees? — 409
13. Why Aren't More Pharma Companies Nonprofits? — 415
14. Corporations Are People Too — 419
15. Can Anything Save Corporations' Tainted Image? — 423
16. Do You Have Skin in the Game? — 427
17. Lawmakers Need a Hippocratic Oath — 431
18. I'm a Better Manager Now that I'm Out of the Job — 435

| | | |
|---|---|---|
| 19. | What the Heck Were They Thinking? | 439 |
| 20. | Failure Hidden in Plain Sight | 443 |
| 21. | Corporate Greed Should Be Low on Our List of Worries | 447 |
| 22. | How Much Should Bosses Care About Employees? | 451 |
| 23. | This Is Most Senior Leaders' Single Biggest Weakness | 455 |
| 24. | Immortality Is a Foolish Wish | 459 |
| 25. | Five Ways to Ensure You'll Never Be Forgotten | 461 |
| 26. | We're All Big Babies | 463 |
| 27. | Skepticism is Safer Than Blind Trust | 465 |
| 28. | What I Learned Negotiating for a Living | 469 |
| 29. | Bucket List, Eh. I'm Starting a F — It List | 473 |
| 30. | The Information Diet | 475 |
| 31. | Status Games You Can Win | 479 |
| 32. | The Boss Toolkit: When My Best Employees Couldn't Prioritize | 485 |

# Introduction

Greetings readers and congratulations! Simply by virtue of being here, you are already on the path to increasing your odds of success.

Success as a leader does not require you to be perfect. Your task is to be self-aware and deliberate in how you approach situations.

Armed with the tips presented here, perhaps you will pick one idea and apply continuous improvement principles to tip the odds of success in your favor. Slowly but surely, you can turn the tide to your advantage.

Your career can certainly make you happy, but too often people make themselves miserable in pursuit of their ambitions.

The happiest people I know are the ones who learn that success is not measured in money:

- Can you say you like, trust, and respect the people you work with?
- Is your work interesting, challenging, and valuable?
- And do you share values with a solid company that has a strategy for continued success?

Then you have all you need to be happy and successful in your career.

These articles are about ways to advance your career while paying attention to what will make you happy. You will find additional approaches to succeeding at work in the companion volumes **Thriving at Work** and **The Pragmatist's Rules for Work**.

Success at work is not necessarily the same as how to live a good life or achieve satisfaction. If you want to explore these topics more deeply, I recommend you spend some time with the **Pragmatic Wisdom** series.

Be well.

## Chapter One

# No One Said Life Is Fair

**Things are this way, and we can deal with them without adding to our burdens by worrying about unfairness**

When I was growing up, my dad had a standard response to my brothers and me whenever one of us complained about the never-ending ways that life was unfair:

*No one ever said life was fair.*

My dad's answer used to annoy me no end because it didn't seem like any kind of answer. "That's not fair!" we complained, and my dad said, "That's right."

With time, I better appreciate the wisdom in this approach.

I am reminded of what Mark Twain once said about his father: "When I was a boy of 14, my father was so ignorant I could hardly stand to have the old man around. But when I got to be 21, I was astonished at how much the old man had learned in seven years."

Is it fair when the fisherman pulls a fish from the sea, or the crow plucks a worm from the field? Is it fair when it rains on your wedding day? When your car gets a flat tire, your train is late, and your flight is canceled? When your incompetent but conniving colleague is promoted before you?

We could expand this list a long time, but I'll let you fill in the blanks in your mind.

## It's never personal

No, it's not fair. But nor do we have to take it personally.

Things are this way, and we can deal with them without adding to our burdens by worrying about unfairness. We can make things better without first making them worse by complaining about them.

Now later in my own life, I realize my dad was a philosopher at heart. He was trying to pass on to me and my brothers an old message. Here's how I've since heard it from that model Stoic, Marcus Aurelius:

> *A cucumber is bitter — throw it away. There are briars in the road — turn aside from them. This is enough. Do not add, 'and why were such things made in the world?'*

Marcus Aurelius knew to remind himself of this fact whenever needed. Though he was Emperor of Rome, he needed it every day.

So take this as your own helpful reminder, from Aurelius, my dad, and me to you: "No one ever said life was fair."

If you can keep this thought foremost in your mind when bad things happen, chances are you'll not only be more successful in your career. You'll probably be happier, too.

Be well.

Chapter Two

# How Not To Get Rich

## The keys to wealth, health, happiness, and so much more, are small steps that you take gradually over long periods of time

Most people think that the way to get rich is to earn more money.

"Well, duh!" I hear you say. "We didn't really need you to tell us that earning more money will help you have more money."

Perhaps. But let me give you another perspective.

I started my career as a corporate lawyer in one of those New York firms that get headlines every year for the outrageous salaries they pay starting associates.

What junior lawyer is worth US$200,000 per year when they know how to do exactly nothing? By the way, those are the current salaries, not what I made when I started!

To the junior lawyers themselves, if they have a shred of self-awareness and humility, they know this is a great scam and there must be some catch. There is a catch, and more than one.

To start, those junior lawyers will work hard, really hard. For me, this is when I first became acquainted with what a 100-hour week feels like. For the mathematically inclined among you, it is more than 14 hours a day, every day, with no weekends or days off.

In hindsight, I can be grateful for those initial grueling days. Why? Because no one else's idea of a long week could compare. When I started working only 60–80 hours a week as in-house counsel, it felt like a breeze. I genuinely considered a 40-hour week to be working part-time.

The other catch is that as outrageous as your starting salary was, the law firm was charging your time out to clients at a much higher rate.

- An annual billing of 2,000 hours, which when I started would have been considered modest,
- at an hourly rate of US$500, also not at all unusual these days for junior lawyers,
- means that your law firm is charging clients US$1 million for your services.

Yes, your firm must cover a lot of overhead, and they don't bill all your time, but that still leaves a tidy profit. The pyramid is highly leveraged on the backs of associates.

You can assume law firm partners are clever businesspeople in touting those headline salaries, which is why there are more than 80 US law firms with profits per partner of more than US$1 million.

Back to getting rich. You would think that earning a salary of US$200,000 per year, let alone US$1 million per year, would be a guaranteed path to riches. Alas, for many their salary is no indication of their likelihood to become wealthy.

Why should this be so, you ask?

Let's say you are a lawyer in New York City, as I was, a common location for such high-earners.

- Similar to most big cities, your taxes are high (easily 50 percent all-in)
- as is your cost of living (say 30 percent for housing, and another 10–15 percent for living expenses).
- You might be left with something like 5–10 percent of your gross income to spend.

**Where does it all go? Many possibilities, among them these:**

- You have a nanny, perhaps a cleaner;

- You take expensive trips because after all, you work so hard, you deserve to treat yourself on the rare times you take off;

- You have a second home because even though you are working crazy hours, you can't expect your family to sit around waiting for you in a small city apartment; and

- Those kids will need to go to college.

The far more relevant questions to ask in determining a person's propensity to become wealthy are these:

**How much of your income are you able to save?**

**Can you manage to regularly spend less than you earn?**

If you can spend less than you earn, and you start to invest your savings in low-cost funds that track the broader stock market, you will be on the path to leveraging the power of time and compound interest.

We have among us people who are well on the path to achieving independence at levels of wealth far below what we usually assume is necessary.

I refer to adherents of the "Financial Independence Retire Early" movement or FIRE. These people are proof that you do not need wealth as it is traditionally defined (in money) to be happy.

One way not to get wealthy is to think that you need a lot of money to be rich. Another way is to mistake your income for wealth and spend more than you earn.

The keys to wealth, health, happiness, and so much more, are small steps that you take gradually over long periods of time.

Spend less than you earn, no matter how much you earn, and you will be on a path to good things. Then it is just a matter of being patient.

Be well.

## Chapter Three

# For a Great Career, Pursue Happiness Rather than Ambition

## Pursuing ambitions can be counterproductive to our job performance. Prioritizing happiness instead brings multiple benefits

It took me more than a decade working as a C-suite executive to appreciate that ambition was not the only way to drive my career.

Let me first describe my journey and then I'll tell you what I learned from it. You might find something in my experience that helps you manage your own ambitions.

I hope you also find that pursuing personal satisfaction can be a powerful driver of your career.

### Steps in my career that drove personal learnings

I became the General Counsel of a billion-dollar public company at age 30, which is a big deal.

I nonetheless thought I needed to progress. For example, to become General Counsel of a bigger company, say an S&P 500 company. I thought that's what a career means: Always planning the next move.

There I was, ten years in. Prodded by ambition, I interviewed for and got offered that next General Counsel position.

It was only when I was wrestling with the decision to stay or go that I carefully reflected on what was important to me.

**What really brought me satisfaction in my job and my daily life?** I realized I valued three things most highly:

1. The **people** I work with — do I like, trust, and respect them?

2. The **work** I was doing — is it interesting, challenging, and valuable?

3. The **company** I was doing it for — do I have the same values, is the company successful, and do I believe in the company's strategy for future success?

I concluded that I would be a great fool to give up what I had right in front of me for mere ambition. I saw that I already possessed all the ingredients for happiness and satisfaction in life.

I thus declined the shiny new job and spent the next ten years being grateful for what I had and doing the best job I could where I was.

Along the way, we grew our share price more than 30-fold, outperforming the great majority of public companies, and several years ago my company joined the S&P 500.

When I stopped being driven by my ambitions I got further than where I originally thought I could.

Then when I turned 50, I decided to give up my General Counsel role entirely.

This was not career suicide. It was anything but. It was a careful, conscious choice I arrived at by following the thought process I describe below.

Initially, I worked part-time while running my company's sustainability program. The switch from law to sustainability was invigorating. Not only that, I got half of my life back to spend on "sunny hours and summer days":

> *Many a forenoon have I stolen away, preferring to spend thus the most valued part of the day; for I was rich, if not in money, in sunny hours and summer days, and spent them lavishly; nor do I regret that I did not waste more of them in the workshop or the teacher's desk.* — Henry David Thoreau

Here are the key things I learned on my journey, and why I came to see ambition as the least helpful tool for driving career success.

## Focus first on finding satisfaction

I learned to focus first on finding happiness and satisfaction in life. This need not (and I believe should not) be tied to rigid career goals.

We are ambitious because we think this will bring us happiness, but we make ourselves unhappy in the pursuit of our ambitions. If we first create the foundation for satisfaction in life, we can approach our ambitions in a different way.

I had this thought after discovering that attorneys have one of the of any job, at least in the United States.

And here's something even more interesting: increasing responsibility and higher income for lawyers has almost no correlation with their happiness and well-being.

That suggests there is something more to satisfaction than traditional career progression.

## Career ambition can sabotage your satisfaction

There is a potential conflict between making progress in your career, which requires you to think ahead and try to change your situation, and being happy and satisfied right now in your daily life.

If you are too focused on the future, you can become unhappy with your current situation and so fail to bring your full effort and talents to your current job.

This is doubly unfortunate, because not only do you make yourself unhappy, but you are less likely to advance if you don't bring your best to your current job.

## Happiness enhances your effectiveness

In contrast, persons who truly value what they have, and give their best at what they are doing, are both happy and are performing well.

Happy, positive people engage well with their colleagues, which makes them more likely to be considered for promotion. Similarly, people who bring their best to their current jobs every day are more likely to be given greater responsibility, which also leads to promotion.

Thus, by not blindly pursuing ambition, you create the conditions for becoming happy. Your happiness, in turn, creates the conditions for you to bring your best to the job. And your daily performance is what drives your career.

## Follow advice that's passed the test of time

It is our human nature that either enhances or inhibits our performance. Our ambitions torment us while finding satisfaction makes us happy.

After I grasped this, I realized I could call upon the best advice for mastering human nature that humankind has developed over millennia.

I took inspiration from the Roman Stoics, as well as Buddhist and Zen philosophers. They each have some excellent advice for us to manage this dynamic.

Here's how I summarize my top three takeaways, along with source quotes that provided me with inspiration.

## 1. Be happy with what you have and don't be sad about what you don't have

Consider these inspirations for how to accept your current situation:

> *It is an invincible greatness of mind not to be elevated or dejected with good or ill fortune. A wise man is content with his lot, whatever it be — without wishing for what he has not.* — Seneca

> *Be content with what you have, rejoice in the way things are. When you realize there is nothing lacking, the whole world belongs to you.*
> — Lao Tzu

## 2. Do a good job in your current job

Next, on paying attention to what is in front of you:

> *If you work at what is before you, following right reason seriously, vigorously, calmly, without allowing anything else to distract you, expecting nothing, fearing nothing, but satisfied with your present activity according to nature, you will live happy.* — Marcus Aurelius

> *Do not dwell in the past, do not dream of the future, concentrate the mind on the present moment.* — Buddha

## 3. Decide for yourself what success means to you

If you follow this line of thought further, you realize that ambition for its own sake may be harmful.

Who said it is necessary or good to chase after bigger jobs, more responsibility, and more pay? Who are you doing it for?

And what will your ambitions cost you in terms of hours of the day, time spent with family and friends, and being true to your deeply held values?

> *No one is compelled to pursue prosperity at top speed; it means something to call a halt instead of pressing eagerly after favoring fortune.* — Seneca

> *Wealth consists not in having great possessions, but in having few wants.* — Epictetus

Modern-day philosophers have carried the torch onward. This bit of wisdom from Steve Jobs helped me take decisions consistent with my values even when those decisions seemed crazy to others, like giving up my General Counsel role at the peak of my power.

> *Your time is limited, don't waste it living someone else's life. Don't be trapped by dogma, which is living the result of other people's thinking. Don't let the noise of others' opinions drown out your own inner voice.* — Steve Jobs

## If you still want career advice...

All this said I do not want to talk anyone out of having ambition or looking for career progression. Rather, I want to help you avoid being blindly driven before the whip of ambition without really thinking about what will satisfy you.

In pursuing happiness you may still meet your ambitions but you are much more likely to become happy. What is it you really want?

Be well.

Chapter Four

# Try Using Economics to Steer Your Life

## The basic rules of competition apply in many areas of life beyond buying goods and services. Knowing this, make decisions accordingly

You might greatly improve your quality of life by applying basic economic principles to key choices you make: Where to spend your time, what goals to pursue, and how to measure your success.

By understanding how supply and demand (or more simply, competition) applies to much of your life, you can compete more effectively. You do this by focusing on areas where you have a competitive advantage, which comes from more than your efforts and abilities. It also comes from where you apply your efforts and abilities.

**Supply and demand help explain the world**

To begin, let's consider a few basic economic principles. We see lots of evidence in the news and public debate that many people don't appreciate these simple rules:

- When demand for goods and services remains constant but supplies are scarce, the prices for those goods and services increase.

- When supplies for goods and services remain steady but demand increases, the prices for those goods and services increase.

- And when demand is high and supplies are short, prices can increase dramatically.

All this is another way of saying that competition for limited resources is real and has an impact on what things cost. When we look at changes in supply and demand, we're effectively measuring how stiff the competition is for the underlying goods and services.

The more people who are trying to buy a car, book a flight, or fill their tanks with gas, the more that competition for limited resources will result in prices going up.

*It's a simple concept, for all that its effects are widespread*

The basic rules of competition apply in many areas of life beyond buying goods and services. When there is massive demand but only limited supply, competition will be fierce.

- This explains why it is hard to get into the top schools, join certain professions, or get jobs in fast-growing companies.

- It explains why some salaries are much higher than others, why it's so hard to get elected to political office, and why very few individuals become models, movie stars, or best-selling authors.

## Competing when the odds are stacked against you, or not

Many of us spend most of our time focused on the same things: money, power, fame, possessions. We have been dazzled by the supposed prizes and are blinded to the opportunity costs and likelihood of achieving them.

Economics offers another way of running the equation to achieve success: Look to places where competition is much scarcer (i.e., demand is lower), but where the rewards are still great.

At its heart, Stoicism offers such a refuge: Little competition for great rewards. These rewards are not the same as others chase. You will not hear a Stoic telling you to pursue a big bank account and a corner office, although these things may come.

Instead, set your sights on attaining wisdom and you will be amazed at how wide open the field is. You do not need to compete for scarce resources, because few others are looking for the same goal.

Not only that, but competition on the path to wisdom does not make your task harder. The more people seeking wisdom, the more you can support and benefit each other. Wisdom is one of the few areas in life where greater demand creates greater supply.

## The reward for seeking wisdom

Best of all, the reward for seeking wisdom is a well-ordered mind following reason. Specifically, with wisdom, you will be satisfied and happy without regard to any of the scarce prizes your colleagues run after. Realizing you do not need money, job titles, or possessions to be happy is incredibly liberating.

The question to ask is: Do you want to be successful as it is traditionally understood, or do you want to be happy? The difference lies in whether you seek to attain wisdom.

You see what I did there. You thought you were getting an economics lesson, but instead, we used economics as a foothold into a Stoic principle. But my goal with both approaches was the same: to explore ways to live a good life and achieve satisfaction.

I can't guarantee you'll become wise if you diligently pursue wisdom as a goal. But the odds are in your favor.

Be well.

Chapter Five

# How Will You Be Remembered?

## If you want to know how you'll be remembered, it helps to understand how people think

First, I will point out an irony. That is, if you are overly worried about your legacy, chances are you will be challenged to leave a positive one.

The best people do not always seem to generate the broadest influence, but their impact on those they do influence is deep.

If you want to know how you'll be remembered, it helps to understand how people think.

A certain percentage of the population will tell you that people are defined by their exceptional moments.

- It is your best accomplishments in a long line of mundane events that people will remember.

Similarly, no matter how impressive your overall record is, these are the same people who will tell you that a person is also defined by their worst moments.

- An off-color joke, an offensive tweet, or a politically incorrect view. Any of these can be taken as evidence of your flawed nature, outweighing an otherwise unblemished life and character.

It is true that many people notice just the headlines, good or bad. Nowadays we can think of these fleeting headlines scrolling across our screens as social media moments.

But only shallow people think what they read in the headlines defines a person or even gives you a semi-realistic idea of what they stand for.

## Would you want your life judged by strangers who know nothing about you?

Or worse, that they judge you by what other people are saying about you? I can't imagine many people would rush to sign up to such a standard. And yet it is a standard that people apply routinely without a second's thought.

It really takes only a brief reflection to arrive at a more well-founded conclusion.

Deeper thinkers know people are far more than the sum of their worst (or best) moments.

People are complex, yet we're capable of change.

If that weren't so, there would be no need for school, no need for training, and no need for a great deal of what humans do.

Strangers don't know a fraction of what makes you special and important. Thus, what strangers think of you based on misleading headlines designed to garner attention is far less meaningful than what people closest to you think of you.

When it comes to the people who do know you, the question becomes what impact did you make on them?

### Were you kind and patient?

Did you listen to them when they were hurting and needed help? Did you help develop them and promote them in their careers?

Did you celebrate their successes, and commiserate with their failures? In short, did you act in ways to make their lives better?

If you had a positive impact on people close to you, rest assured your legacy is secured.

Perhaps not among the masses, who are easily distracted by superficial things. But people you genuinely care about and help are the ones who count.

I remember coming across a quote years ago from the Athenian statesman Solon, who was commenting on how to evaluate the lives of successful individuals. Solon's observation was this:

*Count no man happy, until he is dead* [or until the end is known].

Solon's point was that life is full of reversals of fortune. A person who is riding high now may later have a fall from grace. They may lose their wealth, they may fall ill, they may be caught up in a power struggle with the losing side, and so on.

According to Aristotle, to truly evaluate the success of a person's life and decide whether they achieved their highest good or eudaimonia, you should even extend your evaluation to look at their children's and relatives' lives.

For today, I think we can draw this lesson: You don't know what a person's life means until they have lived it out. You can tell very little from an isolated incident or a snapshot in time.

If you would not be judged by your worst moment, do not be quick to judge others for theirs.

Be well.

Chapter Six

# Regret ... and Other Things That Compound

## The power of compounding applies to our thoughts as much as it does to our actions

Many of you will know about the power of compound interest. Albert Einstein supposedly called it the "eighth wonder of the world" and Warren Buffet said, "My life has been a product of compound interest."

I've already referred to compounding for you in articles describing how to get rich. If you were reading carefully, then you understood that, although you can use compounding to achieve financial wealth, that will not necessarily bring you happiness.

If you want to be successful in your career, one of the most important things you can learn is that you are largely a creation of habits.

- Whether you succeed in your endeavors, feel happy with your life, and become physically and mentally healthy — all these things are driven by habits.

- Or as Raj on the sitcom The Big Bang Theory puts it when asking a girlfriend for honest feedback: "... except for anything I say, or do, or am. Those are my triggers."

Replace triggers with habits, and you grasp the importance of habits.

# REGRET ... AND OTHER THINGS THAT COMPOUND

Without consciously realizing it, the little things we do become things that we regularly do. Things we regularly do compound over time. It is not just financial decisions that compound.

If you look, you will find compounding in these areas of your life as well:

- Small decisions you make each day about how you approach your work will impact the course of your career. Do you make a conscious choice to do your level best each day, no matter what you're doing? Or do you resent doing less exciting or less important work because you know you can do more?

- Your routine daily interactions with those around you will determine the course of your relationships. Do you treat your friends and family as gifts, and cherish them? Or do you take them for granted, and sometimes vent your frustrations on them?

- Anyone who has struggled to maintain their weight knows that it is small, daily decisions about what you eat that drive your long-term health.

- Similarly, if you've ever gotten on an exercise kick, you will have felt first-hand the wonderful reinforcement that comes from sticking with an exercise program and seeing the impact on your fitness.

The power of compounding applies to our thoughts as much as it does to our actions. If you dwell on your mistakes and wallow in regret, you will become a bitter person.

We all know someone who cannot let go of a past relationship or a missed opportunity. Does this make them fun to be around, even to themselves?

Do you want to be a sad, angry person? When you are stuck in the past, that means you are not living in the present.

## Change is possible

My suggestion to you is that your nature is not immutable. Far from it. No matter what ill winds blow your way, you are more than the sum of what's happened to you.

If you wish, you can become a more positive, charitable, kind, and happy person. You don't even need the iron willpower of a Stoic master to do it.

All you need is to recognize that the power of habits applies to your mind and your thoughts. You can then start to adopt habits that move you in the direction you want to go.

The only thing you truly control is what you think. Thus, the path to happiness is not built upon pavers of enjoyment, but from choices: You must decide what you want and stick with your decisions.

You might be thinking, "This all sounds great in theory. But how do I control what I think in practice? Negative thoughts come to me unbidden."

To start, try to recognize when you find yourself dwelling on negative thoughts, or being uncharitable to others.

Also notice when you are being uncharitable to yourself. We are never so strict taskmasters as when we are judging our own actions.

## Focus on the positive

Over time, you will become adept at catching yourself when you start to think negative thoughts. The next step is to consciously focus on something positive, no matter how trivial it seems. You can almost always find a positive in every situation.

Treat it as a challenge to find something good in even the seemingly worst possible situation. Relatively soon, you will have trained yourself to look for the positive. A setback suddenly becomes an opportunity, a hardship, a chance to test your mettle.

This practice is doubly helpful. It will move you in the direction of becoming a happier and more self-sufficient person. It also helps prepare you for the inevitable setbacks and hardships that come your way.

Be well.

# Chapter Seven

# Would You Rather Win the Silver or Bronze Medal?

## Do you understand how much your desires are themselves contributing to your unhappiness?

By now you know this is probably a trick question. But it illustrates a really important point that, if you can master, will help keep you on the path to happiness. First, some background.

Until recently I thought the so-called "replication crisis" was limited to the field of psychology.

The crisis refers to the fact that many published studies of scientific results cannot be reproduced by others who perform the same study at a later time. This depressed me because my undergrad was in psychology. Was it all a waste of time?

As it turns out, many fields besides psychology suffer from the problem that published scientific results are difficult to reproduce by others. Studies in medicine, marketing, economics, and now hard sciences are each falling prey to the problem of unrepeatability.

But there is one lovely little area of psychological research that has seen its results replicated, several times. It concerns the reactions of Olympic medalists to finding out if they've won gold, silver, or bronze.

- As could be expected, gold medalists are quite delighted. "I'm the best in the world, baby. Beat that."

- Bronze medalists are also outrageously happy on average, and good for them.

- If you've any sympathy in you, save it for the poor silver medalists. In some disciplines, their reactions ranged from despair to contempt, to nothing.

"Nothing, really?! You just won a freaking silver medal in the Olympics."

## The space between

What explains this amazing reaction?

The studies refer to the athletes running "counterfactuals" in their heads, i.e. they compare their achievement to *what could have been*.

I've told you before that while people don't evaluate things well in isolation, we are excellent when it comes to comparing two things. The difference in the silver and bronze medalists' reactions can be explained by their comparison groups.

The silver medalist is looking at the tiny distance that separates them from the gold medalist.

- If only they could have eked out a few milliseconds more, they could be the champion.

- In this comparison, they forget that they've just beaten out every other person on the planet but one.

The bronze medalist, by contrast, is looking at the tiny distance that separates them from fourth place and everyone behind them.

- "My goodness," they think. "Only milliseconds separated me from not getting a medal at all."

- They look at all the others they have vanquished to become an Olympic medalist.

In other words, what you feel about a situation depends on where you direct your gaze.

Are you looking upward at what you could have achieved but did not? Or do you consider how far you have come and how many others you have outperformed?

Now for all of you who are not Olympic medalists or hopefuls, guess what? The same phenomenon applies to all of us in our daily lives.

Are you happy with your house, your job, your spouse, your salary, your neighborhood, your schools, your children, your pet, and on and on? It's not an objective standard, but rather a relative one.

If you're reading this, you're living in a time when more people have more freedom, security, and material goods than at any time in human history.

- Some 10 billion people who lived before you had a comprehensively tougher time, not to mention living lives that were "solitary, poor, nasty, brutish, and short."
- And you're complaining because your internet speed is too slow and there's nothing on Netflix?

## Desires contribute to unhappiness

Do you understand how much your desires are themselves contributing to your unhappiness?

Have you realized how little the things you attain actually contribute to your long-term happiness? To make yourself unhappy by wanting things that will not make you happy is not a recipe for success.

By all means, aim for gold. But on the way, don't forget to appreciate what you have already achieved in your life and in your career. And remember how much better you have it than countless others.

Or to say it once more because it bears repeating: Be thankful for what you have, and don't be sad for what you don't have.

Be well.

## Chapter Eight

# It's Good To Be the Boss!

## Of all the things that come with a promotion and a senior title, the one you should spend the most time contemplating is this: Responsibility

There are lots of reasons why it's just great being a senior manager. Here are a few common ideas people have about the benefits that come with the title:

> *Finally, I'll be able to just **make decisions** myself, without having to worry about what my boss or others think.*

> *Ah, I can't wait to have the **authority to implement** my priorities. People will have to do what I say!*

> *People will **listen to me** and respect my opinion because of my position. No more fighting for attention.*

My more experienced colleagues are no doubt laughing out loud right now. Or at least ruefully shaking their heads. And for good reason.

Of all the things that come with a promotion and a senior title, the one you should spend the most time contemplating is this: Responsibility.

- To make decisions is to have responsibility for the outcomes your team achieves.

- To exert authority to implement decisions is to bear responsibility for the resources your team expends.

- And to command authority by virtue of your position is to be responsible for what you say in every setting.

And that's assuming you actually are free to make decisions, exert authority, and have your opinion heard.

Let's explore the real world of your work environment for a moment.

## Freedom

As a senior manager, you are *never* free of others' expectations when you make decisions.

You may be the senior-most legal officer, sure, but you still are bound by fiduciary responsibilities and must interact collegially with your other management peers.

Your tenure will be brief if you are oblivious to the toes you step on when making decisions. Not to mention the CEO and the board of directors are looking over your shoulder at every step.

(Lest you think there is yet a higher level at which you are ultimately free of such expectations, the CEO bears the cross of the board, and the board members ultimately answer to shareholders.)

## Authority

So if you are not really free to make your decisions without considering the context, your fiduciary duties, and your various stakeholders, can we at least grant that you are much better positioned to *implement* your decisions?

To this, let me simply ask "Have you ever observed a parent interacting with a cranky toddler in a store?"

The parent clearly has all the structural authority in the relationship. They can direct the outcome by force. Yet witness how often the child prevails.

And before you blame this on poor parenting, turn now to your workplace. Can you think of a time that you yourself defied or ignored a company policy because it did not fit reality, was poorly designed, or was just plain "stupid"?

One of the things I liked most about working at a company with lots of engineers and scientists is that they are logical and methodological. If you can explain the reason and the rationale for your proposal, they will be faithful allies and excellent partners.

Now instead try to force such colleagues to implement your policy just because you say so and see what happens.

Your work colleagues have improved upon the tricks the cranky toddler employs to such great effect. If you try to force them to your will, you will meet with noncompliance that makes your hair prematurely gray and fall out.

I recently came across a line Desiderius Erasmus wrote in a letter to Sir Thomas More in 1521. The context was Martin Luther's agitation that led to the Protestant Reformation, and whether Church authorities should permit debate or force adherence to the current doctrine:

> *It is no great feat to burn a little man. It is a great achievement to persuade him.*

What was true 500 years ago is still true today: You must persuade, never dictate.

## Being heard

And to our final point, will you have authority by virtue of your position? Will people listen to you as a result of your role?

Here I can give more positive news. Yes, they will, at least at first.

For them to keep listening, you must do both of the following:

- You must listen carefully and ask relevant questions to tease out the real issues, for the full set of issues is rarely contained in the initial request.

- Then you must provide pragmatic advice that demonstrates you understand the context and have placed the company's interests first.

In other words, you have to be good at your job if you expect people to listen to you. Your position just gets you the first "at bat." Everything after that is up to you.

It is unquestionably good to be the boss because it puts you in a position to influence your company.

But if you take your job seriously, you'll soon see that little comes with the title beyond the responsibility to live up to others' expectations.

I am confident you can do it. In fact, I expect nothing less.

Be well.

## Chapter Nine

# Why It's So Important to Develop Principles

## I will save you the decade or so I spent following what turned out to be mostly fads. There is a simpler, better way to grow

Bad advice will be given to the new manager. By this, I mean a great mound of well-meant, but ultimately useless advice.

I will save you the decade or so I spent following what turned out to be mostly fads. There is a simpler, better way to grow.

But to fully appreciate the simple path, you must first understand the pitfalls that lie on the new manager's road.

### Categories of bad advice

Here are some categories of advice I believe are as likely to lead you astray as help you:

- Almost everyone's first-hand explanation of what made them successful
- Almost all articles in management and business journals
- Most psychology or economics research unearthing some surprising quirk of human thinking or behavior

You can identify potentially bad advice from among the following characteristics:

- It is largely anecdote-driven

- It contains statistics expressed as percentages and only few absolute numbers

- It is included in a best-selling book with a dust-jacket blurb from Bono, Bill Gates, or Barack Obama. (Not to pick on these three fine individuals.)

Most of all, bad advice falls in the set of suggestions described as "This worked for Successful Person X or Company Y; try it and you can be successful too!"

Because we humans are fantastic pattern-recognition machines, we seek patterns everywhere and we find them everywhere. This would be wonderful except that we regularly assume causation in the face of nothing more than correlation.

We are easily taken in by anecdotes and stories because they trigger our pattern recognition function. We recognize a pattern, and we are primed to look out for the moral or lesson of the story.

## What to do with others' success stories

You should consider one person's description of success to be an interesting story, nothing more.

That person experienced a unique situation, with unique challenges and opportunities, and brought to bear their special skills and experiences.

That person encountered far more randomness than they realized in each of their settings, their actions, and the outcomes of those actions.

Even if you could replicate their actions precisely (which you cannot because you are your own person), what are the chances that you will be in a similar enough situation and not be influenced by a different set of random interactions?

## Why fads sell

Management and business journals are in the business of selling advertising, which means they need to drive viewers. Surprising and interesting stories attract eyeballs and clicks.

The truth of those stories is of secondary interest. Turns out that if you tell people what they want to hear and occasionally titillate them with something surprising along the way, they'll read your stories.

How about scientists? Can we take refuge among tenured professors, the scientific method, and peer-reviewed journals?

- Alas, you must be vigilant. Most published studies cannot be replicated, in most fields.

- Even studies with some validity are blown out of proportion in the push to publish.

- And reporters describe findings sensationally and without context because they want to grab your attention.

## Focus on your own situation, skills, and experiences

In the business context, such advice from individuals, journalists, and experts is more than not useful.

It's downright harmful because it distracts you from focusing on what you could be more profitably doing.

"And what is that?" you ask. It is to focus on your own situation, your own skills and experiences, and your own challenges and opportunities.

What works for someone else is unlikely to work for anyone else because others are not you and others are not facing what you are facing.

But what works for you is something *you* should focus intensely on: How did you make that decision, why did it work (or often, not work), and what will you do differently next time?

Carefully observe your thought process and your decision-making process. Write down the principles that you are following. Discuss them with your colleagues on your team and refine them over time with the direction you'd like to take.

When I ran a legal team, I described our Legal Team Principles, called the Six Ps, as follows:

- **Proactive** — We address risks as early as possible.

- **Protective** — We protect the company's long-term interests.

- **Pragmatic** — We take informed risks.

- **Purposeful** — We work on high-risk and high-value topics.

- **Plain** — We seek to reduce complexity.

- **Powerful** — We follow continuous improvement principles.

To someone outside our team, this may look like a list of virtually useless buzzwords.

To me, it was a framework helping us decide among many competing priorities. It contained the seeds of our values and our mission. It reminded us to only work on topics that were directly supportive of the company's strategy.

I am not recommending the Six Ps to you as candidates for your own principles. I am suggesting that you spend time first considering and then committing your own principles to paper.

By focusing on how you make decisions and what you are doing in your unique situation, and then describing and improving your principles, you can drown out the distracting noise of others' unhelpful advice.

The only advice I'd like you to consider is this: You know how to improve your own results better than anyone else.

Be well.

Chapter Ten

# Do You Have a "More" Mindset?

When we do not dwell in the past or daydream about the future, we open ourselves to the possibility of finding tranquility and joy

We live in times of abundance and surplus when standards of living are higher for more people than they have ever been.

How puzzling then that so many people are unhappy with their lot. I think you can lay the blame at the feet of our ambitions.

Although striving for material progress served humanity well for centuries by raising us out of widespread poverty into wealth, today it may be causing more harm than good. Let's explore why.

### Why are we so ambitious?

We are ambitious because humans at heart are driven by relative status. We live in hierarchies, which are a fundamental facet of every society.

For a long time, accumulating material wealth was a way to show you were successful. And the more wealth, the more successful, apparently without any rational upper limit.

Thanks to both normal distributions of ability and the Pareto principle, a small percentage of people will be disproportionately successful in whatever dimension you measure, including earnings and wealth.

In the last few generations, and largely because most people no longer lack basic material goods, we've seen some interesting tweaks to the game of jockeying for status.

- Today a person can demonstrate high social status through a commitment to a cause, for example, climate change.
- Other topics that allow in-group members to lay claim to moral high ground include political party or religion, diversity, inclusion, and equity, or anti-racism and critical race theory.

What these all have in common is that they do not require anything other than passion and self-identification to have the desired signaling effect.

The ultimate aim for signing on to some of these causes may be to redistribute resources in different ways. Or to gain power and be able to be in charge of many of the decisions that will arise within working for the causes.

But in the short term, the social signaling aspect is a powerful reward in itself.

The problem with social virtue signaling as a status symbol is similar to that of accumulating wealth: "More" is better and there is no logical stopping point at which one can say enough is enough.

Hence, we see people taking ever more radical positions to demonstrate they care more than others. Our current polarized politics are one manifestation, as are the fights you see in schools over systemic racism training, and in companies over unconscious bias and diversity training.

## The danger of comparing to others

My point is not to criticize any particular cause or social group — they almost all have basic validity at some level.

Rather, I want to draw attention to the idea that if you seek your relative value or worth in comparison with others, you are demonstrating a "more" mindset: If only I had more _____, I would be happy.

Is there another way? How about living fully in the moment?

When we do not dwell in the past or daydream about the future, we open ourselves to the possibility of finding tranquility and joy in what we are doing right now.

## Success can mean saying "No"

I recently came across an example of a person who was successful at almost everything he tried, including things that appeared impossible before he came along and did them.

The genius mathematician, Edward O. Thorp, demonstrated that it was possible to beat the house playing blackjack, and then went on to spearhead the quantitative trading movement in financial markets, becoming wealthy in the process.

His book *A Man For All Markets* is fantastic reading.

More impressive than his many intellectual and financial accomplishments, at least to me, were his decisions to stop playing the game.

Thorp recognized that a "more" mindset could never be satisfied and so thought about what was important to him in life. In his own words:

> *To preserve the quality of my life and to spend more of it in the company of people I value and in the exploration of ideas I enjoy, I chose not to follow up on a number of business ventures, although I believed that they were nearly certain to become extremely profitable.*
> – Edward O. Thorp

The Stoic philosopher, Seneca, would celebrate Thorp, not for his many material accomplishments, but for having identified what was important to him and behaving accordingly.

If that meant leaving money and accolades on the table, so be it. In this way, Thorp serves as one of the many good examples that we can follow.

**You're already there**

The only thing I would wish you to seek more of is satisfaction. Your happiness will come from paying attention to what you are doing at the moment you are doing it.

We do not need to be geniuses to follow in the footsteps of geniuses. They have blazed a path for us, and all we need to do is follow. It is up to us to choose our paths accordingly.

Be well.

Chapter Eleven

# What Should We Wish For?

## Perhaps we should wish for something other than more of the promotions, wealth, and possessions that aren't making us happier

I used to sign farewell cards at work with something like: "I wish you every success in your new endeavors."

Now, when I think back, this was wrong to write.

- A person who is successful at everything has no reason to question the foundation of their happiness.
- They have material wealth, and career success, and seem to have it all.
- But such persons are at great risk of identifying their happiness with those external things.

### Failure and setbacks are normal

What happens when life knocks a pillar out from underneath a person who's known nothing but success?

Say they suffer a career setback, a health issue, or have relationship troubles. It can be devastating. They become unhappy and cannot be happy again until the external situation is fixed.

If getting everything we want carries its own pitfalls, what should we wish for others to achieve?

Let's say you are a caring boss, and you want your colleagues to succeed at work. What does that success actually mean?

- Does it mean they never make a mistake?
- Or is it better that they learn from the small mistakes they make and so become wiser?

## Promotions are not the true measurement of success

Does success mean an employee advances from one promotion to the next, scaling the heights of power? Or would you wish that they come to appreciate the deep satisfaction from doing their existing jobs ever better?

Does success mean they make more money than their peers in other companies? Or are they better off learning early that their worth is poorly measured in money?

## Wish what parents wish for their children

What about what parents wish for their children?

If you ask the kids themselves, many will tell you they want to be rich, powerful, or famous. Sometimes all three.

It takes the age and experience of parents to wonder if a far more valuable gift would be that their children are happy, find love, or make a lasting contribution to society.

I suspect you've noticed people who never seem satisfied with what they've achieved. You may have managed employees who are always itching for more: responsibility, pay, and promotions.

I've noticed the desire for more does not seem to correlate with talent. That is, all sorts of people fall prey to being dissatisfied with their current position, the gifted and the striving alike.

## External wants don't satisfy

It's usually easy for a boss or a parent to offer sound advice to a colleague or their child:

# WHAT SHOULD WE WISH FOR?

- Be careful placing your hopes and dreams in external things like wealth, power, or fame.

- When you set any of these as your goal, you set yourself on a path of guaranteed hardship and likely disappointment.

Goals are a declaration of what you want, not a blueprint for how to get there. Moreover, when you set a goal, you are opening yourself up to a potentially long period of unhappiness until you reach your goal.

You may find that the cost of achieving your goal far outweighs the benefits, but you realize this only after the damage has been done.

Taking the larger perspective, we live in times of great abundance. Most of us have demonstrably more wealth, health, and possessions than humans across the vast march of time. We have also advanced the state of our collective knowledge to unprecedented heights.

How do we explain then that we simultaneously find ourselves irritated and annoyed to distraction?

We chafe and argue with one another and believe we are surrounded by dangerous idiots. We feel that our own success remains out of reach, and we run harder chasing after it.

## A tranquil mind

Perhaps we should wish for something other than more of the promotions, wealth, and possessions that aren't making us happier.

I think we'd do well to give ourselves the same advice we'd give our colleagues and our children: To experience lasting joy — and not just fleeting enjoyment — we must remember that joy does not come from external things but from a tranquil mind.

> *When you are free from doubt, worry, jealously; when your course is the same whether you are pushing into the headwind or blown along by a tailwind; when you delight in stillness as much as you do in motion; when you do not rely on external things, joy is your reward.*

So the next time you sign a farewell card, consider writing something like this:

"I wish you a string of small failures that teach you to be mindful so as to fully appreciate all that you already have, the people you're lucky enough to spend time with, and whatever you're doing at exactly this moment."

Or if that's too long, you can just say "Be well" and hope they fill in the blanks themselves.

Be well.

Chapter Twelve

# Who Are the Most Cost-Effective Employees?

## Because humans are complex and varied, the safeguards put in place to protect us themselves create opportunities for mischief

Can a company rationalize discrimination?

Healthy societies foster freedom of thought and freedom of expression. We can make the world a better place through our ideas, and this requires us to share them. It is in this spirit that I offer today's discussion.

I explain my thinking with a series of hypotheses. You may agree or not with any of them, but at least you'll understand my thought process.

I'll show how an organization could easily justify preferentially hiring and promoting a certain type of employee.

**Hypothesis 1 — It is economically rational for companies to consider their total costs when hiring and promoting employees.**

These costs can include brand and reputation impacts associated with the composition of a company's workforce.

There is a strong argument that having diverse employees leads to better business outcomes (although hard data demonstrating causation is thin on the ground).

Furthermore, companies that lack diversity risk alienating stakeholders.

## Hypothesis 2 — Some employees cost their companies more than others even though they perform the same work.

Costs here include not just an employee's salary and benefits, but also the risks and friction associated with the company managing that employee.

It takes time and costs money to respond to employee concerns, complaints, and lawsuits. Here are several examples.

- Employees may oppose the company pursuing legal business with customers they object to, which could include any "out-of-favor" group or industry. We sometimes see this in younger employees or those who simply may have more of their idealism intact. For as many opinions as individuals have about the world, some employees expect the company's business to reflect their opinions. This is understandable, but the attendant controversy is costly. Either the company voluntarily reduces its business, or it risks losing employees and customers who disagree with its decision not to cut off other customers.

- Whenever an individual is promoted, you can expect some employees to think that other, more qualified, individuals were overlooked. Because individuals' perception of their own performance is biased, any merit-oriented organization will suffer from concerns about these decisions. This puts companies in no-win situations: They either let the issue blow over, which means living with a certain number of disgruntled employees, or they give reasons why the non-promoted persons were not as qualified, making them and their promoters doubly unhappy.

- Next, because individuals' understanding of their own versus others' relative work contributions is incomplete, any merit-oriented organization will suffer from concerns about unequal pay. Paying two individuals differently for what appears to be similar work is unequal pay, so complaints are easy to make. Many complaints are justified. But responding to such complaints is fraught with risk. Companies either demonstrate that individuals' market value and how their contributions differ, demotivating the less valuable employee, or they avoid the argument by simply adjusting pay to eliminate gaps, demotivating the employees making greater contributions.

- Lastly, we have strong laws protecting many groups against unlawful discrimination. In the United States, companies may not discriminate on the basis of race, color, sex, or age, among other things. Call these groups "protected classes." Protected classes can have different costs, as I explain below.

It is necessary and appropriate for individuals to raise legitimate concerns about discrimination. This helps keep companies honest. But because humans are complex and varied, the safeguards themselves create opportunities for mischief. Here's how.

Although most people are honest and ethical, some percentage is not. Behavioral economics predicts that when rewards for cheating exist, some number of people always cheat. They take advantage of loopholes to gain a personal advantage.

A dishonest employee can put considerable pressure on their employer by claiming discrimination even where none exists.

If even a few employees in protected classes exploit legal protection to obtain negotiation leverage, promotions, or settlements, companies' costs rise for all employees in that class.

## Hypothesis 3 — Some people are dishonest, and a few bad apples cause harm to all the rest.

If you think that all employees are completely altruistic all the time and would never take an action that personally benefits them at the cost of their colleagues, I guess you can stop here.

But if you have observed that people sometimes behave selfishly and dishonestly, read on.

Let's assume unethical behavior is evenly distributed across all groups. Protected classes have more opportunities to exploit the laws precisely because they have laws protecting them.

This means that some employees come with higher implicit total costs than others. For example:

- Women as a group spend fewer hours in paid work than men on average. This is because they spend more time on unpaid family-related tasks and because women have traditionally taken more maternity leave than men paternity leave. A pay gap that relates to fewer hours worked is still unequal pay on its face, however, which gives room to complaints.

- Employees respond differently to adverse employment decisions in my experience. Some accept they could do better and try to improve. Others claim any bad outcome must be the result of discrimination and complain accordingly. No company fires a protected-class employee without carefully considering the risk of a lawsuit.

- A similar calculation occurs on the part of employers considering adverse actions against over 40-year-old employees. Although it is relatively easy to avoid an age discrimination claim, doing so requires advance planning and limits companies' flexibility. Hence, over-40 employees have a relatively higher cost from this perspective as well.

If new employees, women, historically underrepresented minorities, and everyone over 40 are relatively riskier and hence more expensive, who does that leave?

## Hypothesis 4 — The sweet spot consists of white men in their 30s who do not otherwise fall in a protected class.

They have been with the company for 5–10 years. By then you know the cultural fit is good. If employees have lasted that long, they usually navigate the workplace well and so are less likely to complain.

They also have enough experience to be productive at their jobs but have not had decades of annual salary increases that make them expensive just with the passage of time.

Considering each of the factors above, white men in their 30s appear to be the employees least likely to complain and cause friction for their companies.

Some of you will be saying, "That's right, and it's because *they have the least to complain about*." That may be entirely true.

But if white men complain less on average, it could also be because they have fewer laws protecting them. That is, they are among the only groups it is safe to openly discriminate against.

Either way, they generate lower total costs for their employers.

Should you take any of this as an argument in favor of hiring more white men? Not at all.

It is an observation that promoting diversity comes with a cost to companies because of the laws that favor protected classes and the fact that some individuals will seek to exploit those laws.

This may help explain why it has taken longer to develop diverse workforces than everyone expected considering the obvious social and reputation benefits to doing so.

## Ignoring financial incentives won't work

Considering all this, can we do anything to improve the situation?

One option is to keep raising the social costs on companies that do not promote diversity quickly enough. This makes it easier for companies to justify paying overall higher costs to compensate for occasional bad actors.

We may also consider raising the costs on those individuals who make false claims because they artificially raise the costs of the entire protected class.

What probably won't work is ignoring companies' financial incentives when they evaluate how expensive different employees actually are.

Be well.

Chapter Thirteen

# Why Aren't More Pharma Companies Nonprofits?

## The shareholder model is absurdly counterproductive in the case of pharma companies

This essay is about the power of incentives. When you look past the surface of things to the incentives that drive behavior, you sometimes find surprising things.

Full disclosure: I believe in the shareholder model of capitalism and the theory that companies pursuing their own long-term profit will drive the maximum benefits not just to shareholders but to society as a whole.

I say this despite having worked for more than a decade on sustainability topics and also believing strongly in the benefits of a broad environmental, social, and governance (ESG) strategy.

Having run a global sustainability program, I am aware of the growing chorus of calls for companies to discard the idea of shareholder primacy as having long since served its purpose.

### The stakeholder framework's fatal flaw

My principal objection to stakeholder capitalism is that we have yet to identify a consistent framework for choosing priorities among competing stakeholders.

A company has many stakeholders, all of whom rightly believe their concerns are paramount. Stakeholders respond to the competition by ratcheting up the pressure on companies to pay attention to their issue.

The public pressure leads to the misallocation of resources in which companies waste money in areas where they do not have the greatest potential impact.

## Shareholder primacy isn't perfect either

I have come to understand two necessary modifications to my belief in the fundamental soundness of shareholder capitalism.

First, we can solve the problems of the stakeholder model by allowing companies to determine in good faith their unique opportunities for the greatest stakeholder impact.

What would happen if we allowed those companies who genuinely want to make positive contributions to determine freely where and how they would do so? I expect we would see much better performance on those metrics.

True, not always in those areas that some stakeholders would prefer. But I ask you what's better in the long run? Second-rate forced compliance on topics the company doesn't fundamentally agree are important, or enthusiastic all-in commitments on selected topics?

Second, some types of business are ill-suited for the shareholder model. The reason is the very thing that makes the shareholder model so effective: incentives.

The normal incentive is for companies to grow their long-term profits, which accrue to the benefit of many stakeholders, including shareholders. The emphasis on the long term is what keeps companies from committing harm to certain stakeholders.

What opponents of capitalism conveniently ignore is that no company is successful over the long term that breaks the law, underpays employees, squeezes suppliers, or cheats customers.

The mechanisms are not perfect, and we see many temporary exceptions that outrage us, but it is hard to argue with the improvements in much of humanity's quality of life that have been brought about by modern capitalism.

## Mismatched incentives are a source of great mischief

That said, is it possible for a company's good faith successful pursuit of long-term profitability to create incentives that are harmful for their customers and for society as a whole?

The staggering cost of healthcare in the United States combined with relatively poor outcomes strongly suggests this is so, at least for some market participants.

Healthcare costs have been steadily increasing such that Americans now pay more than people in any other country for their care. But Americans are not getting healthier. For evidence, we can look at developments in life expectancy, preventable years of life lost, and the leading causes of death.

Here's the mismatch between pharmaceutical companies' incentives and their customers' incentives:

- Pharma companies wish to have proprietary drugs approved so they can exclusively sell them to patients for the greatest profit.

- Customers wish to be healthy and well.

- Drug trials are designed to prove the efficacy of a drug compared to not taking the drug. The trials are *not designed* to prove the efficacy of that drug compared to other interventions, including non-pharmacological inventions.

- As a result, the US Food and Drug Administration (FDA) approves many drugs for use *without any evidence that they provide the best outcome for patients (i.e., health and wellness)*.

Perhaps a diabetes drug does reduce the risk of heart complications in one out of several hundred patients. That small benefit may be enough to warrant approval of that drug to treat patients.

But nowhere must the pharma company describe or even mention that a program of diet and exercise might be vastly more effective at treating both diabetes and cardiovascular risk.

What kinds of patients are the ideal customers for pharma companies? Those who never or only sparingly take medications in favor of lifestyle interventions? Or those who become lifelong customers of a drug?

The patient's desire to become healthy cuts directly against the pharma company's interest in selling its medications to forever patients.

## It's not the employees' fault, but can't we do better?

Now I must point out a great irony. I think the vast majority of employees who work for pharma companies are honest and well-meaning and believe they are making positive contributions to society.

Everyone I know who ever worked for a pharma company expressed personal satisfaction at the strong social benefit they presumed their company delivered.

Almost no one is alert to the fact that, in this special case, their company's incentives are grossly misaligned with their stated values.

Would today's pharma companies be just as effective if they were organized as not-for-profit companies? If we assume employees are genuine in their desire to help cure disease and be a positive force in society, and I do believe this, I see no reason why not.

In contrast, I see every reason why the shareholder model is counterproductive in the case of pharma companies, which leaves me with today's question:

Why aren't more pharma companies nonprofits?

I genuinely have no answer. Let me know if you think you do.

Be well.

Chapter Fourteen

# Corporations Are People Too

## The blanket criticisms of corporations are not based in fact, but when a majority of the public believes the bad press, we better watch out

Effective in-house counsel help their companies address many risks facing their businesses. Today, a key risk is societal doubt about the benefits of corporations themselves.

If we want our companies to be free to pursue business without intrusive regulation, then we need to think carefully about corporate reputations. In-house lawyers can play a critical role in this evaluation.

"Greedy corporations!" We hear this so often it is almost a reflexive response.

Or how about, "All corporations are evil," a Hollywood refrain so common it has led to many young people believing it as a matter of fact.

Certainly, executives of large companies are inherently suspect, the original "fat cats," paying themselves obscene amounts of money.

If you work for a large company, it is easy to dismiss these complaints. After all, you, personally, are a good person, and just about everyone you work with is as well.

You see occasional incompetence, true, perhaps a touch of arrogance, but certainly no evil. Of the many thousands of corporations, a tiny number end up committing malfeasance.

Because of this, it is typically only people who don't work for large companies who hold such derogatory views of them.

## The good and the bad of corporations

What we sometimes underestimate, however, is how many people do not work for large companies. This makes our ignoring the phenomenon risky.

We may know that the blanket criticisms of corporations are not based on fact, but when a majority of the public believes the bad press, we better watch out.

And it is not just investment banks, oil companies, or cigarette manufacturers. Politicians and the media focus a roving spotlight on the particular villains of the day, but no one is safe from their harsh gaze.

The scope of environmental, social, and governance (ESG) stakeholder interests is so broad that virtually every corporation may fall victim to a negative influence campaign at some point.

## Critics and defenders

Is there anyone who will speak out on behalf of corporations?

Each individual company has a strong incentive to stay silent. Why draw attention to yourself? Better to be quiet and hope that the news cycle will turn to another victim.

Milton Friedman spoke eloquently in 1970 about the social responsibility of business. His point then was that businesses brought about the greatest good for society when they focused on increasing their profit.

Academics and advocates are questioning the past five decades of shareholder primacy in the stakeholder v. shareholder debate.

But this debate glosses over the most important point about the role of corporations: Far from being greedy or evil, corporations have been a steady source of significant good in society.

When did we all lose the script?

## Corporations are strongholds

One of the most amazing features of corporations is their potential for indefinite life. This is because while a corporation is comprised of the people who work for it at any given moment, it has a separate, independent existence.

For legal purposes, corporations are people too. The individuals who serve in various functions come and go, but the corporation itself continues on.

I worked for a company with a more than 100-year history. No one involved at the time our company was formed is alive today.

Of course, the company evolved over this time. But the company still is involved in recognizably the same business, selling products meeting a similar need, albeit with vastly improved technology and performance.

I sometimes marveled at how many people worked at my company over the years. How many livelihoods we supported, and how much influence our products had on the world.

Yes, corporations are people too, and what people they are! Capable of coordinating the collective efforts of tens and thousands of people across decades and centuries.

Corporations preserve humankind's know-how and encourage steady improvements in products and services. This has brought untold prosperity and better living conditions to many millions of people across the world.

In most other areas of life, we celebrate the power of collective human action:

- from a simple employee union that brings negotiation power to a group of individuals,
- to massive research efforts (think of the remarkable effort to develop COVID vaccines in record time),

- to even greater scientific feats of human achievement, such as the moon landings or the deployment of the James Webb Space Telescope.

## Rights and the Rule of Law

But also on the individual level, Western society has thrived on the principle of protection of individual rights.

We allow people to pursue their self-interest unreservedly, subject only to operating within the law.

We incentivize risky exploration by allowing people to reap the benefit of their individual efforts. Many ventures fail, but when an individual succeeds, they can become wildly successful.

Allowing and encouraging people to pursue their self-interest benefits all of society.

The rule of law undergirds this system: If you play within the rules, society will protect your person and your property.

There is nothing more fundamental than protecting personal property from predation by other people or the government itself. What you accumulate through your efforts belongs to you.

If corporations are people too, what possible reason can justify changing the rules to apply, for example, an "excess profits" tax?

What undermining of the rule of law warrants telling successful people that, although they played by the rules of the game, they have been too successful?

For every corporation you secretly cheered getting grilled by a grandstanding member of US Congress remember this: It's not just corporations that are people. You are too.

What we do to corporations can just as easily be done to us.

Be well.

Chapter Fifteen

# Can Anything Save Corporations' Tainted Image?

## In the last 25 years, the number of US public companies has dropped by half

Many in society question whether corporations provide sufficient benefit for the supposed harm they cause.

If we want our companies to be free to pursue business without intrusive regulation, we need to think carefully about corporate reputations. In-house lawyers can play a critical role in this evaluation.

Although there have been exceptionally bad actors, corporations' legacy is, on balance, overwhelmingly positive. In the previous essay, I talked about how corporations have contributed to the flourishing of humankind.

I explore here what it is that makes corporations so deeply unsympathetic in the public eye today. And as importantly, whether there is anything corporations can do to turn public sympathy to their side once more.

I think we can chalk corporations' bad image up to two things: Scope of influence and confirmation bias. Here's what I mean.

**They've gotten bigger and bigger**

Because of global networks, large corporations have been getting larger, particularly technology companies.

It is easier for an incumbent to buy a small company and incorporate their novel technology than it is to compete with them. The more technologies and services a company incorporates into its offerings, the more valuable it becomes to consumers.

For their part, smaller companies have every incentive to sell to larger competitors. There is no guarantee they'll succeed on their own and being a public company today is burdensome.

Society puts substantial regulations on companies for fear that the bad acts of a few will become the norm for all. Ironically, this heavy-handed approach has led to ever fewer companies either choosing to go public or remaining independent.

In the last 25 years, the number of US public companies has dropped by half. At the same time, our economies have grown, which means that fewer companies are dividing up ever-increasing markets.

Hence, companies' scope of influence on our lives has increased visibly.

## The bad rap is often exaggerated

This enhanced influence would be unproblematic but for the second point: Confirmation bias.

We are now primed to expect bad behavior from corporations because of prominent examples that politicians and pundits make sure are publicly exposed.

When you expect bad behavior, any example, no matter how isolated, will reinforce your belief and confirm your suspicions.

Thus, a tiny number of incidents has led to overblown concerns. To understand the point, you need only consider the many people who are scared to fly but think nothing of hopping in their cars.

## They need to do more than good deeds

# CAN ANYTHING SAVE CORPORATIONS' TAINTED IMAGE?

What can corporations do? Having attained the reputation as the schoolyard bully or worse, it will not help for corporations to point out their many good deeds.

A year of patient benevolence is undone by pushing down one kid in the playground and taking their lunch money.

I think of this when I read companies' sustainability reports. Page after page of good deeds, which have no effect on the reader, other than for some to suspect the company of greenwashing.

## Know why corporations are important

The reason recitations of good deeds won't help is because society no longer considers the net positive impact corporations have had on society in the past two centuries.

Partly this is a matter of short-termism, as in, "What have you done for me lately?"

Partly it is a matter of being spoiled by good times. We don't personally remember when our quality of life was materially worse and when products and services from household-name corporations changed all that.

Lastly as noted above, we are primed to think corporations are filled with selfish, bad actors, and so extrapolate the acts of a few to all.

Well, what about pointing out what happens in countries when private enterprise is squelched, and the government steps in to provide basic goods and services?

Cuba, Venezuela, and North Korea are clear warning signals for tampering with individual incentives. Surely a reminder of this would bring an ungrateful public around, right?

Sadly, this hope is also misguided. People do not reliably learn from history; they rarely learn from their own experiences and almost never from those of others.

Because of, again, confirmation bias, such as: "I believe corporations are evil and their function would be better performed by the central government. Thus, any evidence to the contrary I simply dismiss. Cuba and Venezuela are a mess, true. But if we were running the show, we would avoid their obvious problems."

## Become a benefit corporation

No, corporations need a radical change of frame. Tinkering around the edges of society's malcontent with a feel-good story in your next corporate responsibility report won't do.

I suggest that for corporations to survive for the next 50 years in a recognizable form, they need to reframe themselves as *operating primarily for the benefit of society*.

Have shareholders vote on converting the company to a benefit corporation. Nothing short of this will snap a jaded public out of its negative view.

Societal benefit looks different today than when Milton Friedman advocated for shareholder primacy.

- Then, shareholders were expected to take net profits and reinvest them in further productive enterprises.

- Today, shareholders have reaped decades of gain from companies' remarkable success and, considering overall wealth, further gains only go to fund lavish excesses.

If shareholders of the largest companies in the world voted to become or similar according to the country's law, individuals would believe companies once again represented a force for good in society.

Short of that, don't hold your breath.

Be well.

PS — If this sounds too drastic to you, don't worry: Companies and shareholders also suffer from confirmation bias, which means they will convince themselves that the status quo is just fine.

## Chapter Sixteen

# Do You Have Skin in the Game?

## Look for where one party has greater upside than downside or a potential gain with little cost and you will find the sources of bad behavior

Spending time with colleagues working at other companies gave me an unexpected benefit.

I realized my fellow in-house colleagues were facing all the same problems as me. No one had a perfect solution to their problems, and we were all muddling along doing the best we could.

In fact, some colleagues had it far worse than me: those whose companies sold products to end consumers, so-called B-to-C companies.

It seems like not a week went by when I didn't say to myself, "Thank goodness you don't have to deal with the individual public as customers." Prompted, of course, by some idiot suing a consumer goods company on transparently frivolous grounds.

Or even when it appeared there might be a sliver of merit, then suing for such inflated amounts that I could never forget where the phrase "deep pockets" came from.

And this was years before the whole environmental, social, and governance (ESG) movement became front-page news. These same companies that had widespread brand recognition were natural targets for the early activists.

- A shareholder proposal at Coke or Nestlé got you much more publicity simply because everyone recognizes the name of your company.

- Still today, the nature of your customer and shareholder base is a great predictor of whether and what types of shareholder proposals will pop up during proxy season.

Working for a B-to-B company that nobody in the public had any reason to know or care about was a great advantage. Yes, my in-house friends at Starbucks and McDonald's ran out of business cards at every get-together. But I read the headlines like everyone else and consoled myself that it is better to be unseen than in the spotlight, at least if you're in-house counsel.

We had our share of issues, no doubt. Many of our customers were big, powerful companies, much more capable of vigorously defending their interests than any individual consumer.

And because these customers bought large amounts of products, when something went wrong, it was almost always worth pursuing.

## The joy of just doing business

Here's the lovely thing about B-to-B businesses: Neither companies nor their business customers have any incentive to push frivolous lawsuits. We just want to do business on reasonable terms.

We typically have long business relationships and want to preserve the relationship. So when a problem arises, it is in both our interests to find a quick, fair solution.

When a business customer decides to sue a supplier, the customer pays for it in the long run.

What all this means is that B-to-B companies' and customers' incentives are aligned. We want to make the best possible products and sell them for a fair price. Customers want to buy the best products for a fair price.

## Lawsuit-happy businesses are another matter

Now consider the B-to-C relationship.

When you buy a treat from Nestlé or Kraft, you are not forming a meaningful, lifelong relationship with either company.

But if you chip a tooth snacking on a cracker, some plaintiff's lawyer will slither out and tell you that you can get thousands of dollars. And best of all, it won't cost you a thing!

In this case, your incentives are not aligned with the company's and are rather exactly opposed. You have no downside risk (also known as "skin in the game") because you suffer no costs if you lose. It's all upside to you.

Your lawyer similarly has almost no skin in the game. True, they need to file a lawsuit, but this is something they've done many times before. They simply change the plaintiff's name on their standard form complaint, update their outrageously overbroad list of requested discovery subjects and topics, and the costs and burdens shift to the company.

Your lawyer knows that the cost of defending even frivolous lawsuits is so high that companies make the economically rational choice to settle many of them. What is a nuisance settlement for *Nestlé* is bread and butter to your lawyer: 40 percent of US$30,000 for doing little more than printing off a copy of a standard complaint is easy money. So it's all upside to your lawyer as well.

## Playing the incentive game

This mismatch of incentives explains a great deal of what in-house lawyers do. Look for where one party has greater upside than downside or a potential gain with little cost and you will find the sources of bad behavior.

Let's assume salespeople are compensated based on the volume of new business they bring in. Will they care as much about the terms of the contract as they will landing a new customer? You know the answer.

## How to identify your greatest risks

Looking at who has skin in the game helps you identify your greatest compliance risks.

Consider how material are the risks that an individual can cause by their actions. No matter what type of company you work for, this analysis usually leads you to the conclusion that senior management creates your greatest exposure.

Senior management has tremendous upside, which encourages them to take risks. They are often well-insulated against downside risk. Yes, they may be dinged on their cash incentive for one year, but their long-term equity incentives still pay off handsomely. Thus, they have insufficient skin in the game.

The time in-house counsel spend rolling out compliance programs to every employee worldwide is largely for show. If we're honest, it's partly a distraction by management to deflect attention from their own incentives for mischief.

In-house counsel's incentives are usually properly aligned with the company's. That is, we don't want compliance problems and we feel the consequences when they occur.

Looking at your compliance program, ask yourself this question: How much time do you spend on window-dressing versus designing incentives tailored to your greatest risks?

Be well.

Chapter Seventeen

# Lawmakers Need a Hippocratic Oath

Passing new laws and regulations without sufficiently considering the likely but unwanted adverse consequences is foolish and risky

I magine a world where your performance was measured, not by outcomes, but simply by your intentions.

*Boss:* "*Hi Sam, come on in. So, annual performance evaluation time already, huh?*"

*You:* "*Yes, Pat, can't wait! It was a great year.*"

*Boss:* "*Hmm, we'll talk about that. I saw on your self-evaluation you gave yourself a 110 percent rating across the board.*"

*You:* "*Sure did! I took that goal of implementing a compliance program in Europe, and I ran with it. Why, I had the most amazing project plan you've ever seen.*"

"*Sam, are you forgetting we got sued by the EU Antitrust Commission for starting up an illegal cartel with our three biggest competitors? I have to testify in Brussels next month!*"

"*Pat, Pat, let's stay focused. On paper, I designed a perfect program. I even called it the Perfect Compliance Program. Why, the training videos alone won awards for most innovative use of Claymation.*"

*"Oh, don't mention those videos to me. Everywhere we showed them management ended up engaging in* more *illegal behavior, not less. It seems like your examples only inspired them to find more ways to bend the law."*

*"That's certainly not my fault. I was only following best practices. And remember, we had that consultant come in and tell us our program ticked all the boxes? No, my intentions were pure."*

*"Since when do we measure performance by intentions, Sam?"*

In the business world, the answer is a clear "never." But when it comes to our politicians and regulators, we all seem to stop at good intentions. Why do I say this? It is because I spent decades managing the unintended consequences of laws passed with the best of intentions.

## Policymaking can be a waste of time

Grandstanding lawmakers and overworked regulators slap a rule in place with a catchy title like the Anti-Money Laundering Act. "See, it's got 'Anti' right in the title; we're taking a stand against criminals." Never mind that the consequences of the law's reporting requirements are that honest companies are now routinely hounded by their banking partners to declare ever more detailed chains of beneficial owners with no appreciable effect on actual money launderers.

## Laws can do worse than simply not achieve their goals

They can lead to the exact opposite outcome than was intended. Consider the cautionary tale of attempts to rein in executive compensation.

One early idea was to limit executive compensation by forbidding companies from deducting pay that exceeded US$1 million. But the law allowed companies to deduct "performance-based compensation" approved by shareholders. The result (predictable in hindsight) was public companies adopting stock option plans and an explosion in equity-based compensation.

Then regulators decided they would require companies to publicly disclose their compensation in painful detail. Even if executives themselves were unashamed, the thinking went, shareholders seeing the details would curtail the worst excesses.

The result was again exactly the opposite of what was intended. How so? Compensation committees benchmark executive pay against peer companies. Where previously there were gray areas and some guesswork, the details became clear to all. Once-missed perks were now added to the calculus.

Worse, the sincere belief that your executives are better than average supports paying above the median. But when everyone does this, the median itself steadily rises. While performance is not notably different, pay has risen steadily year-on-year for decades.

Passing new laws and regulations without sufficiently considering the likely but unwanted adverse consequences is foolish and risky.

So why do we keep doing it? For lawmakers the answer is clear: Their incentive is always to take action, and they have no skin in the game, i.e., they suffer no consequence for bad laws.

## Why do we allow bad policy?

Why does the voting public accept repeated poor performance? After all, we are affected by poorly designed laws and grapple with unintended consequences all the time. Is it because we can't see a better way? I can think of at least three alternatives:

1. **No new laws.** At least prevent lawmakers from making things worse. I welcome gridlock for this very reason. But there are real problems we need to address as a society, so we do want effective lawmaking.

2. **Sunset all new laws.** Let lawmakers pass new laws, but build in a review mechanism. That is, lawmakers must revisit the law's performance after some period, say 10 years, and decide whether to scrap it, keep it, or amend it in light of unintended consequences.

3. **Give lawmakers skin in the game.** Just like executives now must stand behind the company's financials, make politicians personally responsible for the laws they adopt. An easy first step would be making sure lawmakers are subject to the same rules as the general public, which is surprisingly often not the case. Then let's make lawmakers sign up to a modified Hippocratic Oath.

You probably heard an excerpt of the Hippocratic Oath as being "first do no harm." The longer excerpt is actually "I will abstain from all intentional wrong-doing and harm."

Intentional harm includes the reasonably foreseeable consequences of your actions. Just because you didn't want something to happen, you are still responsible if a reasonable person could anticipate that it will happen.

**With all this in mind, the Lawmakers' Oath would read as follows:**

> I will ensure that the intended benefits of all laws I propose are not outweighed by both anticipated harms *and* probable but unintended effects. I will regularly assess the real world actual benefits *and* harms to evaluate the performance of the laws and adjust accordingly.

I don't expect lawmakers to do much better right away. But the Lawmakers' Oath would give voters a way to objectively measure their performance. That seems like a good start to me.

Be well.

## Chapter Eighteen

# I'm a Better Manager Now that I'm Out of the Job

## It takes quiet time and reflection to tease out meaningful learnings from our chaotic days

When you share your thoughts publicly, you wonder how people will react. Will they see what you've written, do they agree with your ideas? Perhaps most importantly, for me at least, will anything you've said be helpful to them in their lives?

I love writing these Career Paths essays. It helps me shape my intuitions, feelings, and more or less well-founded practices into tangible advice. I also appreciate the reach that publishing gives me, as well as the opportunity to interact with readers.

So it was that I found myself responding to a commenter on an earlier article. I noted that I wasn't always able to give good advice in a timely way when I was in my management role and that I was happy to do so now.

### Quiet, strategic thought time can make you great

We're busy at work, and we have many demands on our time. I've found it takes quiet time and reflection to tease out meaningful learnings from our chaotic days.

While working, I knew the importance of carving out time for strategic thinking. I told my team that regularly making time for strategic thought was one of the things that distinguished great in-house counsel from merely good ones.

So we devoted time to strategy. But it was almost always business strategy, or rather legal strategy in pursuit of business goals. Only now with some time and distance from my general counsel role do I see some pretty big gaps in where I spent my time and where I might have invested more time.

## Lessons learned later in life

I learned a lot over the years about managing a team and being effective. But I wasn't always effective at consolidating those lessons and then sharing them with my colleagues.

I find myself saying often these days, "Boy, I wish I had spent more time exploring this idea with my team when I was working!" I just didn't have the time because of the press of daily work. Honestly, I don't think any active manager has the time for considered reflection on many non-core topics.

When I look at how much time I invest now in organizing my thoughts and summarizing ideas, I am alternatively amazed and depressed. I think I'm pretty efficient, and I can write quickly and well. But many are the days that I look up to find 10 hours have passed with my face still lit by a screen and my hands poised over a keyboard.

To be fair, I am writing about many topics beyond those here in Career Paths. Stoic philosophy and how to live a good life. Economics, politics, and psychology. Junk science and the march of human progress. And no one is holding my feet to the fire.

Writing down interesting ideas engages me, as does the idea of helping other people in a way that I would have appreciated when I was younger.

My point is simply this: Getting better at anything takes time, practice, and reflection. Although most of us learn to implement well by necessity, we can do so comfortably without also developing a philosophy or working model that explains and guides our actions. The bigger picture, if you will, comes only upon reflection.

With this in mind, here's another thing I can tell you was a great use of my time when I was working, even though many consider it non-core: Reading widely. It was because I religiously read professional journals that I was able to keep up on so many topics.

# I'M A BETTER MANAGER NOW THAT I'M OUT OF THE JOB

Few people are experts on lots of topics. The good news is we don't have to be. All you need is access to a few good experts on topics that interest you.

If I'm a better manager now that I'm out of the job of managing, I hope I can help you be a better manager now by sharing with you my learnings. What you do with those learnings is up to you.

Be well.

# Chapter Nineteen

# What the Heck Were They Thinking?

## Although it's true we sometimes learn from our own mistakes, it's considerably less embarrassing to use other people's screwups for our teachable moments

I'm a little tired of "best of" awards, truth be told. In my professional life, not a week went by without some law firm being celebrated for an accolade.

In-house counsel seem to do fewer, but we still hand out awards like clockwork such as for best law departments, GCs of the year, and the ACC Top 10 30-Somethings (of which I served as a judge). There are hundreds and hundreds of them.

Now, it's not that the law firms, departments, and individual lawyers who are nominated and who win these awards aren't awesome. They usually are pretty great and deserving of recognition.

The award serves as a temporary boost to the ego, provides a little thrill of recognition, can get you introduced to folks you'd like to know, looks good on your resume, and reassures you that you haven't given up a large chunk of your waking hours for nothing.

The thing is, there's not a great deal awards can teach us. In fact, that a majority of votes went to Person X at Firm Y could mean one of several things.

- Maybe voting was light that year and the marketing department did a great job getting their friends' friends to vote.

- Maybe the judges were lazy or incompetent.

- Or maybe the donation the firm made to the voting committee's favorite charity wasn't completely coincidental.

But let's take even the best assumption, i.e., the winner is a great lawyer who delights their clients. OK, what does that do for me? How does it help me provide a better service?

## I'd rather know what the worst lawyers did

I'll tell you what would be much more valuable to know: Who are the worst lawyers and what did they do that made them stand out?

Flagrant public mistakes can provide great learning experiences. Although it's true we sometimes learn from our own mistakes, it's considerably less embarrassing to use other people's screwups for our teachable moments.

You might be surprised to hear there are far fewer lists nominating "the worst lawyer of the year" or "the biggest legal screwups of the decade." Or maybe you're not surprised. Lawyers are a sue-happy group, come to think of it. Probably not a good idea to go around seeking nominations for your new "worst lawyer" list, although I bet you could get some new advertisers to buy space in your award publication.

The closest analogy I can think of are periodic lists compiled by law firms of the largest fines and settlements companies paid to resolve enforcement actions.

These penalties are the result of sometimes epic misconduct and mismanagement, but it is rare for individuals to be singled out. In just the last few years, each of Airbus, Petrobas, Ericsson, and Telia coughed up more than a billion dollars in fine for paying bribes. Do you know any of the involved parties' names?

It would be really interesting to know what management was thinking in these companies. You don't get to problems that big without senior management malfeasance:

- Either their direct involvement, or

- They knew about it and didn't stop it, or

- They didn't know but should have known.

The thought process in all three cases would be fascinating to understand. Why did they make the decisions they did? Would we have been tempted to make the same decisions?

## The annual "What Were They Thinking" Awards

Because we should be open to continuous improvement from wherever inspiration strikes, I propose we establish an annual "What Were They Thinking?" list for counsel of companies and institutions that experience public crises.

No need to crown an overall winner, and no need to pour salt on the wounds by referring to anything so rude as the "worst lawyers."

And if we're honest, we should demonstrate humility when judging others. What seems like an obvious mistake after a crisis has unfolded was in all likelihood anything but clear at the time. We're talking about smart, accomplished, often well-meaning people who were doing their absolute best in difficult circumstances, not hacks or crooks.

We could use these criteria for counsel's potential inclusion on the list:

- A deliberate decision (or lack of a decision) leading to significant corporate harm. In other words, there has to be one or more avoidable moments we can second-guess.

- The harm must make its way into the public eye. Lots of bad stuff happens that we never hear about. This isn't about surfacing companies' private business.

- Legal counsel either made the decision or was closely involved with those that did and so should have been able to influence the decision.

With this in mind, I quickly came up with the following candidates:

- Disney's counsel in letting the CEO say the company would explicitly fight to overturn a democratically adopted law in the State of Florida that had broad public support.

- Twitter's counsel for suppressing the news about Hunter Biden's laptop two weeks before the presidential election, making it appear as if they were choosing sides on a topic of clear national relevance.

- Boeing's counsel for allowing a circumstance to arise where safety officials say they felt their voices were overridden by business concerns.

- The Motion Picture Academy's counsel on thinking that a 10-year suspension for Will Smith attending the Academy Awards was appropriate while allowing him to retain his award.

Politics is so heated that I have great sympathy for any company that makes a misstep, egregious though they may be. Sometimes the pressure to take a stand is overwhelming. And I would bet there are a lot of companies whose safety officials feel underappreciated and underfunded. The slap and its consequences may not seem to reflect obviously poor decision-making to you.

So I'll offer up one more candidate for the "What Were They Thinking" nominations —

- Credit Suisse's counsel for their inability to control either CS's internal compliance culture or the flow of damaging information to the press. Any company can be hit by a scandal, and follow-on scandals are not that rare. After all, once authorities give you a good looking-over, they are more likely to find more troublesome things. But if your company makes global headlines month after month for a string of scandals over a multi-year period, something's gone terribly wrong.

I'd be interested to know who you think should make the list.

Be well.

PS — When I wrote this, Credit Suisse had yet to collapse and be taken over by its archrival UBS. I felt vindicated, but it turns out no one likes the bearer of bad news, especially if they turn out to be prescient.

Chapter Twenty

# Failure Hidden in Plain Sight

Women are well-represented in the law, or so it seems. Digging deeper reveals some shocking gaps

In-house lawyers are a bit of a secret weapon for companies, but not in the way you may be thinking. Sure, we keep the wheels of commerce rolling smoothly, manage a slew of business risks, and are essential allies in a crisis. What HR teams and management secretly love, however, is how much in-house lawyers contribute to companies' diversity efforts.

Where can we find a group that not only is majority-comprised of women but has excellent management representation, even frequently in executive management? The legal team is exemplary at many companies.*

The reasons for in-house legal teams' outperformance no doubt include our genuine commitment to diversity. But we also benefit from two powerful environmental factors: ample supply and weak competition.

I'll describe both factors and why our very success is contributing to an ugly distortion in the broader legal community. I'll end with a concrete recommendation about what in-house legal teams can do to help move towards balance.

**Supply: A rich palette of talent to choose from**

Law school is the ultimate egalitarian endeavor. At least as it concerns gender parity, women and men have been enrolling in law school in equal numbers for decades. Women enrollees have started outpacing men every year starting in 2016.

What this means is that when in-house legal teams need to hire new lawyers, we are spoiled for choice, certainly compared to many professions.

For reasons I'll explain in a moment, an even greater proportion of female lawyers than law school graduates want to work in-house. What's going on, you wonder, and where's the failure I'm hinting at?

## Competition: Why is in-house practice desirable?

Before we congratulate ourselves on being so wonderful, consider that it might not be us so much as the wretched competition.

According to ABA statistics, more than half of law school graduates enter private practice upon leaving law school. Just about 10 percent start by working in-house. That certainly doesn't look like in-house teams have any recruiting advantage.

But what happens each year after lawyers start to work? A certain percentage leave their law firms and look to move in-house. That reliable recurrence is what concerns us today.

## The depressing truth: Law firms are failing on a grand scale

When I say law firms are failing, I mean they're failing to create an environment in which women thrive and move into more senior roles. Consider this:

- Women constitute not quite half (47 percent) of all associates at law firms.

- Women represent 32 percent of all non-equity partners.

- Just 22 percent of law firm equity partners are women.

From starting in the majority as junior associates, women steadily leave law firms at greater rates than men and are significantly underrepresented in management. Not only that, but male partners have substantially higher average compensation than women partners.

If you ask them, everyone involved will tell you they're unhappy about this. The women for certain, as we'll see in a moment, but the men leading law firms as well.

## In what ways do law firms underperform?

The results of detailed inquiries into the law firm experience are sobering (from the ABA Profile of the Legal Profession 2022): In each of the following categories, vastly more women than men missed out on a desirable assignment, were denied a salary increase or bonus, were denied or overlooked for advancement or promotion, or were perceived as less committed to their career. Women experienced a lack of access to business development opportunities, were mistaken for lower-level employees, and experienced demeaning comments, stories, or jokes.

According to the same ABA study, the three top reasons women say they leave law firms are because of caretaking commitments, stress at work, and the emphasis on marketing or originating business.

Well, there you have it. Suddenly it becomes clear why in-house practice looks so attractive. We offer flexibility and part-time work, we are careful to acknowledge and mitigate stressful conditions, and our lawyers have no pressure to originate business.

## Can in-house lawyers help solve law firms' problems?

Let's assume law firms are making genuine efforts to stem the loss of so many talented women. Whatever they're doing is not working.

No matter how good one's intentions are, perceptions form reality. The statistics about women's daily experiences show what those perceptions are, and they're not good.

A lot of well-meaning people have spent a lot of time both thinking about this and trying to improve. It would be arrogant of us to assume we know their motives or how to create better outcomes.

But we do know that incentives drive behavior. If today's behaviors are not driving the desired outcomes, then the incentives are not sufficiently aligned. It is thus on the incentive side where in-house counsel may play a constructive role.

Because I don't think anyone has an easy fix, it's likely counter-productive for us to try to mandate an outcome. Individually we don't have the leverage and such requests are adjacent to our core work priorities.

Perhaps we can create greater incentives by reminding law firms this issue is important to us. How? *Just ask them about it.* That is much easier and relatively non-controversial.

If the majority of a firm's clients are routinely asking about diversity, law firm management would have a new incentive to keep trying.

## Three questions in-house teams could ask their outside counsel

How about once a year we simply ask our law firms these questions:

1. What are the current diversity statistics for your firm as a whole? How do these compare to the prior two years?

2. What are the diversity details of the lawyers currently working on our engagement?

3. Please describe any commitment to improve your diversity performance you have made. How have your prior commitments been implemented?

## Be careful what you wish for

Note that if we're successful in moving the law firm needle, we're going to make it harder to recruit lawyers to our in-house teams from private practice.

Rather than having a job that sells itself because the competition is terrible, we'll have to convince potential hires how wonderful we are. I am confident we're up to the challenge.

Be well.

\* While this discussion cites data from the US legal market, I've observed similar trends in other markets, including in Europe and India.

Chapter Twenty-One

# Corporate Greed Should Be Low on Our List of Worries

## A thought experiment on what would happen if we tried to promote "fairness" by eliminating "greed." Beware! You may come away feeling differently

Are corporations greedy? I notice that people use the word "greed" carelessly in two misleading ways. First, they imply that greed is unnatural and immoral. And second, they behave as if greed afflicts only one party to a transaction.

### What is greed? Looking beyond the quick answer

Greed is, in fact, a completely natural impulse. Let's say you're holding a garage sale: You've got your front yard filled with unneeded toys, sports equipment, and clothing. Two people are interested in your old bike.

- One says they'll pay you US$100 and the other says they'll pay you US$200.

- Are you greedy if you take the US$200? Or are you simply behaving rationally?

Assuming that transactions between market participants are unforced (that is, consensual on both sides), can it be immoral to allow a transaction to take place exactly as both parties wish?

Before you decide on the morality of market transactions, consider the second point: Which of us is the greedy one? We assume it is the seller who is the greedy party: Greedy corporations raising prices and taking advantage of consumers. But what about the buyers?

If one person at your garage sale bidding on your bike earns twice as much as the other person, and can comfortably pay more, are they greedy for using their superior earnings to their advantage? To give another example, are the young professionals moving to your town and bidding up home prices greedy because they can pay more?

Take two persons earning the same amount of money but placing different values on things. Person A likes to travel to new places and places a premium on their vacations. They could live in a small apartment and be happy. Person B loves to be at home and wants a house with a yard.

When these two want to book a flight, Person A is willing to pay considerably more of their income to get the flight they want. When it comes to their housing, Person B is willing to pay more of their income to get the home they want.

Is Person A greedy? Are they both greedy? Or do their decisions merely reflect different values and choices?

If you believe a seller is greedy for preferring to receive more money instead of less money, by the same logic, a buyer is greedy for being willing to pay more than another bidder to get what they want.

## Subjective and arbitrary standards, including "fairness"

Right now, you might be feeling uncomfortable with your understanding of greed, and for good reason. When we consider either the seller or the buyer to be greedy, a problem arises, because we compare the actual transaction with a hypothetical one that we feel "should have happened," absent some imagined amount of greed, and find the results unsatisfying.

It now should be clearer to us that "greed" is often nothing more than competition for resources playing out in markets with varied buyers.

In fact, there is no objective standard by which to determine when normal price competition goes too far and becomes greed. When challenged to set standards, people usually fall back on another hypothetical and imaginary concept: "fairness." As in, "it's not fair to charge so much."

Because fairness is situational and relative, everyone draws the line differently about what they think is fair. You can easily imagine how chaotic the world would become if transactions were governed by people's imaginary concepts of greed or fairness.

Back at our garage sale, the bidder who offered US$100 for your bike will certainly think it's unfair that someone is willing to pay US$200 for your bike. But is it unfair for you, as the seller, to accept the higher offer? Why exactly?

## Fairness is in the eye of the beholder

Or perhaps the people promoting "fairness" object to something else entirely: that people have different levels of desire for the same goods. Assume both bidders have the same amount of money, but one likes biking more. Is it "fair" that the avid cyclist is willing to pay more for the bike?

Now, consider what would happen if we tried to promote "fairness" by eliminating "greed." As the seller at your garage sale, you could not consider potential buyers' greater desire to own your bike, or their greater ability to pay.

In fact, to be "fair" you'd have to know which person could afford the least or wanted the bike less, leading to absurd results.

- After hearing the bids for US$100 and US$200, the kid next door says "I've saved up US$50, but I also want to go to the movies, so I can't pay more than US$25. I still would like to have your bike."

- Is it fair to *anyone* if you sell your bike to the kid for US$25?

When we apply standards like "Don't be greedy," and "Be fair," it's a short step to conclude that people who have no disposable income are entitled to goods and services for free. Most people recognize that individuals and companies cannot simply give things away or they'd quickly go bankrupt.

People then arrive at the idea that companies should be allowed to earn a "reasonable" profit, but not "excess" profits. Does this sound to you like another way of saying "Don't earn more than an arbitrary amount I decide is fair?" Because that's exactly what it is.

Fairness, like beauty, is in the eye of the beholder. Fairness is relative and situational, which means that what we think is fair changes over time and changes depending on who is doing the comparing. What you think is fair is likely quite different than someone in different circumstances than you thinks is fair.

## A much easier solution

If all this seems messy and complicated, don't worry. There is a fantastically simple and effective solution: Don't worry about greed or fairness but let market forces determine the prices of goods and services. Individuals expressing their individual preferences in pursuit of their own values effortlessly figure out what they're willing to pay.

In every other aspect of life, we give individuals freedom to decide how best to apply their interests and abilities. Some people are naturally talented, while some must work extra hard to achieve the same result. Others squander their gifts and waste their time.

If we value individual freedom, we must accept the necessary diversity of outcomes that comes with it.

Be well.

# Chapter Twenty-Two

# How Much Should Bosses Care About Employees?

Do I need to know what's going on in your life outside work for you to do your best work?

Sometimes you learn important things about yourself accidentally. I learned something about my management style relatively late in my career. We had announced my successor and one of my direct reports commented on the change.

He said, in all innocence, "The difference between your successor and you is that she cares about employees."

Upon first hearing this, I had to laugh out loud. It was so outrageous, but he said it so straightforwardly. Then I remembered my Stoic lesson about how to benefit from feedback: First, consider the source and, second, consider the truth of the statement.

In this case, the source was someone I trusted, which gave me pause. On reflection, I had to concede my friend was probably right.

That makes me sound like a terrible boss, and I suppose I was if my team was looking to me to be their friend providing emotional support. But the legal team was a well-functioning and high-performing team, highly regarded by the business.

This leaves me with the honest question of whether caring for your team is necessary for their, or your, success.

## Some jobs don't teach leadership well

To understand many lawyers' leadership styles, it helps to reflect on our route to leading teams.

Lawyers who spend time in private practice early in their careers usually work independently. Yes, with a supervising partner and one or more senior associates. But junior associates are there to do grunt work and learn by doing. The senior lawyers are incredibly busy with little time and inclination for handholding.

I offer this as a description, not an excuse, for why lawyers typically learn little about team leadership in a law firm. Good role models are thin on the ground.

The lawyers who advance do so largely on the strength of their individual contributions. (And don't feel bad for lonely associates. Partners may feel even less inclined to help partners on matters with which they're not directly involved.)

Now let's say you've gone in-house. You may have started in-house directly out of law school, although I expect many in-house lawyers will have spent some time in private practice. If you did start in-house directly from law school, then everything you've learned about leadership you learned in the company environment.

The good news here is that you've got many more role models for good leaders across the business.

The lawyers leading legal teams have a certain seniority. This comes typically from a mix of private practice and in-house time. The more a legal leader's experience comes from private practice, the less likely they are to have developed strong team leadership skills.

If you've practiced for 10 or 20 years in a law firm, you are probably a great lawyer with impressive legal experience. But you have a steep learning curve in managing your new in-house colleagues.

## I became a boss before I learned team leadership

I only spent five years in private practice before getting hired as the general counsel of a freshly-listed public company. I didn't come with too many bad habits, but I also brought no team leadership skills whatsoever.

Our legal team was small in those days. From the start, I treated my colleagues like trusted professionals. I left them alone to do their jobs, because that's how I performed best and because they knew more about their jobs than I did. I kept interactions minimal because I assumed that would help them work efficiently.

We tackled challenges and grew the team as the business grew. I invested what always seemed like disproportionate time in personnel matters: Budgets, salary rounds, target setting, progress checks, and annual evaluations. To say nothing of hiring new employees, having career development discussions, and finding ways to keep smart, ambitious lawyers suitably challenged but not overwhelmed.

I liked my colleagues immensely and was proud of how much they could do. I made it my personal mission to provide the best working environment I could, which to me meant focusing on strategically relevant topics that were valuable to the company. Our lean team members became awesomely qualified corporate generalists.

Because I was a young general counsel and stable in the role, we couldn't satisfy the ultimate ambition of some. Most who left went on to lead legal teams of their own. I think it says something about our environment that we created so many successful general counsels. It certainly wasn't because I was an empathic leader.

Sure, I got much better at human resource topics. I recognized time spent on employee topics as a wise investment. I am still in touch with almost everyone who spent time in our legal team. For me, this was always in aid of serving company interests.

I reminded myself often that the decisions we made were business decisions, not personal ones.

I could and did counsel underperforming employees, and fired many over my career, though thankfully very few in the legal team itself. I never liked it.

Looking back, my discomfort at disciplining or terminating colleagues probably contributed a lot to my being friendly with everyone but not friends. Otherwise, how could it not be personal?

## Is caring for your employees necessary?

So now back to today's question. Is caring for your team necessary for their, or your, success? My answer is yes, but only to a point.

You must care a lot to be successful. The best leaders I know care deeply about their companies and their companies' fate, so they care about the individuals who work alongside them.

Can I care about your performance and want you to be successful without caring about your personal life?

Put differently, because that sounds callous, do I need to know what's going on in your life outside work for you to do your best work? I don't think so, but I could easily be convinced that more empathy would help an already great team perform better.

If a leader has the emotional bandwidth to delve into their team's private lives, wouldn't that be helpful? Helpful in the sense that people feel an even deeper connection to their colleagues? Feel understood and appreciated for more than their work product?

If it came naturally to me, I would have shown more interest. It doesn't, so I didn't.

I am thankful to my team that everything worked so well for so long. But I am also happy for my team that they now have a boss that cares for them as well.

Be well.

## Chapter Twenty-Three

# This Is Most Senior Leaders' Single Biggest Weakness

## If you are serving in a C-suite role (or aspire to one), today's advice is something you probably haven't considered

I wish I had figured this one out while I was still serving as General Counsel of my S&P 500 company.

Looking back, it seems so obvious to me. But it wasn't at the time. And that's why I can say with confidence this is a weakness many senior leaders share.

I hope by raising this issue and discussing it openly, I encourage currently serving leaders to help themselves become even stronger in their roles.

So now you're wondering, "What's the big issue, James?" It's this:

**Senior leaders have no obvious mentors within their companies**

Senior leaders such as C-suite executives are in lonely roles. There is no one inside the company who understands all the issues that they face. And worse, they have little incentive to seek help from within.

I'll use my experience as General Counsel to illustrate.

The General Counsel cannot discuss many senior management and board-related topics with other legal team members, even senior ones. Confidentiality forbids. And until a person has held the responsibility themselves, they simply don't feel the weight of it the same way.

Other senior executives can no doubt relate. The chief financial officer or head of human resources have similar responsibilities they bear alone. But just as we won't understand the scope of the CFO's role and the intricacies of their concerns, so they do not understand ours.

Our boss is probably in the best position to understand our challenges. But do we really want to air uncertainties, stress, and frustration to our boss? We do not. So, we keep those thoughts to ourselves.

Interestingly, although the reverse is not the case, our boss can get sympathy from us. Every CEO who has felt the urge to vent their frustration at the latest board outrage will find the General Counsel to be most understanding.

## Generic sympathy is nice, but not substantively helpful

We can and do have ways to find a sympathetic ear.

General Counsel probably have friends, maybe even people who mentored us along the way, with whom we feel comfortable airing our frustrations. And periodically letting off steam can be helpful.

Such people can give us generic advice about generic situations. They can also give us advice about managing our emotions and our expectations. We should be grateful for every assistance we get.

But the relief is temporary and anyway is a far cry from providing substantive aid. As in, "I'm facing a really tough decision. Let me tell you what I think and why I'm leaning this way. What are your impressions? What would you do if you were in my shoes?"

## The solution is to talk to someone who knows exactly what you're feeling

Now some of you may be thinking, "That's why I go to industry meetings. The C-Suite club puts me next to other senior leaders for precisely this reason."

I used to think that as well. While those industry groups can be great, the interactions are fleeting and infrequent and everyone you meet is just as frantically busy as you are. In a day or two, they go back to their job, you go back to yours, and that was that.

No, what you want is someone who has not only walked a mile in your shoes but has time to focus on your issues. And you want them when you need them, and as much as you need them.

Yes, I'm referring to an executive coach. But not just any coach. You want as a coach a senior leader who knows from first-hand experience exactly what it feels like to make the decisions you're making. So a former CFO coach for CFOs, a former Head of HR for HR heads, and a former General Counsel for GCs.

Talking with someone who can provide substantive advice as well as emotional support is immensely powerful. Now instead of having to make critical decisions completely alone, you have a sounding board to help you work through the process.

It's obviously so helpful. Why don't more senior leaders use executive coaches? Why didn't I do it?

I can think of three reasons:

1. It never occurs to us to seek out such a coach;

2. We don't know they exist or where to find them; and

3. We're embarrassed to ask for help.

## For smart people, senior leaders can be remarkably stubborn

Let's face it. No one makes it to the seniormost levels of leadership without healthy doses of independence, masochism, and competence.

You get used to doing things yourself (independence). Sometimes that means great effort and sacrifice because the situation demands it (masochism). And you wouldn't keep advancing if you weren't very good at it (competence).

Unfortunately, all three factors mean it rarely occurs to a senior leader that seeking tailored help is even an option.

## Executive coaches who specialize in C-suite roles are rare

Executive coaches are plentiful. Chances are, as a senior leader you've recommended coaching more than once in connection with someone's development.

But coaches who focus on helping C-suite executives are rare. And those who were themselves C-suite executives even more so.

To conclude, there's a final reason senior leaders might not seek out coaching even upon acknowledging it could be hugely beneficial to them.

## Senior leaders don't like to show weakness

Remember the independent, competent, but masochistic executive? There we go again. This reflects itself in our sometimes refusing to take simple steps to improve our lives.

I believe we can break out of this mindset. Ask yourself what you'd recommend to a colleague who wants to develop. Would you look down on them for taking advantage of the best resources on offer?

Of course not. If anything, you'd consider a person foolish for letting their pride or indifference hold back their career.

Don't handicap your chance of being the best executive you can be.

Be well.

# Chapter Twenty-Four

# Immortality Is a Foolish Wish

## A few reflections on why living forever should be no one's desire

What drives the quest for immortality? An admixture of fear and greed. Fear of death. And greed for what seems sweet, for sensation without end. Both are foolish.

There's certainly no need to fear dying. Dying is easy. There's never been a person who failed the test. Willingly or not, they each made way for all of us who followed.

A person's greed for endless life is similarly short-sighted. With enough time, an immortal would suffer crushing boredom, having seen and done everything. Even thoughts and ideas would yield under the weight of time.

Worse, far worse, than an individual eternal's ennui would be the consequence of immortality on humankind. The end of death would mean the end of birth. If we add but a single soul per millennium, our numbers would approach infinity over an eternity.

How incredibly selfish (and arrogant) to think that humanity has reached its peak in us, such that we should not only live forever but be among the last who are born.

Value is found in scarcity. What we can obtain easily without limit, we do not value highly in possessing.

None of us knows our allotment of time, and that's what makes it precious. We strive, we love, and we live in equal measure to our appreciation that our time is scarce.

> *The world is fleeting; all things pass away; or is it we that pass and they that stay?* — Lucian

An ordered mind knows the value of life is precisely that it is limited.

What of those who accept they must pass away, but who wish to leave an indelible mark upon the world? Surely there number some such among authors. "My words will live on after me."

This is an interesting thought. How does it benefit us if some part of us remains after we are gone? Is it fame that goads us, even if it's posthumous? Is it a desire to influence the world, to make it better for all who come?

I suspect it's an ill-defined mix of emotions. We ameliorate the fear of dying by imagining some part of us or our influence will carry on. That, and the desire to make a mark is powerful and does not require that we remain to observe our handiwork.

It comforts me to remember that *everything* exists in a state of impermanent flux.

People will continue to come and go, as they always have. And that's the way it should be.

> *To what shall I compare this world? To the white wake behind a ship that has rowed away at dawn?* — Priest Mansei

Be well.

# Chapter Twenty-Five

# Five Ways to Ensure You'll Never Be Forgotten

## Immortality is easier to achieve than ever

Today I'll tell you how to set up your life such that it continues to be great long after your death.

The Athenian statesman Solon once said, "Count no man happy until he is dead." Until the whole of a person's life has played out, we don't know what misfortune may befall them.

For example, a person may be a famous, well-paid writer, but then suffer a bout of terrible herpes simplex that causes their entire body to break out in a rash, their spouse to divorce them, and all their friends to shun them. (And no, we are not subconsciously wishing that on anyone.)

Never mind herpes simplex, Aristotle took the concept even further. In discussing what made up the best-lived life, one of flourishing or happiness (in Greek, *eudaimonia*), we again judge the entirety of a person's life. But we also include the fate and fortune of their family and those close to them.

For example, a person may make their way to the highest political office of the most powerful country on Earth. But, completely hypothetically, if one son dies from brain cancer and another son is a drug-addled, bribe-taking, prostitute-frequenting, gun-form-application lying, non-tax-paying, (alleged) artist can we say the father is enjoying the most excellent and virtuous life?

No, it's far too risky to leave your eternal reputation in the hands of your potentially criminal relatives. To say nothing of the ones that are just waiting for you to pop off so they can spend your hard-earned money.

If you want to be judged a happy success, you should consider adopting one or more of these approachable paths to immortality (best used together):

1. Schedule stories to be published on your favorite platform for the rest of the century. On some, you can schedule a story to be published for decades from now.

2. To ensure you don't have to actually write all those stories, get ChatGPT to write them for you before it gets banned. (Haha! That'll never happen.) Better yet, pay for a customized AI that mimics your writing style so that no one ever need be deprived of your ongoing wit.

3. Leave your money in a trust that pays out to your relatives and their descendants only if, and to the extent, that they read and comment on your stories.

4. Direct your trust to send flowers to your descendants each year on the anniversary of your death with cards saying things like, "If only you'd been nicer to me, the money for this bouquet could have been yours" and "Maybe next year I'll just give you the money. In the meantime, better keep reading!"

5. Have your lawyers hire trolls in a third-world country (or ChatGPT, whichever is cheaper) to befriend your descendants on social media and tell stories about how they were great pals of yours, and how generous you were to them.

Well, this took a darker turn than I expected, but I can't see an easy way to pull it back, so I'm just going to end it there.

Be well.

# Chapter Twenty-Six

# We're All Big Babies

## The world exists to satisfy our needs and wants, and because of this we will loudly express our displeasure if we are left wanting

I don't mean we are big babies in the sense of still wanting to eat ice cream for dinner, although this is both undeniable and understandable. I mean we are big babies in the sense that babies behave as if absolutely everything was about them.

If something happens that we do not like, we assume there was an intention to cause us harm. If I am offended, you must have intended to offend me.

Now, if this was our only similarity with babies, I would stop right here. But there is another similarity, namely that we think the world should immediately make all unpleasant things go away. I am hungry: Feed me! I am soiled: Change me! I am cold: Warm me! I am hot: Cool me! I am bored: Entertain me! You get the point.

How else to explain microaggressions and safe spaces? We have somehow managed to bring a generation of children into adulthood without ever leaving their babyness behind. And in the process, we have all embraced a bit of our inner baby as well.

I think it is time that we reminded ourselves of a few things. No one said age is a guarantee of maturity. Being an adult is hard, but we're the only ones who can do it. As the Buddha said:

> *No one saves us but ourselves. No one can and no one may. We ourselves must walk the path.*

So the first step to maturing is recognizing that we have to do it ourselves.

But how do we leave the baby self behind? By taking responsibility for our thoughts, which will then help guide our actions. If you want to escape your safe space, and be freed of the pain of microaggressions, take heed of what Marcus Aurelius told himself:

> *Take away your opinion, and there is taken away the complaint 'I have been harmed.' Take away the complaint 'I have been harmed,' and the harm is taken away.*

Though he was Emperor of the Roman Empire, Marcus Aurelius himself needed reinforcement, and I know we do as well. So I offer you this additional reminder on his behalf:

> *Cast away opinion: you are saved. Who then hinders you from casting it away?*

Who indeed is stopping us from being the adults we want to be?

Best of all, I have it on good authority that even as an adult you can still have ice cream for dinner every now and then.

Be well.

## Chapter Twenty-Seven

# Skepticism is Safer Than Blind Trust

Your life improves when you understand the pervasive effect of incentives on human behavior. Skeptics can still be happy

Three advanced degrees, thirty years of work experience, and daily confirmations splashed across the headlines. All pointing to the vital role incentives play in our affairs. Still, I yearned for optimism and to trust my fellow humans.

Regular readers know I decry the folly of living in the land of wishful thinking. Of mistaking what we want to be true for what we experience. It's folly because continuing to trust in the face of regular disappointment doesn't make us kind. It makes us easy targets.

We stop being victims when we start being vigilant.

We can lessen the power of incentives over us, not by pretending they don't exist, but by accurately perceiving them.

### Incentives drive human behavior, predictably and consistently

Humans are motivated to seek what they want (or at least think they want) and avoid what they do not. Understanding this explains most of what happens in life.

Don't let the simple formulation mislead you. This law holds great predictive power.

- People seek personal gain and place less weight on harm to others. Positive incentives predictably drive individual behavior.

- Fear of personal consequences prevents some behavior that harms others. Negative incentives only partially limit harmful behavior.

Concretely, people do things to make money and gain status or power (positive incentives). They avoid things they fear will get them in trouble — legally, financially, or reputationally (negative incentives).

What confuses us is that people sometimes appear to behave altruistically, they do things that demonstrate personal character, and they are not always villains.

This is a distraction. Incentives are always at play. When people behave well, it's not that they've become saints but that the incentives were aligned to encourage that behavior.

Nothing sets you up for victimhood more than mistaking examples of good behavior for evidence that most people are good.

## When incentives are misaligned, bad things happen

The worst outcomes arise when large gains await those who face little risk of consequence for bad behavior.

Humans have significant control over the incentives at play. Individuals thus create opportunities for outsized gains at little risk. Think of every management team that first sets the business targets on which their bonus depends, then jiggers the business to meet those targets.

- Marketers push us to satisfy needs we didn't know we had

- Politicians incentivize us to fear their opponents

- Activists sensationalize science to influence narratives and gain power

- Content creators compete for our attention and falsehoods spread faster than truth

- Companies sell harmful products like alcohol, cigarettes, and junk food while glamorizing them to consumers

- Pharma companies propagandize doctors to peddle pharmaceuticals that turn us into lifelong consumers

- Criminals exploit loopholes in regulation and enforcement to steal our money

Everywhere we turn, incentives are at play. Someone's always playing an angle. If you don't spot the angle, you're the sucker being taken for a fool.

## Does spotting the incentives turn one sour?

When you learn to spot misaligned incentives that drive selfish behavior, you see them everywhere. This can sour a person on their belief in humanity's fundamental goodness.

But it doesn't have to. Consider a spider, snake, or shark. Consider a hurricane, an earthquake, or a flood. All of these things exist in nature. They each wreak harm and havoc. So what? It's not personal, so why should you take them personally?

You don't need to consider a tornado to be aimed at just you to benefit from getting out of its way. You don't need to impute ill will to a hungry shark to see the wisdom in getting out of the water.

People respond to incentives. So what? Just because I won't let you hold my wallet doesn't mean I think you're a bad person. It just means I understand incentives.

## I'm sold, James. How do I learn to spot incentives?

Here's a simple frame to identify relevant incentives about 80% of the time. Ask who gains and whether they could gain at your expense.

Another person's gains do not necessarily come at our expense. I may be perfectly happy spending my money to buy your product. (Although it is instructive to think carefully about why we want the product at all.)

Be alert for situations where someone benefits regardless of whether you benefit.

- When the financial advisor has sold you an annuity you may or may not need

- When the gym has signed you up for an annual subscription whether you set foot in the building
- When you pay an extra $10 a month to show your support for a community and get a gold star for your efforts

"Wait, wait!" I hear you cry. "I bought the annuity to get a guaranteed income stream." Sure. Was it the best product for you compared to other products? Did you realize your broker got a 9% fee for selling it to you?

"Well, I signed up to the gym to get healthy. How is that not in my benefit?" Come talk to me in a month.

"I show my support for the community here because I am the kind of person who selflessly supports others to make the world a better place."

Wonderful! I'd like to invite you to read more of my work. It's guaranteed to make the world better.

Be well

Chapter Twenty-Eight

# What I Learned Negotiating for a Living

## More important than winning, I learned when not to win

My team and I negotiated every kind of contract you can imagine. More than 10 million of them over the twenty-year period I served as General Counsel of an S&P 500 public company.

From tiny supply agreements to executive compensation deals. Sales agreements no one ever looked at again and acquisitions you've read about in the paper.

I learned how to get what I wanted most of the time. I was ruthless because I thought it was necessary. It took me years to gain the wisdom to approach negotiations mindfully.

I'd like to give you another way to think about getting what you want.

### How I became a negotiation juggernaut

Although I possessed a fiercely determined streak from early on, I blossomed as a negotiator thanks to our Chairman and CEO.

He was one of those rare people who possessed a genuine reality distortion field in the sense that he often expected us to deliver impossible things. Just flat out, "No, that's not possible, not today and not in a million years."

What made him special or, now that I think about it, what made the team around him special is that we found a way to deliver on his impossible demands. Routinely, and far more often than we had any reason to expect.

Is it stressful going into a negotiation with a preposterous set of demands? Unbearably so. But the first time I achieved one of those herculean tasks, something happened to my view of the world and my self-confidence.

I learned I could do the impossible and that is an amazing feeling. Suddenly, merely difficult challenges seemed trivial in comparison.

## What I learned from negotiation success

My negotiation success taught me several lessons that I've put to good use elsewhere in my life.

- My doubts are an unreliable guide to my capabilities
- I don't truly know what I can do until I commit to not failing
- It is thus appropriate to set my sights on Olympian heights
- It is also fair for me to ask others to deliver the seemingly impossible

It's not about what you ultimately achieve. It's about realizing that you should not place any limits on your or others' performance.

## What a negotiation win won't teach you

Winning feels good, especially when it's against long odds. That winning feeling tells you nothing, however, about whether your goal was a worthy one.

We once pursued a competitor in an intellectual property infringement case. Mercilessly and relentlessly. We bent the world to our view and decisively won our case. Bankrupting our competitor, leading to their sale to another market participant, and creating the seeds for an even stronger future competitor.

Or consider one of the times we failed in a negotiation. This happened sometimes with monopolists (think software providers) or some of our largest customers.

They could, and often did, simply insist that we accept their terms. No discussion and certainly no negotiation.

Imagine how it feels being forced to submit to someone just because they have the power. Do you feel unfairly treated and taken advantage of? Check. Not only that but burning mad. And likely looking for a way to balance the scales again.

These are suboptimal outcomes for everyone, despite the initial appearance of winning. Focusing too much on a perceived win can blind us to the large set of outcomes that are better for one side without harming the other.

So what's a sounder way to approach negotiations?

## Consider your negotiations (and your life) in context

My epiphany came when I realized that no negotiation is a one-off. There is always a before and an after.

If you are selling to a customer, do you expect to have an ongoing relationship with them? What will happen to that relationship if you press every advantage, just because you can?

Even the deals that seem entirely transactional, in the sense that the parties will never cross paths again, create ripples in how others perceive you. People will notice and interact with you accordingly.

And how you behave in negotiations comes to shape how you perceive yourself. Do you always win, no matter the cost? Or do you demonstrate kindness by being alert to opportunities to help others when it costs you but little?

These negotiation principles apply to our lives more broadly. We can pursue whatever we want in life. If we're willing to pay the cost, we can achieve just about anything we set our minds to.

My advice is to be careful viewing your goals as transactional or one-off. What you do to achieve your goals will affect what your life looks like once you've achieved them.

I still believe I can get whatever I want in a negotiation. But now I think more about what I should want before I go about getting it.

Be well.

# Chapter Twenty-Nine

# Bucket List, Eh. I'm Starting a F — It List

## Letting go is so much more rewarding

**What is a F — It List?**

The F — It List contains not things I will never do, but things I commit to letting go.

1. **Jealousy.** About others' accomplishments, beauty, fame, etc. I celebrate success, knowing that another's success does not diminish mine or anyone else's.

2. **Dressing Well**. I'll have underpants and matching socks on. But no fashion statements will I make. And I'm OK with that.

3. **The Need to be Right**. It is so liberating to be able to think, and to say out loud, "But I could be wrong." I still have opinions, but I hold them less strongly.

4. **Looking Good Running Shirtless**. If ever this window of opportunity was open to me, I failed to notice it. Now when I notice runners who grabbed it, I smile and remind myself of item #1.

5. **The Need to Win**. I am competitive like crazy, and I credit it with carrying me far in my career. But I don't need to win every match. In fact, it's so much less stressful to acknowledge that coming in second (or third, or fourth) is totally fine.

6. **Feeling Guilty About My Sweet Tooth**. I know my enjoyment of chocolate (and cookies and ice cream) is just a collection of learned behaviors that I could unlearn. But I commit to the mighty task of letting go of the feeling I should.

7. **Everything Going According to Plan**. The unexpected is a gift, if we only look at it that way. When a plan goes awry, I now say, "Oh, what interesting opportunity has this change offered up?"

8. **Regret**. Our lives are the cumulated result of countless choices. I was active and thoughtful in all of them, certainly the big ones. Not everything went to plan (see item #7), but I will never make it worse by beating myself up.

9. **Worry About Things Outside My Control**. The Stoic key to happiness is understanding the distinction between what is within our control (or partly in our control) and what is outside our control. When you focus your thoughts on what you can control, great things happen.

10. **The TV Remote**. Just kidding, I'm never letting my spouse get ahold of that!

If you've ever daydreamed about your own bucket list, how about complementing it with a F — It List?

Be well.

# Chapter Thirty

# The Information Diet

## The information we regularly consume is the biggest driver of our mental health

Although it's information that drives our mental health, we act as if what *happens* to us is formative.

If we devoted the same attention to our information diet as the food we eat, we could cultivate positive mental states. The three pillars to doing this are as follows:

1. Understanding why the information we consume is important to our well-being

2. Being aware of which types of consumption are harmful and which are beneficial

3. Creating an environment that allows for beneficial consumption

My thoughts on this are shaped by my psychology training, three decades practicing corporate law, and studying philosophy. More personally, by interacting with friends and colleagues around the world and seeing how their lives played out.

Here's what I've learned about people:

> Humans (short def.) – tell useful stories; also harmful ones.
> Most people do not distinguish sufficiently between the two.

From the same starting points and with similar abilities, some are happy and thriving while others are mired in difficulties. Why the difference? It comes down to their information diets.

## 1. Why the information we consume is important to our well-being

No one questions the importance of what we eat and how we exercise our bodies as fundamental drivers of physical health. Is it so hard to credit the information we feed our minds as influencing our mental health?

The stories we tell ourselves and each other define and amplify human incentives: What should we seek and why? What should we avoid and why?

Stories here mean all the ways we share information, from conversations to books to online content. Watching a video of a person mastering their guitar finger positions reinforces a positive incentive, just like seeing some fool singe off their eyebrows using gasoline to start their barbecue nicely demonstrates a negative incentive.

For much of human history, we shared information to improve the human condition. The great outpouring of human creativity forms the marketplace of ideas. Good ideas spread and become part of what we all know and understand.

Bad ideas also spread. We've put the name propaganda to it in the 20th century, but the concept of influencing how people think is older than that. For as long as people have lived and worked collaboratively, it has been beneficial to influence others' thinking because doing so influences their actions.

In other words, **information is never neutral**. This is so even if the messenger isn't trying to manipulate. Information changes minds, forms beliefs, and drives behavior.

You might have heard it expressed this way: As you think, so shall you become.

## 2. Harmful vs beneficial information types

Contrast drinking water sourced from a mountain spring with runoff from a chemical plant, the ooze leaking from a landfill, or a cup of tea laced with polonium. In the first case, pure and untainted. In the others, processed, polluted, and poisoned.

Think of the information you consume as similarly vital to your mental health and evaluate it in terms of purity and processing.

- **Purity** is a function of the source — is it new and untested or does it come from ancient wisdom, handed down for millennia?
- **Processing** is a function of how the information has been put to the service of an agenda. Does this come from a business that is selling you something or a politician who wants your votes and your money? Does it come from an entertainer who wants your attention?

You may have heard of the Standard American Diet, filled as it is with ultra-processed, addictive junk food. The same could be said of our information diet: Social media dominated, attention-driven, low on nutrition, highly processed, and addictive.

Our information diet should be free of such ultra-processed junk. Just as we're told to seek out natural, unprocessed, whole foods, we should seek out unadulterated sources of information.

Information that humans have been consuming and returning to for hundreds or thousands of years is much more likely to be healthy for us. This store of human wisdom has been digested, interpreted, and found nourishing and fit for human consumption.

This is not to say new information is necessarily harmful. We add valuable information to our stores every day. But to ferret out the worthy examples, we must sample mountains of dreck. Each week, month, and year that safely passes perform this filtering for us.

- We read Adam Smith with confidence today because his ideas have withstood the weight of time.
- We read Milton Friedman with admiration but some reservation because only a half-century has passed.
- We can readily identify those current economists as hacks whose words serve a partisan purpose.

## 3. Creating an environment that allows for beneficial consumption

Be careful of your exposure, particularly the media you choose.

We have no easy defense mechanisms to protect ourselves. Other than the passage of time, there is no food taster to tell us how much poison is in the dishes on offer. There is no test for foodborne viruses; our "fact-checkers" do a disservice to the name.

No government agency is coming to the rescue. The politicians and bureaucrats are among the worst propagandists seeking to control their unruly citizens. Social proof is no salve because trusted experts have fallen to partisan tribalism.

And we individuals are deeply untrustworthy. People will happily believe obvious falsehoods if they signal social status and demonstrate group membership and fidelity. What is a concerned person to do?

Here are affirmative steps to develop a healthy information diet:

- Consider going an Information Fast: Cut out ultra-processed information designed to lead us astray, including all legacy media and most social media.

- Commit to consuming more information from time-tested sources.

- You may consult guides who help you interpret that information, but only once they've proven themselves trustworthy to be part of your diet (i.e. not processed with an agenda).

Good luck in crafting your information diet.

Be well.

# Chapter Thirty-One

# Status Games You Can Win

## Use the top 10% method to live a good life, make better decisions, and be happy

Good things await those who make the right comparisons in life.

We can't turn off the comparison machine that's always running in our heads. The next best thing is choosing comparisons that make us feel great instead of feeding sad thoughts.

**Why not play games you can win?**

Feeling that we have status and a sense of self-worth is vital to our self-esteem, which drives many positive outcomes in life. The trick is to choose which status games we play rather than being inadvertently forced to play others' games.

Daily life offers so many options. Why not choose to play status games we can win? Let's consider "winning" as getting to the top 10% of a particular game (as we define it) because that level of performance will drive self-esteem.

It is simple to create games that suit this purpose. Examples:

- I have never been more than an average runner, in terms of speed, that is. So I focused on simply sticking with it. By running the Zurich marathon every year for 20 years in a row, I became one of just a handful of people who did so. Who cares how fast I am?

- Same thing with completing the World Marathon Majors and even getting a Guinness World Record in the process. That was similarly a function of simple determination and persistence. While others worried about finishing in under four hours or three hours, I just kept going.

If you can't compete on speed, compete on duration. If you can't win along one dimension, choose another that suits your abilities.

If this sounds delusional, as in, we're making up competitions that no one else even realizes or cares about, you're right. But if it makes us feel accomplished, it's a happy delusion that serves a purpose.

## Your game hacks: Be Pragmatic, Stoic, and Machiavellian

As I'm using the terms here, the guidance is simple:

- Pragmatic means focusing on what works
- Stoic means looking within
- Machiavellian means being tactical

## Be pragmatic ... or you can do stuff that doesn't work

Even assuming it's well-intentioned, most advice doesn't work. It's too generic (or too specific), too hard to implement, doesn't solve the underlying problem, only works temporarily, etc.

When I set up a global legal team for a new public company, I had to sift through mountains of advice. I found myself forced to adopt pragmatism as a guiding philosophy. No matter what others said, the only metric I valued was this: Does it work?

Does it work for me and my company? In our context, at this exact moment in time, with the specific challenges we're facing? If not, scrap it. If yes, figure out why and do more of it.

After some time, I began experimenting with pragmatism in my private life. What made one person succeed while other similarly situated people failed? Can others do it as well?

This may sound harsh but most people are not good role models, except as object lessons in what not to do. They waft through life like insects borne on the wind, flitting from one colorful flower to the next. Worse, many people act in demonstrably harmful ways, sabotaging themselves.

Whatever is important to you (health, wealth, career success, relationships, etc.), start by finding people who are good at it. Make them your focus. Spend time with them.

To give a personal example, I wanted to get fit after realizing in my early 30s I was overweight and unfit. I started hanging out with accomplished runners, which transformed my life.

## Be Stoic — first for tough times and later for making times of your choosing

We will face tough times in our lives. Knowing this means we need not live in fear or lament when the tough times come.

Stoicism initially helped me by encouraging me to embrace hard things. I relished pushing boundaries and discovering I could do more than I first thought.

The combination of pragmatism and Stoicism results in profound effectiveness. For many years, I championed effectiveness at work and in private life.

If the story ended there, it would be perhaps interesting but unimportant. What shifted the plot was, ironically, too much success. How many people upon achieving all they once sought, ask themselves: "Is that all? I thought it would feel better. What's missing?"

What was missing, for me and I suspect for many, was meaning, the why of it all. That question led to another round of pragmatism — asking who is happy and satisfied in life and why. What are the things that contribute to living a good life?

How wonderful that answering this question led me right back to Stoicism. This time beyond the superficial finding that we can endure tough times to the underlying vein of wisdom: What we see is a function of where we look.

Put differently, our experience in life is shaped by how we think about it. And we have ultimate control of our thoughts. This allows us to not only overcome any situation but to determine what environments we find ourselves in altogether.

## The power to look at what we want

Just like we are surrounded with mounds of advice, most of it ill-suited to our needs, we are invited to make comparisons that don't make us happy. Rather, the comparisons pushed on us are designed to make us feel lacking.

Marketers have made an art (and a giant industry) of emphasizing what's missing in our lives. They tell us that if we want to be happy, we must buy their products, drink their beverages, and download their apps. The immediate impact of this dark art is to make us unhappy.

Online influencers emphasize what we're missing by highlighting what they're enjoying. Lifestyles of the rich and famous satisfy our voyeuristic instincts while driving dissatisfaction.

This comparison group is hopelessly large, often the whole country if not the entire world. What are the chances you are the luckiest, wealthiest, most attractive, and most accomplished person among millions or billions?

Would you rather play games you can win or games where you're almost certain to be the sucker? Put that way, few would knowingly choose games they're designed to lose. Yet accepting what marketers and social media offer sets us on the path to disillusionment.

## Be Machiavellian by choosing battles you can win

Now we come to the beating heart of it, dear reader. If finding happiness is a meaningful pursuit, then directing our thoughts is a path to doing so.

The comparison machine constantly running in our heads is the greatest risk to happiness, always threatening to lead us astray by spotting how often we fall short.

We can put happiness in our hands by grabbing control of the comparison machine. Stoicism tells us we can choose how to direct our thoughts and Machiavellism points the way forward: We shall only play status games we can win.

Find areas where your current or achievable performance automatically puts you in the top 10%.

This approach works because it feeds the comparison engine. The engine is blind. It doesn't know whether some accomplishments are worth more than others. It only knows whether you're excelling in the areas it's been trained to look at.

Here are some ways to collect status by playing this game:

- **Education** — Did you do well in school or earn an advanced degree?

- **Work** — Are you working, does your company value you, do you have management responsibilities?

- **Finances** — How do your earnings and savings compare to the rest of the globe? You'd be surprised how little it takes to be in the global top 10%

- **Physical aspects** — Are you tall, do you have blond hair or blue eyes?

- **Fitness** — Do you have a healthy weight, are you mobile, have you made it to the age of 40?

- **Anything else** — Do you have a fine sense of humor, a huge collection of matchbooks, or come from a tiny country? Anything that makes you uniquely you can serve as your path to relative status.

It does not matter what you choose to focus on, just that you measure up relatively well. Unhappy people look too long at the areas where they fall short. Happy people appreciate what makes them stand out.

To live a good life and find happiness, learn to direct your attention to the ways you are lucky enough to already be winning. I've never met anyone who wasn't in the top 10% at something — what's your game?

Be well.

## Chapter Thirty-Two

# The Boss Toolkit: When My Best Employees Couldn't Prioritize

## Was I a terrible boss? It sure looked that way, but I had a purpose behind my behavior

What do you do as a manager with a promising employee who isn't getting their work done? Although there are many causes, I found one reliable cure: Pile them high with more work.

It's counter-intuitive and risky because, in the near term, you're just adding to their stress and risking a blowup or burnout. But if you trust your instinct that your employee has potential and is up for it, challenging them is a pragmatic way to help them develop their prioritization skills.

Although it looks cruel, the employee and boss each benefit from the practice because it usually makes the employee into a great performer.

### When perfectionists hurt themselves

I hired many junior lawyers over my career. I came to dread the first six months after they joined.

These were smart, hard-working, and high-performing professionals, used to excelling at whatever they tackled. Ironically, those attributes made them terrible in-house lawyers, at least initially.

Company lawyers perform best when they deliver what the business needs. While this may sound obvious to you, for lawyers it can be a real shift in mindset. Our training teaches us to be careful and precise. Words matter and details matter. So we obsess over every little thing.

The problem is that the business neither needs nor wants obsessive nitpicking on much of what its in-house lawyers do. Negotiations, contracts, and risk management — they all benefit from a careful approach, but not an obsessive one.

Or as you may have heard in other contexts, good is good enough.

In the case of the junior lawyers we hired to review commercial contracts, it was a disaster to see them spending a week reviewing and marking up a single agreement to make it near-perfect when they should have been capable of handling five or 10 contracts a day.

## The solution is to make perfectionism impossible

The simplest way to do this is to pile on the work. Don't give them one contract at a time, give them five, ten, or even twenty. Then set aggressive deadlines that they must meet.

Let them work it out.

Initially, this will create immense pressure and stress. That's when their risk of burnout is greatest. They'll start by maintaining their old, impossible standard of perfection and working all the hours of the day.

Some will quickly figure out productivity shortcuts. This comes from experience, practice, and expediency.

- They realize much of the work is repetitive, so comments on one type of clause will work on all agreements with that clause.

- They experience better results negotiating some clauses than others, so learn which types of clauses are more easily dealt with.

- And they get a sense (from colleagues and you, the boss) of what types of clauses the business cares about and which ones are less important. That naturally guides their efforts.

Other employees need help in seeing the shortcuts. This is also when you can give guidance as the manager. After loading up an employee and letting them try to manage the workload, observe who struggles.

Sit down with your underwater employees and review an agreement with them. Show them how you would do it and why. If they are as intelligent and talented as you suspect, they will quickly grasp the principles.

## Isn't there another way?

I've learned that the gentle explanation rarely works in the absence of pressure. For all those wondering why the boss doesn't explain to employees the process in advance, the boss does but the employee doesn't listen or the lesson doesn't stick.

The pressure of impossible deadlines (under the old, perfectionist system) makes the brightest students pay the closest attention.

It is not kindness to let employees flounder. It does employees no favors to hold them to lower standards. Good employees don't mind working, especially when they feel that what they're doing is both challenging and valuable.

So I say it's correct to put employees under pressure to teach them to prioritize. They'll thank you for it later.

Be well.

# Problem Solving and Communication

Career Paths Vol. 5: Master All Challenges That Confront You

James Bellerjeau

A Fine Idea

Copyright © 2025 by James Bellerjeau

All rights reserved.

No portion of this book may be reproduced in any form without written permission from the publisher or author, except as permitted by U.S. copyright law.

An earlier version of several of these articles was previously published in the ACC Docket (https://docket.acc.com/). Copyright © 2023, Association of Corporate Counsel. Reprinted with permission. All rights reserved. Visit www.acc.com.

# Contents

| | |
|---|---|
| Introduction | 493 |
| 1. Don't Mistake Certainty for Correctness | 495 |
| 2. If You Ask the Wrong Questions… | 499 |
| 3. A Conversation Is the Worst Way to Communicate | 503 |
| 4. Can You Freely Speak Your Mind? | 507 |
| 5. Keep Your Cool | 513 |
| 6. Do You Want to Hear the Truth? | 517 |
| 7. Try Not Telling People You're an Expert | 521 |
| 8. Can You Think Your Way to Success? | 525 |
| 9. I Miss Shaking Hands | 529 |
| 10. Observations From a Social Media Noob | 533 |
| 11. Swiss Cheese Your Way to Safety | 537 |
| 12. Dealing with One-Issue Stakeholders | 541 |
| 13. No One Cares as Much as You Do | 545 |
| 14. Identifying Problems Worth Working On | 549 |
| 15. Identifying Solutions That Will Work | 553 |
| 16. Why It's So Hard Being a Good Corporate Lawyer | 557 |
| 17. The Day You Became Smarter | 561 |
| 18. Write Better Emails Today | 565 |

| | | |
|---|---|---:|
| 19. | Maybe Don't Go to that Meeting | 569 |
| 20. | Persuade Like Aristotle | 573 |
| 21. | Listen Up Already! | 577 |
| 22. | What Lawyers Can Teach Us About Writing Well | 581 |
| 23. | What the Government Can Teach Us About Writing Well | 585 |
| 24. | Two Editing Checklists May Save Your Story | 589 |
| 25. | Breaking News: Lawyer Settles Oxford Comma Debate | 591 |
| 26. | If You Scheduled Your Day Like an Airline | 595 |
| 27. | How to Spot a Bad Lawyer | 601 |
| 28. | How In-house Counsel Reinforce the Rule of Law | 605 |
| 29. | When the Best Course of Action is Inaction | 609 |
| 30. | If We Are What We Eat, Be Worried | 613 |
| 31. | How Being Humble Can Help You Be Wrong Less Often | 617 |
| 32. | Disagree Without Being Disagreeable | 621 |
| 33. | The World's Worst Persuasion Tactic: Insults | 625 |
| 34. | How Not to Be a Sloppy Second Guesser | 629 |
| 35. | I Think, Therefore, You're Wrong | 633 |
| 36. | Thriving In A Low-Trust World | 637 |
| 37. | How To Win an Argument | 641 |
| 38. | How To Get What You Want | 647 |

# Introduction

Greetings readers and congratulations! Simply by virtue of being here, you are already on the path to increasing your odds of success.

Our focus is on how to solve the many problems we'll be confronted with in our lives. An optimist assumes they'll never face obstacles. A pessimist worries that they will never get past them. A pragmatist knows that obstacles are both inevitable and opportunities to shine.

We pair communication with problem-solving because poor communication will make most problems worse and good communication holds the key to solving many others. We'll confront head-on the inescapable truth that it is the lies we tell ourselves that represent some of the most harmful kinds of communication.

Drawing on hard won experience and the lessons of philosophers across time, we'll explore what allows the skilled problem-solver to overcome difficult situations and thrive.

Although I'll cover a lot of ground with these lessons, you should consider them foundational rather than comprehensive. There are additional approaches to overcoming obstacles and succeeding at work, which you will find in the companion volumes of the **Career Paths** series.

Be well.

## Chapter One

# Don't Mistake Certainty for Correctness

## We can be just as wrong about something when we are convinced it's true as when we're uncertain

It is easy to see when someone else is being pigheaded. The most obvious sign is that they disagree with you.

The ones who particularly get our goat, though, are the ones who zealously defend their position against all reason. These people refuse to be swayed by all the facts and evidence that point to them being wrong.

Don't they see how their certainty just makes them foolish?

No matter how often we observe this in others, I find it fascinating that the fewest among us make the link to *how we are perceived* when we are certain about something ourselves.

After all, when we're certain it's because we're right. When other people are certain it's because they're idiots who don't know how to think.

### Is it possible you are right all the time?

I suppose it's possible some people are true savants, making correct assessments of all situations all the time. Based on decades of careful observation, I'm guessing the number of such persons is small.

Sadly, the odds are good that you and I are not among the perfect savants.

For starters, anyone who has been married must readily concede that *no one is right all the time.* You need only consider all the times your spouse correctly pointed out you were wrong about something to know the truth of this.

And we can be just as wrong about something when we are convinced it's true as when we're uncertain.

I do need to add one small caveat for the women readers. Many men have learned the wisdom of the phrase "Happy wife, happy life." This generates in men a greatly increased propensity to use the phrase "You're right, dear."

Your spouse saying you are right does not necessarily mean that you are right in fact, although you probably are if I'm being honest. But that is a topic for another day.

## What happens when we're certain we're correct

Being convinced we're right, however, carries with it several heavy burdens:

- We become closed to new inputs and tend to seek out evidence to confirm our existing beliefs (confirmation bias)

- We make worse decisions because we stop seeking out new or contradictory information

- To justify our bad decisions, we shift blame to other people and factors outside our control

I have had the good fortune of having my many errors happily pointed out to me by friends and family. And they've been doing it for years!

Interestingly, my conviction is still as strong as ever, no matter how many times I am proven mistaken. When we think we are right, we can't help but think we're right.

## How to be passionately wrong less often

Knowing the dangers implicit in this facet of human nature, is there anything we can do?

In my case, the frequent reminders of my fallibility have brought me one very useful practice that I try to apply whenever I can: I leave open the possibility that I may be wrong.

I still believe what I believe is true, but I will now often add to the end of a statement the words "but I could be wrong." That phrase is almost magical in its import. It accomplishes many things.

When you add "... but I could be wrong" to the end of a statement:

1. It means in your mind you are not committed to the absolute truth of what you just said. As a result, you can listen to what others say.

2. It means the person you are talking with does not consider you closed and is more likely *to listen to you*. This creates the condition for a dialogue in which you are as interested in learning something as you are in making a point.

3. Because you are less emotionally committed to what you said, it means you are less likely to feel compelled to defend it against all attacks. If it is just something you are discussing and not a personally-held belief, an attack on the statement is not an attack on you.

If you like the idea that being certain is no guarantee of being correct, then you are already on the path to better decision-making.

If you further agree that small changes made consistently can create great results (continuous improvement), then perhaps you will try out saying "But I could be wrong" yourself.

Be well.

Chapter Two

# If You Ask the Wrong Questions...

## You likely have many unexamined ideas and beliefs about why things happen the way they do

Have you heard the proverb, "There are none so blind as those who will not see"? We've all experienced it, usually when arguing with some idiot who disagrees with us on a perfectly obvious point.

Today I will explain the psychological grounding behind the phenomenon and give you some tips for how to avoid selective blindness yourself.

If you want to become well-informed on a topic, conducting broad research is essential.

Looking at the first few links in a Google search will give you a certain set of information, true. This will likely be mainstream information, meaning that either Google is promoting it or it is consistent with the majority view, or both.

Either way, you will probably not be widely criticized for parroting what most people already believe or can find in a quick search.

Because we do not like feeling uncomfortable, our natural tendency is to seek out information that conforms to our existing beliefs and to ignore conflicting information.

There is a more pernicious problem in conducting research, which is this: We are our own worst enemies. Being confronted with information that conflicts with our existing beliefs makes us uncomfortable, a situation referred to as cognitive dissonance.

Because we do not like feeling uncomfortable, our natural tendency is to seek out information that conforms to our existing beliefs and to ignore conflicting information.

## Wellbeing ≠ Being right all the time

One way to counteract this tendency is to leave open the possibility that we may be wrong. In other words, not to tie our psychological well-being to being right all the time.

I discuss ways to do this in the preceding chapter. Not needing to be right is a helpful, if modest step.

Now I hear some of you saying: "This doesn't apply to me, at least not all the time. When I am doing research, I don't usually have a preconceived idea of what the answer is. I can't be affected by cognitive bias."

Not so fast, my friends. You may not have thought deeply about the issue you are researching, but you nonetheless are likely to have ideas about it.

"What do you mean? How can that be?"

Our understanding of the world and how it works is a complex, multi-layered construct, built up over the whole of our experiences. Some beliefs are at the forefront of your consciousness, and so you think of them as your core beliefs or values.

But you likely have many unexamined ideas and beliefs about why things happen the way they do. Humans are amazing pattern-recognition machines, so much so that we regularly and easily see patterns where none exist, finding causality in random correlation.

Even when you approach a topic with what you think is an open mind, you are coming with a lifetime of experiences that have shaped not only what you believe, but the very process of how you form new opinions.

Even if you don't cling to the need to be right, it can hurt when your belief system does not match up with new evidence.

A far more powerful way to counteract your cognitive biases is to *actively seek out information* that conflicts with your current view.

You will not do this by accident. It requires deliberate effort. But that effort does not have to be burdensome.

Some of the smartest people I know view it as a game. They love finding contradictory information because it means they've learned something about the world or themselves.

In this light, discovering you were wrong about something can be a gift. Thinking about it that way is a fine way to remove the potential sting of cognitive dissonance.

## Do you want an interim test of what I'm talking about?

Some of you may have noticed a little frisson of displeasure when I suggested above that Google promotes certain views (and thus, by definition, must suppress others).

Because that is inconsistent with what many of you think about Google, i.e., they're just a search algorithm and they don't put a thumb on the scale. You either dismissed it without realizing it or you didn't even notice I wrote it.

Okay, don't believe me. Check for yourself. I'll wait.

There is an alternative search engine called DuckDuckGo. Search for something in Google, and then do the same search in DuckDuckGo.

- See how much overlap there is, and whether you detect any skew in the results.

- It will be easier to see the effect if you use a more polarizing topic, say "Trump indictment."

## Identify blind spots

To sum up: We are biased, pattern-recognition machines, predisposed to confirm what we already believe, even if we don't know we believe it.

By reminding ourselves that we are fallible, and making a game of trying to identify our blind spots, we can improve the chances that we are looking at the world with relatively clear eyes.

These steps will help ensure that we not only ask better questions but that the answers we get are useful to us.

Be well.

# Chapter Three

# A Conversation Is the Worst Way to Communicate

## It seems to me that there are more people shouting at each other than ever before

I suggest that a conversation is the worst way to communicate, at least if you are personally taking part in it. Why should this be so, you ask?

For a person to learn new information, they need to be open to receiving it. In a conversation, this means actively listening to what the other person is saying and making a conscious effort to understand it.

In my experience, people rarely demonstrate such purposeful listening.

You may see active listening occur in some professional settings, where there is some formalism to the exchange. For example, in a mediation where one side talks and then the other side talks, or where there is a clear hierarchy with one person speaking first and then others responding.

Outside such formal exchanges, the typical conversation is fluid, fast-moving, and unstructured.

- As a participant, you are expending a significant portion of your mental processing power planning your response.
- You are thinking about what will you say when the other person finally

stops blabbing and lets you get a word in edgewise.

In contrast, **listening** to a good conversation can be a pleasure. This is why interview podcasts of two people talking are so popular.

It is much easier to pay attention to what both sides are saying when you are not a participant in the conversation and when you do not have to think of a response. Plus, because you chose the podcast and are listening to it for pleasure, you are a willing participant.

## Listen to understand

If you want to increase your chances of being heard by your conversational partner, try approaching your next conversation with only one goal: listening to the other person and understanding their point.

Make an effort to summarize and repeat back what you heard and ask your conversational partner if that is what they meant. You may be surprised by how much this increases their willingness and ability to listen to you.

And if you are not trying to talk over the other person, the conversation feels more like a true give-and-take and less like a shouting match.

In fairness, communication is difficult under the best of circumstances, regardless of the means used. You would think that it would be easier to communicate with people in written form.

"Surely if I write something down in a short, simple memo, everyone will understand what I mean, right?" Sorry, no.

Here's what really happens when you send out a memo:

- At least a third of your audience will not see or even bother to read what you have written.

- Another depressingly large portion will not take away what you intended. This is because people read and hear what they want to see, not what is objectively in front of them.

- Most of the minority that read your memo and understood your intended point will forget your message within moments of reading it. There are just too many other sources competing for our scarce attention.

Does this mean that it is pointless to try and communicate? Not at all. My learning from the last few decades of communicating with large groups is this:

1. Keep your messages short.

2. Repeat them.

It typically takes three to five repetitions of a message before you reach a majority of the audience.

If we are honest, part of the reason no one listens to us is that we have nothing important to say.

Most of what we do as humans is fleeting and leaves no lasting impression. A conversation is one of the most fleeting of all, with even the participants in disagreement over who said what the moment the conversation is over.

One reason people get so animated in conversations is that they care what other people think. We are social animals, after all, and it bothers us when others' opinions differ from ours.

The Stoics argue that we should know our own minds and be confident in the wisdom of our decisions. Not all the advice or input we will get from our fellow persons will be accurate or appropriate.

## A better way forward

I was drawn to this topic because of what I've seen in the public discourse recently. I don't know about you, but it seems to me that there are more people shouting at each other than ever before.

And ironically, the more heated the conversation, the less likely it is that anyone is being convinced, let alone influenced, by anything the other side says.

I am reminded of a saying from the Buddha, "Better than a thousand useless words is a single word that gives peace."

I can't guarantee that you will find peace by learning how to listen better. But you will find yourself having better conversations and communicating better.

Be well.

Chapter Four

# Can You Freely Speak Your Mind?

Do you think you live in a country that protects freedom of speech? How about at school, at work, or on the Internet?

The questions for this chapter are, "Can you freely speak your mind?" and "Do you?" If you want to be successful in your career and life, you must be able to answer both questions with a clear "Yes."

I think many of us when asked these questions would instinctively say "Of course!" At least, I suspect you would answer this way if you live in most places in Europe or the United States. Perhaps today's article will cause you to question your conviction.

**How has the Internet impacted freedom of speech?**

We hear much about how we live in times of economic and technological miracles. Particularly with the rapid spread of the Internet across the globe, I assumed that freedom of speech had also been seeded far and wide.

I was wrong.

The organization Freedom House performs surveys on the level of internet freedom in 70 countries around the world. They look at things like Obstacles to Access, Limits on Content, and Violations of User Rights.

A recent report makes for depressing reading. (See Freedom on the Net 2023.) Among other findings:

- Global internet freedom declined for the 13th consecutive year, as "attacks on free expression grew more common around the world."

- Governments are using generative AI to drive disinformation campaigns: "At least 47 governments deployed commentators to manipulate online discussions in their favor."

It seems that economic and technological progress is not inevitably correlated with greater online freedom.

Looking at the ten most populous countries in the world, which together represent 59% of the global population, only the United States, is considered "Free" in terms of Internet Freedom.

- The U.S. represents just 4.2% of the global population.

- The other countries are rated either "Not Free" (China, Pakistan, and Russia), representing 23% of the global population,

- or "Partly Free," representing 32% of the population.

This paints a dark picture, so I went looking for other bastions of freedom. I found them in Europe, excluding Eastern Europe, where we find another 450 million citizens living in societies with Internet Freedom, almost 6% of the global population.

Beyond that, we can add relatively large countries like Japan, South Africa, Argentina, Canada, and Australia, together accounting for not quite 4% of the population.

What I take from these numbers is simply this: *The great majority of the world's population does not experience anything like the freedom of speech that most of us take for granted.* Our ability to access information and express our thoughts is an aberration, not the norm.

## Don't rest easy if you're in a Free or Partly Free country

Even if you are lucky enough to find yourself in those havens of democratic freedom in Europe or the United States, should you rest easily? I'm not so sure.

According to Freedom House again,

> *Even in more democratic settings, including the United States and Europe, governments considered or actually imposed restrictions on access to prominent websites and social media platforms, an unproductive approach to concerns about foreign interference, disinformation, and online safety.*

Some of you will be tempted to dismiss this as fearmongering by disgruntled political minorities. I've had conversations with several people who insist that talk of censorship and self-censorship is greatly exaggerated and largely imaginary.

"I am fully free," so they tell me, "To speak my mind on any topic at any time."

I suspect these people are making the same mistake that I did before writing this article: Assuming that their personal experience is representative of the larger world.

## Universities illustrate well our changed times

I'll pick one slice of society to explore the point, our universities. If there was one place where we could traditionally expect to find freedom of thought, freedom of expression, and an open environment, it would be the university.

In 2014 the University of Chicago published the "Chicago Principles," which set out the University's commitment to protect and promote free expression. In their view, "without a vibrant commitment to free and open inquiry, a university ceases to be a university."

> *In a word, the University's fundamental commitment is to the principle that debate or deliberation may not be suppressed because the ideas put forth are thought by some or even by most members of the University community to be offensive, unwise, immoral, or wrong-headed.*

This is an admirable principle that defines what freedom of expression means in practice and they seem to mean what they say.

So how do we explain the anecdotal evidence of speakers being "shouted down" or canceled for views that some students find offensive? The newspapers are peppered with such stories. Are these isolated examples or a sign of a dangerous trend?

Luckily for us, the Foundation for Individual Rights in Education has been conducting annual surveys of college students about free speech on their campuses. The 2024 survey included more than 55,000 students at 254 colleges and universities. As such, it gives us a good sense of current attitudes on free speech in the United States.

Here are some key findings from the 2024 College Free Speech Rankings:

- "More than half of students (56%) expressed worry about damaging their reputation because of someone misunderstanding what they have said or done…. Twenty percent reported that they often self-censor."

- "More than 2 in 5 students (45%) said that students blocking other students from attending a speech is acceptable to some degree, up from 37% last year."

- "[M]ore than a quarter of students (27%) said that using violence to stop a campus speech is acceptable to some degree, up from 20% last year."

I am blown away by these findings. Please read them again and consider the implications.

The University of Chicago is not the norm, but itself increasingly an outlier. The students we assume should be most open-minded are rather a self-censoring, censorious mob.

## Are things any better in the workplace?

If so many students report self-censoring their views in an environment expressly committed to the freedom of expression, can we expect a different experience in the workplace?

At work, there is generally no upside to speaking your mind on non-work topics, and potentially a great downside. Namely that you may be fired or at least have a complaint filed against you by someone you've offended.

Companies are filled with what I'll call "optimists," by which I mean people who have an incentive to tell favorable stories.

- This includes people who draft budgets, submit forecasts, and fill out self-evaluations.

- It covers managers who set financial targets and employees who report on their contributions to results.

- Marketing professionals live in a world of optimistic hyperbole.

- It is a rare Board of Directors that hears an unpopular truth.

## In-house lawyers are in a unique position to help

In this sea of Pollyannas the in-house lawyer faces a stark choice: Tell people what they *want* to hear or tell people what they *need* to hear.

The truth is painful. Often what the lawyer points out are harsh realities and obstacles to quick progress:

- That path is illegal, and the alternatives take more time and may cost more money.

- That behavior is inappropriate, and we must discipline the star employee.

- We are indeed subject to this new regulation, and we must spend money to ensure compliance.

You will be greatly liked if you tell people what they want to hear. You may even initially find career success by following this path because it takes time and bad luck for most legal problems and non-compliance to come to light.

I don't recommend basing your career decisions on luck.

The best lawyers are the ones who know their true value to their companies, which is to *always and only speak the truth*. When most around you say what they think will benefit them or what others want to hear, a person who only says what they believe to be true is a treasure indeed.

You must not let fear of disappointing others hold you back. Yes, you are discussing difficult situations, where something bad has happened or could happen. But it's rarely your personal fault, just the situation itself.

## Speaking truth to power will bring you influence and respect

Every senior manager and CEO I know is (typically rightly) paranoid that they are getting bad information from their subordinates. One reason you see CEOs asking multiple people the same question is that they are trying to triangulate the truth through a thicket of self-interested answers.

If you tell the CEO what you think they want to hear, you will be missing a great chance to become one of their inner circle of trusted advisors.

- The CEO has plenty of potential lackeys but relatively few truth-tellers.
- If you are someone the CEO trusts will always say what you believe, they will seek out your perspective more often.

You will annoy others by being scrupulously honest. This is because, in the land of liars, the honest person is hated by those with something to hide. For example, when what you say contradicts someone who spun a different story. Or when someone gets in trouble as a result of your noting something inappropriate they did.

One important caveat: Speaking the truth does not mean you always divulge everything you know. Knowing when to speak, and to whom, i.e. exercising discretion, is also part of the successful lawyer's repertoire. The point is that *when* you speak you must be honest.

This advice holds true no matter what your job. To understand why, ask yourself this: If you live in a country where it is still possible to freely speak your mind, what do you think will happen if you do not?

Be well.

# Chapter Five

# Keep Your Cool

Long-term success as a senior manager requires you to keep your cool in many settings, including handling information overload and remaining calm when others have lost their cool

There is so much to make us mad. The people who are trying to get us to spend more time online consuming their content know it.

News stories drip with disbelief and outrage. To skim through the headlines of even a non-partisan newspaper these days is to subject yourself to a heart rate workout.

The free access to information is, of course, to blame.

Why should this be so you ask? Back in the 1950s, the political scientist Herbert Simon noted that information consumes its recipients' attention:

> *a wealth of information creates a poverty of attention, and a need to allocate that attention efficiently among the overabundance of information sources that might consume it.*

In other words, because we have so much content potentially available to us at any moment, creators employ ever more fantastic methods to get us to stop on their stories.

Long-term success as a senior manager requires you to keep your cool in many settings, including the two I'll discuss here: Handling information overload and remaining calm when others have lost their cool. Let's consider both points.

## Information overload

Even if you become reliably good at detecting misinformation, you still face an overwhelming amount of *legitimate* information relevant to your business.

Which regulations are the ones you need to focus on with high priority, and which can you put lower down on the list?

- There are hundreds of thousands of laws, rules, and regulations that apply to businesses in every country.

- If you are working in a multinational context, the number of applicable rules runs into the millions.

- Authorities themselves enforce these rules selectively in the sense that they give greater attention to certain topics at different times.

Authorities' priorities are driven by politics, public perception, and the gamut of emotional responses that characterize human behavior generally.

- Companies make convenient scapegoats for politicians looking to distract from their own poor performance.

- We are also seeing more countries using targeted enforcement against non-local companies for purposes of geopolitical positioning.

- The European Union's antitrust enforcement, or individual member countries' digital service taxes, are recent examples.

Amidst all this, you are bombarded with law firm and consultant advertising. Each firm tells you the issue they're hawking is the most important in the world, and that you must immediately drop everything or face humiliation and ruin.

So how to choose among many competing possible priorities? Guess correctly, and you will help your company safely navigate the complex minefield of public expectations and compliance.

Wrongly deprioritize even one significant topic, however, and you be held responsible for not "setting the right tone" and instead contributing to a culture of non-compliance.

The stakes are high, in other words, when you choose where to focus your limited attention.

## Remain calm

Keep your cool. Take fear, and emotion, and excitement out of your decision-making if you can.

Hone your BS detector so that you can more easily tell when someone is selling you something that is unambiguously good for them, and only potentially good for you.

Collect reliable indicators to separate fevered headlines from real-world changes.

- Are companies in your industry taking up the topic?

- Have any peer companies found themselves in trouble?

- Do enforcement authorities have any teeth, and have they shown themselves willing to combat companies?

I read widely and considered multiple sources for every potential new issue. I wanted to see people with different perspectives and different agendas talking about it.

Over time, I learned which publications, and which authors within them, had a better track record of focusing on relevant topics. Your systems for detecting significance among much noise will vary, but you must develop and test them if you want to be more than just lucky in your career.

On to our final point, which is easy to describe: No one welcomes a panicky lawyer to their party.

In a crisis, a person who keeps their cool helps the whole team stay focused. True, you are operating under the same uncertainty, and you are feeling the same twisted gut, as the others. But you focus on what can be done, and on what the company needs to do next.

I suggest keeping calm amidst bedlam is also one of the easiest things for you to do.

- It's easy when you remember that you are simply playing a role, among the many roles you already play.

- Your role in a crisis is to be the level head, the sage counsel, the unflappable member of the team.

- Act that way, and you will not only start to feel that way, but others will believe you are that way.

And a person who keeps their cool when others are losing theirs is seriously cool. Try it and see if you don't agree with me.

Be well.

Chapter Six

# Do You Want to Hear the Truth?

## Although we are blind to many of our imperfections, our colleagues' vision is perfect when identifying our flaws

In an earlier chapter, I explored with you the question of Who Can Freely Speak Their Mind? Here, we tackle what may be a tougher question: Do you want to *hear* the truth?

Although this one may make you uncomfortable at times, stay with me to the end and I bet you'll feel better.

You will decide for yourself what you think. Let me lay down a few pieces of evidence that suggest to me we often just don't want to hear the truth:

- The formula for maintaining your weight is simple and widely known: Eat less and exercise. Yet diet books remain a significant chunk of total book sales, and new diets are introduced each year.

- The secret to happy relationships is no secret: Pay attention to the people closest to you, communicate well by listening more than you talk, and express your emotions in terms of how you feel and not what the other person said or did. Yet the offices of psychiatrists and marriage counselors are filled with angry couples and sad individuals.

- The path to advancing your career is open to all: Do a good job in your current job before you reach for the next, focus on continuous improvement in all areas of your life, and volunteer often while remaining open to opportunities.

- Yet of the 10 percent or so of the workforce that turns over every year, many are people frustrated that their aspirations have been thwarted. How many more remain within their companies but suffer from the same discontent?

I could go on because there are many more examples to choose from. I picked topics that we usually think of as anything but simple to demonstrate that *it is we humans that make topics complicated.*

Why? I'm not sure, but perhaps it is because we really would prefer an easier answer.

*I can't lose weight because of my genes, or hormones, or because corporations make unhealthy food.*

All true, but these are factors conveniently out of your control.

*I am unlucky in love. Perhaps it's because my parents moved too often, and I have had to change schools once too many times. If only I had the right clothes, or haircut, or social media presence. It could be because my company expects me to work evenings and weekends — I have no life outside work!*

All true, but also apparently outside your control.

*I have not progressed my career, even though other, less-qualified, people are promoted ahead of me. Management is biased, and the company is not as committed to diversity as they pretend. I have to work twice as hard to get the same chances as others, and I'm tired of it!*

True, true, true.

## Focus on what we can control

Now, I don't want to make you feel bad by suggesting that what happens to you is your fault. Many things that happen to us are completely outside our control.

Stoic advice is for us to focus on what we *can* control. This starts with how we feel about what happens to us.

The Stoic solution is simplicity itself but because it requires self-knowledge and self-discipline, the great majority ignore it and seek salvation in external things.

Because you are here with me reading this, I am confident you are interested in expanding your self-knowledge. As such, let's explore the question of whether we want to hear the truth from another angle.

Notwithstanding how useful it can be to learn something about ourselves, how do we typically respond when someone offers us "constructive criticism" in the workplace or otherwise?

- Do we listen carefully and thank them for taking the time to give us feedback?

- Do we thoughtfully consider both the credibility of the person giving us advice and the objective validity of their advice?

## Truth can be painful

If you're anything like me, that is not your instinctive response.

I have a raging monster inside me, tethered on the flimsiest of leashes. When someone offers me "feedback," I know to expect the monster to feel a flood of emotions. These range from shame, to fear, to outrage.

Through practice, I've learned to take note of these feelings (I cannot suppress them, and don't bother trying), while trying to listen carefully.

I am not yet gracious enough to thank the person at that moment for the gift of their observations, but at least I no longer try to counter their unprovoked attack by vigorously defending my virtue or letting the monster out to go on the offensive for me.

I think we don't want to hear the truth because the truth is often painful. We are none of us perfect, except perhaps in our mother's and grandmother's eyes.

Although we are blind to many of our imperfections, our colleagues' vision is perfect when identifying our flaws. Others see what we cannot.

In every other work setting, we acknowledge gaps and weaknesses and take steps to compensate. But when it comes to hearing truths about ourselves, we shy away.

Is it possible to overcome the resistance to hearing the truth about ourselves? I believe so.

I try now to ask myself two questions when confronted with feedback.

- "Does this feedback come from a person I trust?" If so, why wouldn't I listen to them now?

- And regardless of the source: "Is it possible that what this person is saying is true?" If so, should I not take it into consideration and act accordingly?

In this way, we can apply our continuous improvement principles based on what is *actually* true.

And because so few people are willing to undertake this exercise, you will find doing so is something like a superpower.

Be well.

## Chapter Seven

# Try Not Telling People You're an Expert

## When listening to the advice of an expert, any expert, add "... but they could be wrong" to the end of their statement

Have you ever noticed how often we answer the question "What do *you do*?" with a statement of *what we are*?

As in, "I'm a teacher," "I'm a nurse," or "I'm a lawyer." This no doubt conveys important information, which is why we do it.

But there are at least three reasons why you might not want to identify yourself by your profession:

- Unreasonable expectations,
- Clouded self-image, and
- Unwarranted assumptions.

Ironically, these are among the same reasons why people are usually proud to tout their professional credentials.

Let's explore the dichotomy, after which you can decide how you'll refer to yourself (and think of others) from now on.

**Unreasonable expectations**

Here's something that happens to many recent law school graduates. Upon hearing that you've passed your qualification exams, a friend or relative asks you a ridiculously specific question about a narrow area of tax or inheritance law.

When you say you don't know the answer and they are better off talking to a specialist, they say with some puzzlement and possibly suspicion, "But you're a lawyer, aren't you?"

Have you experienced something similar?

I suppose, compared to the layperson, the chances are much higher that you, the lawyer, would know the answer to a specific legal question.

But, because of the breadth of the legal field, it's unlikely the average lawyer will retain detailed knowledge about many areas beyond those they regularly use.

Or consider the poor soul who rashly identifies as a doctor in a social gathering. All too often they must field similar questions about a strange itch or recurrent dizziness because, after all, they're a doctor aren't they?

This is more than irritating to both parties in the conversation. Over time I think such exchanges can be corrosive to clear thinking.

If the people you interact with routinely come to you expecting that you know the answers to a lot of hard questions, you may be tempted not to disappoint them.

Indeed, most lawyers and doctors profess a self-confidence that is out of proportion to their actual track record. This is because compared to the layperson, the professional knows a lot. They certainly know enough to spout BS alongside good advice without anyone knowing the difference.

Others' high expectations are valuable if we force ourselves to live up to them. But beware of giving in to the temptation to believe others' expectations without doing the hard work necessary to be a real expert.

## Clouded self-image

A related risk to identifying ourselves by what we say we are, rather than what we know or do, is that we get a false sense of what we are. This is because others' expectations of us shape how we see ourselves.

Take surgeons, whose self-image sometimes becomes greatly distorted over time. Not all surgeons are brain surgeons. Much of surgery is (reassuringly) repetitive and routine, making its practitioners more akin to experienced mechanics.

True, much of surgery beyond brain surgery is also difficult. But do we value the difficulty of the task itself or that human lives hang in the balance?

And does the fact that lives hang in the balance reflect solely on the difficulty of the task or also the fact that hospitals make mistakes at distressingly high rates?

I am not picking on doctors. We could talk about mistakes made by any professional group and find that they are not at all rare (even if they are less likely to be fatal).

My point with this discussion is to suggest that *professionals are people too and people are fallible.*

It is therefore risky for us to put too much stock in our own favorable press when it comes to assessing our actual performance.

## Unwarranted assumptions

Professionals are presumed to be experts in their field and, as laypeople, we give them great deference. Professionals know this and come to rely upon it, even when demonstrating humility would be welcome.

The history of many professions is filled with cautionary tales of well-meaning but misguided individuals who were utterly wrong about vital topics. Medicine, psychology, economics, and even the annals of physics, are littered with the errors of our forebears.

Again, this is not to criticize any particular profession. It is to keep in mind that *professionals are just people.* Everyone is a fallible, biased, opinionated, and emotional creature.

I am reminded of the meditation practice called, "Just like me." As a way of developing compassion, the practitioner calls to mind the fact that everyone has fears, dreams, and desires and is, in many ways, "just like me."

There is another benefit to remembering that even professional experts are "just like us" in being fallible humans.

- We are less likely to be duped by credible-sounding experts trying to trick us.

- We are more likely to apply our own critical thinking to a situation and seek out additional information.

I described a while back how helpful it is to remind ourselves that *we are fallible* by adding, "But I could be wrong" to the end of our statements of belief.

My suggestion today is that when listening to the advice of an expert, any expert, add "... but *they* could be wrong" to the end of their statement.

If you want adulation, for your assumptions to go unchallenged, and to enjoy the deference reflexively awarded to experts, by all means, continue to introduce yourself as a lawyer, a doctor, or a similar expert.

But if you truly want to get better and to be recognized for your actual contributions, when asked what you do, try saying something like the following:

"Hi! My business card says I'm a — — — — — — . But I do many things in life, some better than others. And just like everyone, I'm not always an expert at everything I do."

I wonder which version of you people will come to respect and appreciate more over time.

Be well.

## Chapter Eight

# Can You Think Your Way to Success?

## I made my aspirational list, put it aside, and didn't think of it for years. Looking back, I see that sheet of paper changed my life

I can think of many times in my own life when I firmly believed I would benefit from magical thinking or the power of thoughts alone.

The sports world is filled with elite athletes who practice visualization or mental imagery. This is the practice of imagining yourself performing the sporting activity as you would like to do it in the real world.

For example, if you have an important race coming up, you can visualize yourself performing the race in your head.

- There you are at the starting line, feeling calm, full of energy, and ready to go.

- You envision yourself clearly as you start running, with smooth and quick strides, conserving your energy.

- You imagine what you will feel and how you will respond when you notice some tiredness, or perhaps a stitch in your side.

- And look, here is how your neck, shoulders, arms, and legs will all be flowing and relaxed as you head into the final stretch.

It becomes palpable.

## Using mental imagery

From Olympians on down to us average plodders, in sports as diverse as golf, weightlifting, running, or chess, studies have demonstrated the startling power of first playing out realistic scenarios in your head. *Psychology Today* writes about this mental imagery exercise.

It seems that our thoughts can produce similar mental patterns as the actions themselves. As a result, visualizing your specific performance in a specific setting can impact your later physical (and mental) performance.

Remarkable, but also easy to understand, I suppose, when we consider how important one's mental attitude is to performance.

You may have heard the phrase attributed to Henry Ford, "Whether you think you can or think you can't, you're right."

Visualization — and confidence — are key to producing the desired performance. By mentally going over your race or event, you are seeing yourself perform as you would like.

You are training yourself to "think you can" by seeing yourself do it in your head.

## Mindfulness

I'll provide two more reasons why we might keep an open mind about the power of the mind to impact outcomes in the real world.

And I will wrap up by speculating on the thread tying all this together and offering my formula for how to turn thoughts and ideas into personal success.

First, some of you know I am sharing elements of Stoic philosophy in the **Pragmatic Wisdom** series. One key lesson is that one's state of mind is crucial in determining our path through life. By focusing on what we can control, and particularly on our thoughts, we can live a purposeful life.

You've probably heard the term, "mindfulness." Steering our thoughts and actions is part of what it means to be mindful. How could I embrace Stoic wisdom without at least being open to the idea that our thoughts have the power to shape our lives?

## Articulate

Second, one of the spookiest things I ever did was write down on a single piece of paper a number of life goals: Personal, professional, financial, social, and fitness related.

It was Christmas break in 2006. I made the list as part of a career development exercise in which I considered my situation 10 years before, the present day, and where I wanted to be in 10 years.

I made my aspirational list, put it aside, and didn't think of it for years. Looking back, I see that sheet of paper changed my life.

Without realizing I was doing it, I started to knock off one item on the list after the other. By now I've accomplished more than 90 percent of the things on that now almost 20-year-old list.

I don't know about you, but I rarely complete task lists of any kind as well as that one. Mind you, these were not little goals. Many were so ambitious as to be almost comical to my 2006 eyes.

Some 10 years ago, I started to take out the list about once a year and update it. I'd check off goals I accomplished and add new goals. I might spend an hour on it, that's it.

I kept the original sheet of paper because it was already clear to me something magical (and kind of scary if I'm honest) was going on. I know it wasn't the piece of paper itself, but it was hard not to be superstitious.

I think writing down goals all those years ago helped me in two ways: I personally acknowledged what I wanted to achieve and I expanded the scope of what was possible for me to achieve.

Just writing down goals made them not only tangible but doable, and they became goals I thought I could achieve.

Did writing down goals cause me to pay more attention to them in the coming years and take action as a result? No doubt.

That's part of how we move beyond *knowing* an idea and *implementing* that idea. We have to take some concrete steps to move from thought to action.

## The power of magical thinking

My experience suggests that even a small step may help get you started. Once you are on your way, if you just keep putting one foot in front of the other, then nothing will stop you from reaching your goals.

So go ahead and believe in your own magical thinking, so long as you take at least one step right away toward achieving your goals.

Be well.

# Chapter Nine

# I Miss Shaking Hands

Very belatedly, I have come to see the wisdom in my Swiss colleagues' practice of starting and ending meetings

When I started working in Switzerland, I was struck by what seemed like an annoying, old-fashioned custom.

In most business settings, a person joining a meeting is expected to individually greet each person in the room. You would say hello, shake each person's hand, and perhaps give the three cheek kisses to women, left, right, left.

And you were not done with the ceremony. Upon departure, the proper procedure is to once again shake the hand of each person in the meeting. You can understand why I soon learned to come to meetings early and leave late.

Does this seem anachronistic to you? I resisted. I never got comfortable with cheek kisses, which requires a European flair and elegance I do not possess.

Although the custom waned, with the advent of the #MeToo movement, I advised management that cheek kisses were not OK anymore. (Did I have my own ulterior motive in relegating check kisses to the compliance bad list? Maybe.)

As to the procession of handshakes, for some time I tried an airy wave at larger groups of people instead of individual greetings. This was probably an unwelcome move by a relative newcomer to a country.

Then again, as a stranger in a strange land, my colleagues probably had but minimal expectations for me.

## Why the handshake is so important

The Swiss themselves are resoundingly successful in doing business in foreign countries.

I sense they hold themselves to a high standard, from learning the local language to spending time understanding and following local customs and practices.

Plunk a good Swiss manager down almost anywhere in the world, and he or she will thrive. I saw this over and over again, and I am deeply impressed.

The common thread between the handshake ceremony and success in foreign settings may be a simple acknowledgment of, and respect for, others as individuals.

- You hear Americans described as individualistic, and I agree.

- But the difference is that Americans prioritize themselves as *individuals*, while Swiss customs indicate they value *others*.

It is certainly both acknowledgment and respect to take a moment to shake each person's hand. Maybe this helps set the tone for productive meetings because each person feels individually welcomed. You are there for your personal attributes and so you feel more comfortable contributing.

The contracting process helped me evaluate the importance of handshakes.

I'm not ashamed to admit I love contracting and I hope I've gotten good at it. I've certainly had a lot of practice, overseeing more than 10 million commercial agreements. Of course, only a tiny fraction of those had in-depth review and negotiation, but it's still a big number.

I started teaching contracting principles to Master of Law students several years ago. When I was creating materials, I thought about how businesspeople make deals and have done so for centuries.

- You signal agreement by shaking hands. The handshake represents so much more, though.

- On an individual level, it signals trust, personal commitment, and a certain responsibility for the relationship going forward.

## Honor the spirit of an agreement even if legally you could challenge it

In observing my business colleagues in practice, I realized that handshakes are powerful.

If a person agrees to something and shakes hands on it, the agreement becomes more meaningful than the strict enforceability of the words from a legal perspective.

This translates into better contract drafting by following a simple principle: Always ask for what you want, and make sure the business parties acknowledge what's been agreed upon, with a signature or a handshake, or both.

An example: It was important to me that we limited our liability when selling our products. I wanted to use the same simple and clearly written contract clause in all jurisdictions, even though in some countries this was not always enforceable as written.

However, we found that our business partners almost always honored the spirit of the agreement even though they could have made a legal argument challenging its enforceability.

Why? Because we could say to them, we had a deal. You signed the agreement (handshake or not), and the deal is clear. The lawyers in the background would make their arguments, but the business sense, the unwritten honor code, usually prevailed.

## Connect with others

I hope you agree there are many solid business reasons to respect the handshake. It took the pandemic to drive home how important the handshake is on a personal level as well.

How many times did you catch yourself holding out your hand in greeting or farewell, only to realize that social distancing forbids it? I did this over and over, and it made me realize that the handshake is key to forming emotional bonds.

You like people more, and they like you more, when you make a connection. Yes, we can still do this with words remotely, but a handshake is simple, quick, and effective.

I miss handshakes, and I look forward to their return.

Very belatedly, I have come to see the wisdom in my Swiss colleagues' practice of starting and ending meetings. The next time I go to a meeting, I will gladly shake everyone's hand.

Just don't expect me to kiss anyone.

Be well.

Chapter Ten

# Observations From a Social Media Noob

If you find yourself connecting with the majority of your audience, feel free to ignore the small and grouchy minority

Have you ever noticed that the professionals most likely to attract interest on social media are often the least inclined to use it?

I am thinking of business owners and senior executives who have fantastic experience and know-how that others would love to hear about. The problem? They're usually so focused on their priorities, and so busy in general, that they spend little or no time on social media.

That was me not long ago. I spent the first 25 years of my career almost entirely focused on the job in front of me. When I went in-house, I saw the value in interacting with other in-house lawyers, so became active in ACC. Good call. As much enjoyment as I got out of the interactions, I could justify them by the business benefit I got from meeting with peers.

As for social media, I barely gave it a moment's thought. I created a Facebook profile and then largely deleted it because of privacy concerns. I think I went more than a decade without once logging in. Later I set up a LinkedIn profile — isn't that what professionals do? —and then let it languish.

At least I would check in on LinkedIn every couple of months and, if someone I knew sent me an invitation to connect, I would accept. I think I created my first post in 2021, although I've since gotten quite a bit more active. Still, when I tell you I doubled my connections in the last year you should not be impressed.

Being relatively new to the game, I have been carefully observing how others behave, what seems to work well, and what gets people in trouble. I think I've identified some parallels to other professional pursuits that may shed some light on basic human nature. Understanding this, perhaps we can improve our performance not just on social media but in other areas of our jobs and our lives.

I've still got questions, though. Maybe you can help me understand.

## Is it possible to post anything of substance without attracting detractors?

In my experience, a certain percentage of people simply disagree with you, no matter what point you're making. (I'm not talking about cat videos or people-are-amazing clips. Everyone loves those.) Looking at polls from Rasmussen Reports over the last few years, it seems around 25 percent of those polled reliably express downright bizarre opinions.

This is consistent with something I noticed when I started teaching about 10 years ago. I would prepare diligently for my classes and tried hard to be informative and entertaining. I watched other great lecturers and applied continuous improvement principles. And yet, no matter the topic or the class, I would simply not click with maybe 10 percent of the group, sometimes more.

## Could it be me?

Yes, of course, there could be style I could adopt that would click with the other 10 percent or so of the class. But seeing the phenomenon now repeated in other domains, whether I'm trying to be serious or funny, supportive or critical, I've come to believe that perfect communication with 100 percent of your audience is simply impossible.

Repeating my classes over multiple years helped me realize it might not entirely be my fault. That's because the critical feedback from year to year differs significantly, even though I deliver the same (or hopefully continuously better) lectures. This is not surprising when you think about it. From psychology we know that people are emotional, irrational, biased, and suffer routinely from cognitive dissonance.

At any moment, a certain percentage of any large group is going to see the same story unfold but take away a very different meaning.

As a result, I've learned to expect dissonant responses on social media, and I don't let it bother me. Well, at least I try. It helps me when I remember that many more readers are either neutral or positive than will ever let you know. In other words, there are many viewers who silently appreciate your point. I've had many conversations with colleagues and been happily surprised when they refer to a post or an article they saw. I didn't know they were there.

## What is the ratio of lurkers to posters?

I think lurkers, or passive viewers to make it seem less creepy, outnumber posters by at least 10 to one. And of the posters, a small but vocal minority who feel passionate about certain topics often dominate the public space. Let's posit that one percent is grouchy, nine percent positive, and 90 percent silent.

You will measure your communication effectiveness your own way. But don't be too hard on yourself. If you find yourself connecting with the majority of your audience, feel free to ignore the small and grouchy minority. One of the very best things I learned on Facebook was the power of blocking people determined to be jerks. I've only had to use it once, but the benefit to my wellbeing was immediate.

If only I could find a way to do the same in real life.

Be well.

## Chapter Eleven

# Swiss Cheese Your Way to Safety

## Any in-house counsel worth their salary knows that learning from the mistakes of others is free tuition in the school of life

Has your company ever gone through a serious problem or crisis? If you have *not yet* dealt with such wrenching times, you should prepare now.

If you have experienced the pain of a compliance failure, you likely want to learn more about the best way to handle it. And you are surely motivated to ensure similar mishaps don't happen again.

Any in-house counsel worth their salary knows that learning from the mistakes of others is free tuition in the school of life. Knowing the pitfalls, however, is the easy part.

Getting people to pay sufficient attention to potential problems before they arise is much harder. Or, as I've said elsewhere, "We do not lack for knowledge of what to do, we lack the will to do it."

I'll help you find the will to act by making your task easier.

While serious problems in companies can arise without warning as a result of single acts, such instances are thankfully rare. We don't need to spend much time on them because, for truly one-off failures, it's difficult to anticipate them so challenging to maneuver in advance.

## Most significant problems are the result of multiple issues

In my experience, most significant problems are born of multiple causes in the sense that they result from several, cascading failures.

Often one or more of these failures sets off warning signals to vigilant watchers. The first lesson: Be aware of any signs of crisis considered averted.

When one of your monitoring systems nips an issue in the bud, be thankful. But look carefully at what allowed the risk to arise at all. Something is not right.

Small problems by definition don't cause significant harm. It's tempting therefore to ignore them to focus on bigger issues. But small problems have a way of growing when you're not looking.

A mantra I repeated often with my team was: "Don't let small problems become big problems." So study your small problems and understand root causes wherever possible.

In diagnosing your non-catastrophic failures, consider what standards of behavior you expect of your colleagues.

Do you expect employees to first remember all relevant rules and then to understand and follow them correctly at all times? If so, you may be new to the job. (Or you may have better colleagues than I did; I liked mine a lot despite their failings.)

So, we need to assume that people are imperfect. They will be distracted, make mistakes, and sometimes try to subvert our systems. Although people are wonderful as individuals, in groups they are predictably and depressingly unreliable.

Some people, perhaps most people, will not follow all the rules all of the time. People make exceptions for themselves and happily refuse to follow rules they don't agree with.

## The Swiss cheese strategy

If we expect mistakes and noncompliance from the start, we can design our systems to anticipate them.

For one, we pay more attention to incentives. Can we design incentives to directly encourage the behavior we want and discourage otherwise expected but unwanted behavior?

Further, we usually seek to build in redundant protections, assuming that one or even several layers of defense may be insufficient. And in redundancy lies the Swiss cheese strategy.

Simply put, consider each of your defenses as a slice of Swiss cheese* in the sense that it has holes in it. Each slice of your compliance system will stop some problems, but not all.

So you layer on another slice of cheese, aligned slightly differently, which stops many of the issues that made it through the first line of defense.

But again, perhaps not all. So you add a third slice of cheese.

Take your contracting process as an example of the strategy in operation:

- You will have carefully prepared standard terms and conditions, and maybe some standard agreements, the first line of defense. But you won't be able to use your agreement in every transaction.

- So then you prepare a contracting guideline as a second layer. Your guideline sets out in simple and clear terms the must-haves and nice-to-haves in every deal. But your team won't negotiate every point successfully and will make exceptions.

- As a third line of defense, you may require nonstandard terms to be approved by successive layers of management. The approval requirement serves two purposes: It means teams try harder to get compliant terms to avoid having to ask for approval and it gives management a chance to influence the deal.

The beauty of this system is that each of the individual defenses may be simple and inexpensive. After all, they don't need to be perfect. Just add another simple and inexpensive layer. Simple systems are easier to explain and implement, meaning you get less resistance.

The Swiss cheese approach of layering redundant and backup systems greatly reduces the chances that one or a series of small problems will grow into something catastrophic.

And here you thought the Swiss just melted their cheese.

Be well.

* My Swiss friends are yelling at the screen now saying, "There are literally hundreds of types of Swiss cheese! What do you mean 'Swiss cheese'?" To an American's eyes, not to mention taste, Swiss cheese usually means something resembling Emmental, with large yellow slices containing eyes or holes.

Chapter Twelve

# Dealing with One-Issue Stakeholders

## For your stakeholders to stop shouting and listen to you, they must feel that you have listened to and understood them

In the corporate world, we often encounter stakeholders who care deeply about a particular issue.

These stakeholders use their focus and passion to drive attention to their topic. They write letters to regulators and the board, file shareholder proposals, and generate publicity, all of which create pressure on companies to act.

In-house counsel and their companies are at a disadvantage when dealing with such vocal advocates. The advocates have just one issue, and they are willing to do almost anything to promote their cause.

We, in contrast, have hundreds of issues to deal with, and many pressing priorities. We simply do not have as much time to devote to the topic as they do.

When confronted with one-issue stakeholders, no one cares as much as *they* do about *their* issue.

I don't want to digress today into the debate about whether companies should be primarily shareholder-focused or stakeholder-focused. It's sufficient to observe that the stakeholder model suffers from a serious defect.

Namely, there is no consistent and accepted mechanism for deciding priorities among competing stakeholder interests. Hence, the shouting we see among stakeholders to make the most noise, so companies pay heed to their squeaky wheel.

## How should a company react?

When all the wheels are squeaking all the time, what is a responsible company to do?

One answer is to simply ignore the noise and develop your strategy top-down, quietly, without being influenced by externalities. After all, management and the board surely know best what the company's strengths and weaknesses are, and where the most promising opportunities lie.

The risk here is that by ignoring stakeholders you only arouse them to greater heights of frenzy. What do people do when they think someone has not heard their message? They repeat it, and more stridently each time.

True, sometimes they get tired or veer off to pursue a more receptive target. But particularly with passionate stakeholders, and that's most of them, ignoring a stakeholder request in favor of your own priorities is a risky path.

So, what to do?

## Listen

*Listening* to stakeholders is a good idea, even though it can seem like a waste of time.

True, we already understand the issue well because we've heard it many times before. Listen, nonetheless. You might still learn something new.

More importantly, by listening you take away the stakeholder's immediate need to escalate.

You can make even more progress if you then acknowledge the importance of the topic. Perhaps you will express your desire to see positive change.

For your stakeholder to stop shouting and listen to you, they must feel that you have listened to and understood them. A stakeholder is someone who has an interest in, and is affected by, the company's decisions. So, it is right to listen to and genuinely seek to understand their concerns.

Only now are you in a position to safely raise the issue of competing priorities. But be careful.

In my experience, it never goes over well when you say some issues are more important than others. Even though this is demonstrably true, no one wants to hear that their issue is not the most important one. A disappointed stakeholder is likely to take out their frustration on you, the messenger.

## Focus on the impact your company can have

What I've found works better is to focus on the *impact* your company can have. That is, where can you make a substantive difference?

Preserving access to clean water is no doubt important, but if you are a software development company you may have less of an impact here than, say, a mining company. Explain what areas you are focused on, and why.

The conversation goes something like this:

**Stakeholder:** *Passionate advocacy, i.e., request for your company to immediately and completely change its business model and upend everything that made it successful.*

**Company (calmly):** *Thank you for raising your concern. We hear you and understand your issue. We agree that [topic] is an important and relevant issue that the world needs to tackle.*

*Our company is focused on X, Y, and Z of the UN Sustainable Development Goals [or similar]. We focus on these particular areas because, given the nature of our business, the location of our operations, and the partners we work with, we feel these are the areas where can have the greatest impact.*

### Environmental, social, and governance (ESG) strategy

It helps if you have already publicly described your environmental, social, and governance (ESG) strategy and can refer back to it in the conversation. Your strategy will outline where you can have the greatest impact and, thus, where your focus areas are.

If you have not developed and published an ESG strategy, I can only recommend you do so. Otherwise, you are at great risk of a one-issue stakeholder dragging you to their level and defeating you with their persistence.

Be well.

# Chapter Thirteen

# No One Cares as Much as You Do

## Your ambitions exceed your abilities not because of any failing on your part, but because everyone is focused on their own priorities

I will tell you why you need to be a one-issue stakeholder if you want to be successful. The reason is that no one cares as much as *you* do about *your* issues.

This rule applies universally across your entire life. It operates at work and in your personal life. On every topic you can think of, you care the most about the things that affect you.

**Everyone else is a one-issue stakeholder**

Your doctor may be wonderful, talented, and caring. You are still one of hundreds of patients, and for the doctor, there is a commercial aspect to your visit that colors the encounter. Thus, you must be your own zealous advocate in managing your health.

Your contractor is a whiz with every kind of power tool, sticks to their quotes, and answers the phone. You are still one of many clients, and for the contractor, your project is a job to be completed and an invoice to be paid. They do not have to live in the house after the renovation and will not notice every fleck and imperfection the way you will.

Your kid's teacher is patient, experienced, and magic with the class. Your child is one of a room full of students, and for the teacher represents a source of work and aggravation. There is homework to review and tests to correct, but the end of term looms with graduation all but certain. Whether your child performs to her maximum potential is no doubt a matter of some interest, but no teacher's concern will match your own when it comes to your child.

## What does it mean, practically?

I don't mean to depress you by hammering home the point. Understanding that no one cares as much as you do about your issue gives rise to two important implications:

1. Implementing your initiative (say writing consistently and growing your followers organically) requires *much* more effort than you think it should.

2. You can successfully pursue fewer initiatives than you would like at any given time, also due to the first point. This is because you'll be spending more time and effort driving progress on each initiative.

## Why success is elusive ... but approachable

Your ambitions exceed your abilities not because of any failing on your part, but because everyone is focused on their own priorities. Be realistic, therefore, in your expectations of how quickly you will advance in pushing your priorities. There is no shortcut. There are no exceptions.

Take your talent and your energy and devote them to being a tireless advocate for one (or a few) initiatives at a time. And then plan on doing it over and over again for everything in your life that you consider important.

If you find this image disheartening, let me leave you with this thought to cheer you up again.

- Each time you persist and persevere, you will become more effective.

- You'll learn which of your strengths to leverage in what settings, and which of your counterparts respond best to what pressure.

- Your tasks become easier, therefore, whenever you succeed.

Your colleagues will not be as patient as you. They will mistake busyness and effort for progress, although these are not the same. You will recognize that only progress is progress, no matter the desire and effort. Because of this, you will succeed more often.

Over time, the combination of your focus, persistence, and successful implementation makes you unstoppable. That is worth fighting for.

So go ahead and care about your issues, the more the better.

Be well.

Chapter Fourteen

# Identifying Problems Worth Working On

## What can you do that no one else will do, or do as well?

Let me start with a fundamental truth that experienced employees know all too well: Identifying problems is easy.

New employees are typically astounded at how many problems they quickly identify when starting a new job.

Guess what? You are not the first person or the only person to detect things that aren't working perfectly. I tell new hires that identifying problems is the easiest thing for an employee to do.

If you stop at merely identifying problems, you won't be much use to your colleagues or your company.

Employees who go on to add real value become just as adept at proposing solutions to the problems they identify. But, as we'll discuss in Identifying Solutions That Will Work (the following chapter), it turns out that *proposing solutions* is also not the hard part.

### Driving change is the hard part

The hard part in driving change is as follows: Identifying which problems are worth focusing on, and which solutions are worth pursuing among many possible approaches.

Doing so requires a blend of strategic thinking and real-world pragmatism that most people only gain through experience. Let me explain why this is so.

We typically have a rich buffet of problems always laid out before us. Faced with this abundance, many people choose to address problems they feel are manageable. That is, smaller problems with relatively quick solutions.

Is someone requesting your input via email? That's easy. Take a few minutes and respond to them. This type of problem-solving can be quite satisfying. You are checking items off your list and making visible progress.

The typical workday also requires us to deal with mundane topics. Few people can avoid the many minor interactions that make up modern work.

Hence, the abundance of advice we see on how to work more efficiently. If we are going to spend a fair amount of time dealing with little problems, it is useful for us to learn how to solve them quickly and well.

The expedient path to problem-solving is nonetheless a risky path.

Notice first how the number of small problems never diminishes. Each task we accomplish provides a fleeting burst of pleasure but is rewarded by two more tasks.

Next notice how often we spend our entire day in a succession of what we thought would be brief moments of quick answers. The many little things we chase after mindlessly eat up the day.

## Focus on what can make the greatest difference

If you are purposeful, you may have carefully thought about your important priorities. These are the strategic things that you believe will have the greatest influence.

Ask yourself how much overlap there is between the small daily problems you usually spend time on and your strategic priorities. If you are like most people I know, the answer is not much.

Another risk is that the further you advance in your career, the more you will find people looking for you to help solve *their* urgent problems.

# IDENTIFYING PROBLEMS WORTH WORKING ON

This is only natural, but you must be aware of this key fact: Other people's problems are not necessarily your problems. And helping solve other people's problems is often not the best use of your time.

If solving other people's problems is not the best use of your time, do you have a clear sense of what is? Take a moment and write down what you think are among your greatest potential contributions to your company. How do you (or can you) add value?

## Your greatest value may be that you helped avoid problems

Especially for lawyers, keep in mind that your greatest contribution may be avoiding negative outcomes.

People overweight additive initiatives, like acquisitions, introducing new products, or entering new territories. But, often, tremendous value hides in helping ensure your company and colleagues do not, pardon the phrase, f — things up.

We know there is great value in strong governance and effective compliance. But our business colleagues do not default to preventive measures unless prompted.

## Summary and method

In sum, problems large and small always clamor for our attention. The things we spend time on by default may be a necessary part of our day, but they are unlikely to be the most important problems.

It is helpful for us to carefully consider the ways in which we add value because this helps us identify potential problems worth focusing on.

I recommend taking the process in separate stages.

First, devote quality time to identifying a long list of problems that your team or your company is facing.

- At this stage, just identify problems.

- Try hard not to consider how easy each problem would be to solve, but rather rank them according to how valuable it would be if they were solved.

Then put your list of problems aside and consider the ways in which you add value.

- What can you do that no one else will do, or do as well?

- Your contribution may be in the form of focusing on things others do not, being willing to devote more time to a project, or in the special skills and abilities you possess or can nurture.

Now you are ready to take your short list of potentially strategic problems and match it up against your list of your unique value propositions.

If you're lucky, this will reveal a few overlaps where you would be well-positioned to focus your efforts.

Be well.

## Chapter Fifteen

# Identifying Solutions That Will Work

## I've seen talented managers devise solutions that would unquestionably address a strategic problem but still fail to make progress

Before we consider solutions to problems, we need to evaluate which problems are worth our attention. I discussed this in the prior chapter.

Although we are tempted to pursue problems with quick solutions, we create enduring value by focusing instead on strategic problems. This essay addresses how to devise effective solutions to our strategic problems.

Just as with identifying problems, proposing solutions is easy. You are not the first person or the only person to come up with any number of solutions to the problems you've identified.

Here's the thing: Strategic problems typically have no easy solutions. They wouldn't be strategic problems otherwise.

I've seen talented, successful managers devise solutions that would unquestionably address a strategic problem but still fail to make progress. Why is this?

Otherwise promising solutions fail for many reasons, most prominently:

> 1. Underestimating historical and cultural factors supporting the status quo, and

2. Focusing too much on the benefits without considering the costs.

Let's explore both points.

## Figure out what caused the problem

Before we can safely dive into problem-solving mode, it is critical to ask how the situation developed and why.

Although some problems develop spontaneously, there are very often explanations behind the things that appear screwed up to us today. It helps to understand how we got here before trying to set a path to a new destination.

Change requires effort, and significant change requires extraordinary effort.

Because people are creatures of habit, we tend to keep doing what we have been doing, even if we know it's expensive, inefficient, or downright harmful. Ask anyone who has tried to change their eating, exercise, or spending habits.

The burden of change today is magnified when the reward is distant in time. The more we must change for a speculative future reward, the harder the challenge.

Thus, the first reason potential solutions fail is that we don't account sufficiently for human stubbornness, which tends to preserve the status quo. The obvious correctness of a solution doesn't help overcome this.

In a work setting, successful implementation means you must be willing to either (1) invest extraordinary effort in pushing your solution, or (2) identify and piggyback on existing initiatives and cultural currents underlying the behavior you want to change.

## Determine who can help you implement the needed change

Even if you can invest extraordinary effort, you are well-served to spend time understanding your company's culture.

- Who among your colleagues has a respected voice and will support you?
- Are there other successful initiatives already underway to which you can add your own initiative?

Think of your company as a slow-moving river of molasses. Don't try to push your boat against the flow, or uphill. You may be able to gradually shift the course, but remember you are dealing with incredible momentum.

Now to the second reason solutions fail, which is not sufficiently considering the costs. These costs include the active resistance from those who are disadvantaged by upsetting the status quo and the unintended consequences our solution gives rise to.

It is because of these factors that even successful projects regularly take twice as long and cost twice as much as planned.

## Plan ahead for obstacles and how to circumvent what you can

You can forecast likely costs more accurately by conducting pre-mortems. That is, assume your project has failed (or stalled, or taken longer, or cost more, etc.). Now describe all the reasons why.

This will help you plan for those obstacles, and perhaps avoid some of them. But mostly it will help you come up with a more realistic assessment of what substantive change behind your initiative will require.

You should be sobered, if not depressed, upon concluding your pre-mortem exercise.

Significant change requires extraordinary effort, which comes at the cost of all the other things you cannot pursue. If you are grand in your expectations, be humble at least in your estimate of how quickly you will proceed.

## Know the costs of the solution

Recognize that when we push solutions without a clear understanding of costs, we do worse than impede progress. We lose time and waste resources pursuing solutions that are bound to fail, making an eventual effective solution that much harder to implement.

I'll end with an example to illustrate the dynamic. Most people agree that human-caused climate change is a serious, global concern. The solutions seem obvious to policymakers: Immediately and drastically cut carbon emissions, while shifting to renewable energy.

A short reflection using our new model reveals, however, why the obvious solutions are destined for failure.

- We have not given enough weight to the historical context: particularly that today's first-world economies developed on the back of low-cost energy delivered by fossil fuels. Today's developing economies are naturally interested in their own advancement, which cannot be accomplished cost-effectively with renewables.

- Consumers in many countries have grown accustomed to their current quality of life, which has been fueled by decades of steady or declining energy prices. Achieving net-zero carbon emissions requires immediate cost and real sacrifice for the foreseeable future in return for a very long-term, speculative payoff.

- Should we assume that most people will suddenly decide to put future generations' interests above their own? I suppose coordinated altruistic behavior by large groups of people is possible, but it goes against all historical precedents.

Climate change may well be the most important project for the world to work on. I predict we won't make great progress until we are considerably more transparent about the costs.

Only then will individuals and societies be willing to consider whether the costs are worth the benefits. Importantly, seeing the true extent of the costs will trigger a search for alternative solutions that may be equally effective but easier to implement.

Being transparent about costs is one of the best ways you can improve the quality of your problem-solving. Showing true costs seems risky, but the payoff may be a solution that works. That's worth taking a risk for.

Be well.

## Chapter Sixteen

# Why It's So Hard Being a Good Corporate Lawyer

## Even if you're not a lawyer, pity for a moment the career path they are facing

If you want to become a good in-house lawyer (that is, a lawyer who works for a corporation) you face a number of problems. Let me depress you for a few minutes by describing what some of those problems are:

### Law school didn't teach you practical skills

To start with, your law school did not teach you many practical skills and tools necessary to be effective. Here's a quote from the New York State Bar Association Task Force on the Future of the Legal Profession:

*We used to think that being a good lawyer simply meant knowing the law. Today, we are more likely to think that good lawyers know how to do useful things with the law to help solve client problems.* — New York State Bar Association Task Force on the Future of the Legal Profession

So it's not enough to know the law; you have to know how to *do* useful things with it to solve your organization's problems.

Now, the law school method of how to teach someone to become a lawyer is largely unchanged for the last 150 years. I hope we'd all agree that the practice of at least in-house counsel has moved on since then.

Law firms and bar associations believe law schools should pick up the slack, not them.

But for the sake of argument, let's say law schools are doing what they should because someone has to teach you about the substantive law, and how to think analytically.

## Law firms can't prepare you for in-house life

Your next problem is what happens after you graduate from law school. Let's assume you start working at a law firm. Law firms are good at many things but law firms simply don't know everything that an in-house counsel needs to know.

There are entire areas of skills that are relevant in-house that are not relevant in a law firm. And as we've seen, they don't think it's their job to train lawyers for in-house practice.

So you won't get your in-house training in a law firm either.

## You can't count on high-quality company training

Now let's assume you've made the switch to a company, government agency, or another organization, and you're actually practicing in-house. All clear, right?

Unfortunately, your search is not over because it is a rare organization that trains its in-house counsel in a systematic way across all disciplines that might be relevant. What training exists is either ad hoc or narrowly focused.

- Ad hoc training often takes place in smaller teams that don't have the resources to do systematic training.
- And in the bigger organizations that do have training resources, lawyers often become specialized, so your exposure to broad issues is limited.

## You'll learn most by doing

What this means is that most of your learning is on-the-job training, or learning by doing. This can be very good indeed but, under the *best of circumstances*, it can take years and years of experience to become truly effective as in-house counsel

— at least from the perspective of having broad awareness and skills across many topics, i.e., being a corporate generalist.

Ultimately, whether you become a well-rounded generalist who is capable of not just handling the daily work but anticipating challenges and strategically planning ahead is largely a matter of luck. The right organization, the right team, the right time, etc.

With this depressing background out of the way, how do you improve your odds of getting ahead? Here's my personal view: The best thing you can do is to become highly valuable to your organization starting with what you're doing right now.

In other words, do such a good job where you are with what's in front of you that your legal team, your business colleagues, and everyone you interact with, all think "Now there's a person I'd want to work with again if I ever got a chance."

In the next few chapters, I am going to lay bare my best secrets on how to outperform at work as part of a series on **Master Skills for Communicating at Work**.

## You can cut to the front of the line

Although it took me years of experiment and practice to develop this guidance, I want you to cut right to the front of the line. Why am I sharing these secrets with you? It's because I saw the wonderful impact they can have on a company and its culture.

- Initially, I saw the benefit among my team members, who became some of our most appreciated employees.
- The interesting thing was when people saw how effective our communication practices were, they clamored to have them spread across the company.

It's because I know how hard your job is and appreciate how much you do that I want to help you be more effective.

Stay tuned.

Be well.

Chapter Seventeen

# The Day You Became Smarter

## Part of the Master Skills series on how to crush your job with better communication — five tips to write clearly

I wasted a decade or more sharpening my legal skills until I realized the secrets to great performance lay elsewhere.

And they weren't even hard to learn.

I'd like to spare you that lost time and share the secrets. This and the next several chapters comprise the Master Skills on how to communicate better.

- Write plainly and clearly (this chapter)

- Taming the email monster (Write Better Emails Today)

- Avoiding time-wasting meetings (Maybe Don't Go to that Meeting)

- Influencing others (Persuade Like Aristotle)

- Engaging with others (Listen Up Already)

If you want your work colleagues to be amazed at how much smarter you've become overnight, **write everything in plain language** that everyone can understand.

## Lawyers are notoriously bad communicators

Although this advice applies to any manager, it is particularly helpful for lawyers.

Why is that? Because our non-lawyer colleagues expect us to be confusing, poor communicators. We're famous for our impenetrable legalese.

When you show up with your simple and clear messages, you will stun people. They will understand what you're saying. Because of this, they will think you're brilliant, far out of proportion to your actual legal chops.

Do you know how a layperson determines which of two people is the better lawyer? One or more of these factors typically comes into play:

- A better-looking suit;
- Billing at a higher hourly rate than competitors;
- The lawyer lets slip that they graduated from Harvard or Yale;
- They return calls; and
- They can string together a comprehensible sentence.

For years, I thought the secret was returning calls. Colleagues so appreciate responsiveness that it really seemed like a genius way to generate goodwill. And it is.

But it's not enough if you also want people to think you're smart.

You probably know this, but in-house lawyers must never rely on the first three factors because they all serve as barriers to our business colleagues liking us.

Although Machiavelli assured us in The Prince it is better to be feared than loved, being liked is a good middle ground. This means your path to legal stardom lies in being a great communicator.

For our purposes, let me modify Machiavelli with the following five rules for clear writing:

## 1. It is better to be understood than complete

You spent a long time becoming a legal expert. Don't show off all that you know. Don't go down every hypothetical pathway for the sake of completeness. Start with the most likely scenario and describe it simply.

Being understood also means you use simple words and omit extra words. I love words and I know lots of fancy ones. But simple words get your point across better.

Short sentences work better than longer ones. Same for short paragraphs.

## 2. It is better to be kind than precise

This means knowing your audience and giving them just what they need.

How much detail must you give for a reader to understand the point? Sure, you had to look up all sorts of laws and regulations to answer the question, but does it help your reader when you list them chapter and verse? Normally not.

If you think some readers may want more detail, offer it in later sections or even an appendix. The reader who is interested in the detail can continue, while the ones who trust your answer can stop.

## 3. It is better to be first than last

What I mean is this: Make your last sentence into your first sentence. Nothing demonstrates a stellar communicator so much as starting with the answer or conclusion.

I know that's not how lawyers' minds work. We start with the facts, determine the relevant law, perform an analysis, and only then come to our conclusion.

Keep right on doing that. But once you've reached the end of your analysis, simply move your concluding sentence up to the top, and you'll go from average lawyer to superstar in one easy stroke.

## 4. It is better to be active than passive

You should give every sentence a subject. Don't hide behind ambiguity.

I know sometimes we don't know who the actor is. But we lawyers have let the passive voice take over all our writings. And the passive voice does more than make our sentences dull. People don't understand passive sentences as well.

Our bad habit is deeply ingrained. I encourage you to root it out, sentence by sentence.

Good news for everyone who can't stop from writing in the passive voice right away: You can more easily spot passive sentences upon a second reading. That leads us to our final point.

## 5. It is better to edit than write perfectly

I told you upfront the secret to good communication wasn't hard to learn. Knowing the secret doesn't mean you will write perfectly all the time.

Despite years of practice, I catch myself reverting to old habits often. The solution is to read and edit what you write, which thankfully is much easier than writing perfectly.

Simply check your next document against these five rules and you'll be a better writer than almost all your colleagues.

And you can bask in their amazement at how much smarter you've suddenly become.

Be well.

PS — I was inspired to write this by two brilliant sources on clear writing; I hope you go on to inspire your colleagues by your example: The US Security and Exchange Commission's Plain English Handbook (including the preface by Warren Buffet), which contains numerous tips that are useful no matter what language you use, and Scott Adam's blog, The Day You Became A Better Writer.

## Chapter Eighteen

# Write Better Emails Today

## Part of the Master Skills series on how to crush your job with better communication — ten tips for better emails

Just to mention it, maybe you shouldn't write so many emails.

I share below how to make your emails awesome but that assumes you need to write one at all. Sometimes you don't.

You know emails are terrible for emotionally charged situations. Did you also know that the best predictor of how many emails a person receives is how many they send?

If you find yourself plagued with emails, consider the anti-Nike approach: Just don't do it.

But I get it. Emails are unavoidable, often necessary, and sometimes useful.

When I managed a global legal team, I loved being able to pass on assignments at the end of my day knowing that colleagues half a day behind me (or ahead) would still have time to handle them. I imagined that the sun never set on our hard-working team.

Allowing for asynchronous communication, as in I write when I have time and you respond when you have time, permits us both to maximize our productivity.

Thus, I start with the premise that you must write at least some emails. So, let's write the best possible emails, shall we?

## 10 Secrets to Better Emails

### 1. Use clear subject lines

Your subject line should describe the topic and whether the message is for information only or whether action is required. Edit outdated or unclear subject lines when you respond to emails you receive.

### 2. State your purpose early

The very first sentence of your message should tell readers what you want from them.

If you are requesting specific action or follow-up, make sure the deliverable is clear.

### 3. Set deadlines

Always set a deadline and highlight it in bold or another color. Be realistic in setting deadlines, recognizing that your colleagues have other priorities.

### 4. Only include necessary information

Give only the background information or context necessary for your reader to understand your message, no more.

Delete unnecessary text, including prior messages, as appropriate.

### 5. Avoid jargon

Do not use legalese, terms of art, acronyms, or other abbreviations that your reader may not know.

### 6. Have a good review process

Review the content of your message to ensure it is short, simple, and focused.

Consider asking a colleague to review important messages to check they are clear.

## 7. Keep your distribution narrow

Have a specific reason for each person you send your message to. Only send emails to persons who must act on the message.

The broader your distribution, the less likely an individual reader feels it was intended for them.

## 8. Separate emails to smaller groups

If you have to send emails to a lot of recipients, consider sending multiple individual emails to smaller, relevant groups of people.

## 9. Keep emails to five sentences or fewer

Challenge yourself to write concisely. See five.sentenc.es/ for inspiration. It's not always possible, but the challenge of reducing a long reply to five sentences helps clarify your key points. You can usually eliminate a lot.

These tips are powerful because people can implement them easily. You just have to want to do it and then be mindful of what you are doing.

Thus, I will end with my final tip for writing better emails:

## 10. Don't hit send before reviewing your emails against this checklist

It is hard to write emails perfectly the first time. But editing them is easy.

I wish you happy editing.

Be well.

# Chapter Nineteen

# Maybe Don't Go to that Meeting

## Part of the Master Skills series on how to crush your job with better communication — ten tips for awesome meetings

Nothing sends a signal that you carefully manage your time like declining a meeting invitation. Short of just saying no, which I understand will be a shock in many organizations, how about asking what you would be there for:

*I see you invited me to meeting X. Based on the agenda, I am not sure I can add value. What specifically do you expect me to be able to contribute?*

When we created a training program for middle management on personal and leader effectiveness, we asked what caused employees the most frustration and wasted time.

The top two answers by a wide margin were too many emails and time-wasting meetings. I share here the secrets to holding effective meetings. You likely spend a significant part of your day attending meetings. Many of them will be unproductive.

Although meetings do not have to be a burden, changing your company's culture will take time. Start by setting a good example with the meetings you hold. If you are lucky, others will be so impressed that they will adopt your good habits for their own meetings.

## 10 Ways to Improve Your Meetings

### 1. Have an objective

Only schedule meetings when necessary. Don't have a meeting just because it's routine. Have a specific objective for every meeting. If you can't articulate a clear objective, you aren't ready for a meeting.

### 2. Use a goal-based agenda

Stick to a goal-based agenda for all meetings. Specify what you hope to achieve for each item on the agenda. Make a note of off-topic items raised during the meeting but don't let them derail the agenda.

### 3. Distribute material in advance

Meetings are more efficient if participants come prepared. Distribute the agenda and materials at least one day in advance and earlier if possible. Remember your colleagues all have other priorities.

### 4. Invite only necessary participants

Only invite participants who need to be there. You may decline meeting invitations if you will not add value. Ask the organizer to clarify your role if unclear.

### 5. Use cost-effective locations

Your meeting is not an excuse to travel to an exotic location. Unless the purpose of the meeting is pleasure, best to keep meetings and pleasure separate.

### 6. Use only time needed

Don't schedule 30- or 60-minute meetings just because that's what your calendar defaults to. Try scheduling 15- or 20-minute meetings instead.

Start meetings on time and end on time. If you accomplish your objectives early, end early.

## 7. Have proposals ready

Have proposals ready for decisions that need to be made at the meeting. Use the meeting time to discuss the proposals rather than the background so you can take action following the meeting.

## 8. Eliminate distractions and focus

Keep participants focused by asking them to put away phones and computers during the meeting — as needed, one person can take notes. Break every couple of hours to allow time for participants to respond to urgent calls.

## 9. Distribute notes and action items

Send notes and action items that come from the meeting promptly following the meeting.

These tips are powerful because people can implement them easily. You just have to want to do it and then be mindful of what you are doing. Thus, I will end with my final tip for holding effective meetings:

## 10. Don't send that invitation before reviewing your agenda and materials against this checklist

With practice, you will become skilled at making the most effective use of your colleagues' time. If you follow this checklist, you are much more likely to hold effective meetings that do not waste time.

But remember that the best meeting might be the one you never attended.

Be well.

Chapter Twenty

# Persuade Like Aristotle

## Part of the Master Skills series on how to crush your job with better communication — five ideas on the path to persuasion

If you want to know which students will become successful lawyers, it turns out the law school admissions test is not the best predictor. A few years ago professors Marjorie Schultz and Sheldon Zedeck identified 26 lawyer effectiveness factors that serve as better predictors of career success.

The whole list makes for interesting reading. Here I focus on one set of skills the professors grouped under the "Communications" heading:

- **Influencing and advocating**. Persuades others of position and wins support.

- **Writing**. Writes clearly, efficiently, and persuasively.

- **Speaking**. Orally communicates issues in an articulate matter consistent with the issue and audience being addressed.

- **Listening**. Accurately perceives what is being said both directly and subtly.

You can be well-liked, rigorous in your analysis, and correct in your conclusions. But inevitably, someone whose pay depends on disagreeing with you is going to challenge your views. It thus will come as no surprise to all of you working in the real world that being persuasive is pretty important.

With all this in mind, I was annoyed that no one told me the secret to effective persuasion is no secret at all. That, in fact, it has been known for over 2,000 years thanks to Aristotle's *Rhetoric*.

I spent the better part of 20 years watching, teasing out best practices, and honing my own skills at being the Gerry Spence of the boardroom.

## Time-tested advice with modern tweaks

One of the things I learned is that no matter how strong your persuasion skills, you can get better. Although I bet you're already pretty good, today I will give you a condensed version of time-tested advice on how to persuade, together with a few modern tweaks.

I personally put the lessons here into practice every time I have to teach or present. Here are five elements Aristotle believed were critical to effective persuasion,* to which I will add a few observations:

### 1. Ethos (Credibility)

Ethos is that part of your talk where you give the audience insight as to why you are credible. This can come by virtue of your position or from your specific experience.

I find you build credibility by never lying or shading the truth, even when it hurts your case. Admitting a weakness upfront is a great way to show you can be trusted.

It also helps to be transparent about your interests. People know you are representing a position, so go ahead and tell them what you want.

### 2. Logos (Appeal to reason)

Having set the stage about your credentials as a person, this is where you use facts and data to form a rational argument.

Everyone likes to think they are logical, rational thinkers. So help them see a clear path to your point of view. Think of it as a fact-based hook for people to hang their hat on, something that allows them to agree with you.

## 3. Pathos (Human emotion)

Notwithstanding what we just said about the appeal to reason, the most powerful persuasion is carried on the wings of emotion.

And the single best vehicle for arousing emotions is the story. The bulk of your presentation therefore comes in the form of storytelling. This doesn't have to be a fully-fledged plotline. You do well to call upon a simple anecdote or episode from your life.

## 4. Be tangible

Particularly when you are trying to get your audience to accept or understand a new idea, analogies and metaphors are great tools. They give the impression that the new thing is really just something the audience already understands. And they make otherwise abstract ideas tangible and vivid.

## 5. Be concise

People have short attention spans, now more than ever. Don't fight it. Instead, make your argument short and simple. Start strong and end strong.

In the business context, I assume your audience knows you and knows why you are there. Don't waste time and valuable attention on introductions, background, or other unimportant topics.

I say jump right into the heart of your story and grab the audience's curiosity. Storytelling is so important to persuasion that I start with it always, even when I have to take pains to later build credibility and the logical argument.

Practice your prepared remarks enough so that you can speak fluidly. Speak written remarks out loud at least once, even if only to yourself. This will help you catch awkward phrases that don't sound right.

Be animated, speak with energy, and show interest and enthusiasm in your subject. Your excitement shines through to your listeners. But don't let your enthusiasm carry you away. Speak clearly and pace yourself. Get a friend to point out your "ums" and "ahs" and similar empty words.

Watch your audience carefully for clues as to how you're doing. Help them keep the thread of your story by stepping back on significant transitions:

*This is where we are. I just discussed X, and now I am going to move on to Y.*

I hope the law and the facts will always be on your side. When they are not, you need to be the best persuader in the room. And that is more a matter of preparation than anything else.

I hope today's discussion arms you well for the battles ahead.

Be well.

* I was inspired to take up the discussion of Aristotle's Rhetoric by the HBR article The Art of Persuasion Hasn't Changed in 2,000 Years.

# Chapter Twenty-One

# Listen Up Already!

## Part of the Master Skills series on how to crush your job with better communication — active listening explained

When I teach law students about effective communication, I start by telling them the most important skill is none of what they're usually taught. It's not writing clearly or learning to be a great presenter. It is listening.

Teaching lawyers how to listen is surprisingly hard. It's hard because it seems trivial. Everyone in my classes thinks they already know how to do it. Ironic, isn't it, that the greatest barrier to learning how to listen is that people don't listen to the lesson?

For all the articles saying listening is important and giving advice about how to do it better, I find few digging into details about *why* listening is so important.

They'll say listening well builds trust, encourages openness, or shows respect. Listening does do these things but they're not the most important reason to listen well.

On a human level, we have a deep need to feel heard and be understood.

- Good listening builds a connection between you and the other person.
- That connection, in turn, allows both participants to engage in a conversation that tackles meaningful topics.
- We are far more likely to listen to someone whom we feel is listening to

us.

That's why if you want to be a great communicator, you need to create connections by listening.

## A good listener stands out

The great majority of modern interactions are superficial, fleeting, and of little consequence. In the work-from-home era, we're having fewer in-person conversations. Emails, social media, and Zoom calls punctuate our days.

Thus, when someone slows down and appears to be willing to take time for a deep conversation, it stands out.

The traditional advice for listening better is to practice what's called "**active listening**." First developed as a tool to help clinical psychologists be more effective counselors to their patients, active listening has become mainstream in the business context.

Unfortunately, the message got garbled in translation on the journey from psychology to business.

## Active listening tips

I say this because there seems to be no consistent description of how to practice active listening. Most systems suggest listeners follow these steps:

- Pay careful attention, listening to verbal and non-verbal cues.

- Do not be judgmental or criticize what the person is saying, simply listen openly.

- Think about what you hear and seek to clarify your understanding.

- Repeat back what you heard and ask the person to confirm if it is correct.

Probably the biggest difference between active listening and what normally passes for conversation is the focus on the initial speaker.

As the listener, you do not seek to introduce any new thoughts or ideas until you have luxuriated in the first person's thoughts. Explore their topic, look at it from multiple angles, and make sure you have really given their thoughts proper air time.

You may never get to raise your own thoughts because, after all, this is about listening to the other person.

Contrast this with a normal conversation, which is you waiting for the other person to take a breath and stop blathering so you can get a word in edgewise.

Turns out, however, that the advice for clinical psychologists on listening to patients doesn't transfer perfectly to the business world.

## Active listening in business

When we evaluate who is the most effective listener in the business context, we want something different:

- Paying attention does not mean silently listening. The best listeners ask constructive questions. This demonstrates that they are following along and understand what the speaker is saying.

- Withholding judgment is not enough. Effective listeners give positive feedback that encourages the speaker to be open. They do not necessarily agree with everything the speaker says, but nor are they trying to win a debate.

- A good listener also gives suggestions that make the conversation flow back and forth. They serve as a sounding board for the speaker's ideas and help develop and improve them.

I usually end these Master Skills articles by urging you to follow the checklist of steps I've outlined. I won't do that here. Indeed, my advice for you is not to get hung up about whether you're actively listening or exactly what steps to follow.

While I hope the tips above inspire you to try some new things out, a single step will make you stand out as a super-listener: simply paying attention and focusing on the other person without immediately trying to introduce your own point.

Because listening is becoming a lost art, people will notice when you really pay attention to them.

Be well.

Chapter Twenty-Two

# What Lawyers Can Teach Us About Writing Well

## Writing in plain language is a pleasure

Your readers love it when you write in plain language. Plain language means text they understand on the first reading.

Bryan Garner is a towering figure in the legal world. He's written many books on how to write persuasively and clearly. But his wise words are known mostly to lawyers.

I share the best of his plain English writing tips here. These are taken from his book *Legal Writing in Plain English*. I think you'll agree his tips can make us all better writers.

**Framing your thoughts: The most productive hour**

Have something to say — and think it through. Of all the things you might mention, what are the most important points? Practice leaving out everything that doesn't help you make your point.

Plan your writing projects in a four-step process, and keep the steps *separate*:

    1. Brainstorm lots of things you want to say (10 minutes)

    2. Outline a sensible order for those thoughts (5 minutes)

    3. Using the outline, write a quick draft (25 minutes)

4. Edit your draft (10 minutes).

## Organize your material

Order your material in a logical sequence and keep related material together. Divide your document into sections and use informative headings.

- Headings and subheadings help you organize your thoughts
- They make it easier for your readers to follow your argument
- They make your text skimmable
- They signal transitions
- They provide a road map when collected into a table of contents

## Crafting sentences

Omit needless words. This enhances your clarity, makes readers faster, and gives your writing impact. You will struggle to write concisely at first. You can fix this in editing.

Keep your average sentence length to about 20 words. But also use variety, i.e. some longer and some shorter sentences.

Keep the subject, verb, and object together at the beginning of the sentence. This is how we think. When we read a sentence, we're looking for the action.

Prefer the active voice over the passive. If you're active, you do things. If you're passive, things are done to you. The active voice brings you several advantages:

1. It usually requires fewer words
2. It better reflects chronological sequences
3. It makes the reader's job easier
4. It makes your writing more vigorous and lively

End your sentences emphatically, with a kick. What you end with you emphasize. Choose wisely.

## Choosing words

Root out jargon that you can simplify.

Use strong verbs. Minimize is, are, was, and were. Turn — ion words into verbs when you can.

Simplify wordy phrases. Watch out for "of." Can you kill half of them?

Make everything you write speakable. It's OK to use contractions. Readers like the sense that a writer is talking directly to them.

Be well.

Chapter Twenty-Three

# What the Government Can Teach Us About Writing Well

Writing in plain language is a pleasure

Your readers love it when you write in plain language. Plain language means text they understand on the first reading. I summarize here the key points from the best government guidance on writing.

"Wait, did you say the *best government* guidance? I thought governments were terrible at communicating clearly." That's normally true, but they've been working hard to get better.

President Obama signed The Plain Writing Act of 2010. It requires U.S. federal agencies to communicate clearly in a way that the public can understand.

The government prepared guidelines to help agencies write better, and it is those guidelines that I summarize for you today. I think you'll agree they can make us all better writers.

### Write for your audience

Writing for your audience means using language your audience understands and feels comfortable with. What is their current level of knowledge and expertise?

Put yourself in your reader's shoes and provide them with only what they need to know. What are they trying to accomplish? How does your writing help them? This includes anticipating what questions your reader will have.

Address the user: write as if you are speaking with one person. Use personal pronouns like "we" and "you." More than any other single technique, using personal pronouns like "you" pulls users into the information and makes it relevant to them.

## Organize the information

Make your writing easy to follow. Organize material in a logical order.

- Put the most important information at the beginning. Include necessary background information towards the end.
- Similarly, put general information first, and specialized information or exceptions later.
- Consider likely questions.

Use a table of contents for longer documents. Add useful headings to guide the reader through your document. Make your headings descriptive and informative.

Lists make it easier to see all the steps in a process. Use a lead-in sentence to explain your list.

## Choose your words carefully

Use simple words and phrases. Choose simple expressions over complicated ones.

- Avoid jargon and legalese.
- Minimize abbreviations and definitions.
- Avoid hidden verbs, which are verbs converted into nouns.

## Be concise

Write short sentences and break up longer sentences into smaller units.

Keep the subject, verb, and object close together.

- Don't put modifiers between these parts.
- Put modifiers at the end of the sentence or in a new sentence.

Check your prepositions, such as "of," "on," and "to." They often mark phrases you can shorten.

## Keep your writing conversational

Use the active voice. Specify who is performing the action.

## Design for reading

Use an easy-to-read font, like Times New Roman.

Put your headings in bold text and use uppercase and lowercase letters, not all caps.

Use standard bullets, and not more than two types.

Highlight important concepts using **bold** and *italics*.

Use tables for complex material

Take a fresh look at your document when you are done.

- Is it easy to follow?
- Is it visually appealing?

Be well.

Chapter Twenty-Four

# Two Editing Checklists May Save Your Story

## Writing well is hard. Editing well is easy

Your readers love it when you write in plain language. Plain language means text they understand on the first reading.

Here are simple editing tips originally developed for lawyers to write in plain language. You'll probably agree lawyers need the help. More importantly, these tips can help all of us write better.

**Checklist of Basic Edits**

1. Check punctuation, misused words, spelling, etc.

2. Convert the passive voice into the active voice

3. Use stronger verbs in place of "be" words (is, are, was, were, be, been)

4. Change words ending in — ion to verbs where you can

5. Check every "of" to see if can be rephrased to eliminate it

6. Try to cut each sentence by 25% or more

7. Read your work aloud. Does it read naturally?

If you want to advance to masterclass level, particularly for longer pieces with multiple points, apply these advanced editing tips.

## Checklist of Advanced Edits

1. Have you achieved the tone you wanted?

2. Does your central point emerge clearly and quickly?

3. Is there a strong counterargument you haven't addressed?

4. Can you spot a bridge at the outset of each paragraph?

5. For each block quotation, have you supplied an informative lead-in?

6. Can you phrase your points more memorably? Should you use bullets instead?

7. Have you kept citations out of the main text? Doing so improves readability. You should always cite sources but use footnotes or endnotes instead.

Be well.

N.B. – Inspired by *Legal Writing in Plain English* by Bryan Garner.

## Chapter Twenty-Five

# Breaking News: Lawyer Settles Oxford Comma Debate

### It's not a question of style or personal preference. A simple rule of thumb to avoid exposing yourself to needless risk

If you have an opinion about the Oxford comma, let it be an informed opinion.

I am informed that people have been fighting about it since The University of Oxford was founded in the 12th century, a full three centuries before the comma itself was even invented.

More recently, I spent 25 years writing and reviewing SEC filings.

- When companies make a mistake in these public documents they face legal liability.
- Expensive lawyers like me thus spend hours checking every sentence to ensure companies' disclosures are clear.
- This work taught me more than I ever wanted about the Oxford comma.

Here's my simple rule of thumb about the Oxford comma that you are free to use yourself:

If you are a corporate lawyer writing SEC disclosure documents, use the Oxford comma or risk getting sued for malpractice.

## What's the fuss about the Oxford comma?

Simply put, when you list three or more items in a sentence, people debate including a comma (the Oxford comma) before the last item. They argue it changes the style of your writing and the look of your sentence.

People who did not go to law school lose sleep worrying about all the ink needlessly spilled when using a comma in sentences where it may be plausibly omitted.

"Think of the children!" they cry.

## Is there a difference between using it or not?

The truth about the Oxford comma is that it's much more than stylistic. That's because the comma serves a specific purpose. And the clauses mean very different things when you use the comma or omit it.

When a sentence is ambiguous or its meaning is disputed, judges apply simple rules of construction (i.e. interpretation) to resolve the dispute:

- When you include the comma, it means you are describing a list of three or more distinct items.

- When you do not include the comma, it means the final two items in the list are examples of the previous item on the list.

## What if I'm not a corporate lawyer writing SEC documents?

I feel sorry for you. The next best thing is to imply to others that you do important stuff for a living.

How? You signal your importance to the cognoscenti by punctiliously using the Oxford comma.

If small-minded people challenge you, I recommend adopting a superior tone and explaining that there are at least two reasons to use the Oxford comma.

- First, you eliminate potential ambiguity when you include the comma. That alone is reason enough to use the comma and should satisfy most doubters.

- If the person insists on hearing your second reason, tell them this. In the large majority of cases, you are in fact describing a list of distinct items. Only rarely are you modifying the prior item in your list with examples.

True, you're probably not facing millions of dollars in legal exposure by skipping a comma. But can you really afford to take the risk?

Be well.

# Chapter Twenty-Six

# If You Scheduled Your Day Like an Airline

## If you let your aim point downwards, even a little bit, don't be surprised if you end up in places you don't want to be

Well, that didn't take long. No sooner are we back to business travel than the airlines remind us why flying is so maddening.

To illustrate, let's assume your boss has started scheduling meetings the way airlines schedule their flights. How would that look?

Boss's Assistant: *"Oh hi, Peony. I'm calling about your request for a meeting with Gorgon."*

You: *"Great, thank you, Agonia! We have a big decision coming up, and I need Gorgon's input. How does next week look?"*

*"Ha, ha, ha! You're so cute. Let's see, I have some availability in three months' time."*

*"What, really? I need only a few minutes of Gorgon's time. Isn't there an earlier time available?"*

Heavy sigh. *"Well, there is a slot in two weeks, but ... ."*

*"I'll take it. I really need to talk with Gorgon."*

*"I'll send you an invite. Bye Peony."*

## A few days before the meeting

*"Hello Agonia. I'm calling about the meeting invite you sent for the 10th."*

*"Yes. Do you have the meeting reference number?"*

*"What? Er, it's the meeting with Gorgon starting at 3 pm on the 10th."*

*"I need the reference number. We categorize Gorgon's meetings by reference number. It's clearly listed in your meeting reservation."*

*"Oh, that's new, hold on, let me look … Agonia?"* Calling back *"Hi there, Agonia. We got disconnected somehow."*

*"What can I do for you Peony?"*

*"I found the meeting number. It's C&xD*çRiuP."*

*"Sorry, I don't have any meeting scheduled with that number."*

You, repeating number: *"Wait, is that a ?"*

*"I have it. What can I help you with?"*

*"Well, I'm a little confused. It says here my meeting lasts for two hours. I only need 20 or 30 minutes at most."*

*"Gorgon is keen on making efficient use of employees' time. The last thing he wants is for you to be late for your next meeting. Best to stick with this schedule, because then you can be sure to finish on time."*

*"I guess so, but I'm not sure how that makes efficient use of my time. Anyway, never mind that. The meeting invite says I should come to Gorgon's office at 1 pm already. That's two hours before the meeting starts!"*

*"Yes, and be happy you're not visiting from one of the international offices. International employees have to come three hours before their meeting is scheduled to start."*

*"But why?!"*

*"Well, we also want to make efficient use of Gorgon's time. Once an employee came five minutes late to a meeting, and it threw off Gorgon's schedule for the whole*

morning. We never wanted that to happen again, so now we require employees to come two hours early to make sure the meeting will start on time."

Muttering under your breath. *"What's this about checking my meeting readiness the day before the meeting?"*

*"Gorgon just wants to make sure you're ready for the meeting. It helps if you send everything in advance, including your slides, the project charter, the names of the other executives involved, and the meeting minutes."*

*"But I don't have any of that! I just need to talk with Gorgon for a few minutes to get some input. He knows what this is about."*

*"If you'd like, I can reschedule the meeting for a later time when you'll be ready ... ?"*

*"No, no! I guess I can send something in advance. Let's just leave it."*

## The day of the meeting

Arriving on the executive floor, you see a line of faces standing in the hallway outside Gorgon's office. You recognize two colleagues.

*"Sade, Maddie! What are you doing here in the hallway?"*

Maddie: *"Waiting for our meeting with Gorgon. Mine was scheduled for noon, but he's running behind again."*

Sade: *"Ours was yesterday afternoon, but that got cancelled. Technical problems or something."*

Recalling that you saw Gorgon leaving at 3 pm yesterday with golf clubs, you say: *"Oh, sorry to hear that. Who are all these other people? And why are you all in the hallway?"*

Maddie: *"Agonia only lets us in at the time our meeting starts. We used to be able to wait in her office, but once someone talked too loudly on their cell phone, so now we only get to go in once our meeting is called."*

*"Gosh, it's not so comfortable out here. I'll just sit on the floor over here and try to get some work done."*

## Two hours later

*"Peony? Time for your meeting."*

You, getting to your feet and whispering to yourself, *"Finally!"*

*"Come on in. We pride ourselves in making sure Gorgon's meetings start on time. Take a seat along this wall. We put in an extension cord so you can charge your laptop while you wait. Not sure it's working after someone spilled water on it, but it's the thought that counts, right?"*

You, noticing that most of the people who were waiting in the hallway are now waiting in Agonia's office. *"Agonia, I thought my meeting was starting."*

*"Your meeting did start, dear. It's just that you won't see Gorgon for a little while yet because of congestion from earlier meetings. I'll give you an update on the schedule as soon as I know more."*

You, thinking to yourself, *"I'm so glad I brought my power bank today."*

Two further hours go by. It is now a little after 5 pm.

*"Peony, Gorgon will see you now, quickly, hurry."*

You, grabbing your things and rushing into Gorgon's office. *"Gorgon, hi. I'll keep this brief. I put everything you asked for in the slides and summary memo. I recommend we go with Option A, although Option B would cost us 10 percent less."*

Gorgon, looking blank. *"I don't think I saw your summary. Maybe you can send it by email, and also drop off a hard copy with Agonia. I've been really busy."*

You, looking at Gorgon's spotless desk and empty office, are at a loss for words.

*"Anyway, I'm running a bit behind today, so if there's nothing else ... ."*

Agonia enters. *"Come along Peony. Look at that will you, we started on time and finished on time, as promised! We are keeping up our perfect track record."*

You, unable to help yourself, *"Agonia, I got here two hours early, waited in your office for two more hours, and now we finished 15 minutes late. How is that on time?"*

"Well Gorgon is so busy, we agreed with the CEO that any meeting that starts and ends within 15 minutes of its scheduled time will count as an on-time meeting. Isn't that wonderful!"

"What? Wait, why are we going out this back door to the fire escape? I left my coat in your office."

"Oh, just come by again tomorrow to pick it up. We found that it was confusing to have people coming and going from the same door, so now we have departing attendees leave this way."

"But security only lets people onto the executive floor if they have a scheduled meeting! I need my coat."

"Your meeting invite did say to keep your belongings with you at all times, Peony. But don't worry, schedule another meeting and I'm sure everything will be fine."

People can get used to almost anything if it is presented in small steps. It is only by looking back at the cumulative effect of many small changes that we realize how far we've come.

We often don't realize how many aspects of our lives are affected by this. Prices raised a few percent at a time, the amount included in a package shrunk ever so slightly, and online terms are just a bit less favorable with each revision.

If you let your aim point downwards, even a little bit, don't be surprised if you end up in places you don't want to be.

This is the flip side of continuous improvement, where small positive changes made steadily over time lead to impressive results. Let's call it dissolution by degree.

Pay attention to what you accept in your performance.

It may be too late for airlines, but it's not too late for us as we manage our careers.

Be well.

Chapter Twenty-Seven

# How to Spot a Bad Lawyer

## The rule of law must benefit everyone equally or it is meaningless. And the time for us to be especially wary is when we feel most strongly about a cause

The comedians among the public are itching to answer something like: "Did they graduate from a law school?" Or: "Are they admitted to practice law?" Lawyer jokes are rampant because lawyers, sadly, live up to and exceed the public's worst expectations of us.

I'm thinking beyond sleazy personal injury lawyers and slithery prosecutors. I will explore with you here how we feel at heart about one of the hardest legal duties: Staying objective in difficult circumstances and upholding the rule of law.

**The law is supposed to apply equally to us all**

We learn in school about the rule of law and how preserving it is vital to maintaining a democratic society. We tell ourselves we operate in nations of laws, not nations of individuals, where laws apply equally to all.

So what is a lawyer to do when the facts point one way and the law another, when our potential client is truly odious, or when our personal beliefs go against what the law dictates? The answer is clear, at least for a law student, but in practice, lawyers' behavior is anything but.

Let's take a few examples to illustrate.

Let's say you work for a famous civil rights organization, dedicated to defending free speech. Does it matter whether you only take cases from people whose speech you agree with?

- In the era of Trump-inspired lies, what if you refused to defend someone's right to free speech specifically because you disagreed with their viewpoints? Well, you wouldn't be much of a defender of free speech, would you? That's precisely the position the ACLU finds itself in today.

Now consider Harvey Weinstein, a deeply unsympathetic person. Accused of forcing himself on a string of vulnerable women, he is what comes to mind under the definition of "odious client." But does a client's unpopularity justify refusing him a defense? In today's charged atmosphere, many otherwise serious people think it does.

- Harvard University law professor Ronald Sullivan came under intense criticism for agreeing to serve on Weinstein's defense team, with Harvard firing him as faculty dean of an undergraduate house. (Sullivan ultimately withdrew from the defense team.)

- One commentator at the time wrote, "The reason we think of civil rights lawyers as doing 'good work' is because they chose just causes." (Nathan J. Robinson, Lawyers are Responsible for their Choice of Clients)

**Nothing could be more wrong**. In its heyday, the ACLU defended the KKK and was proud to defend pornographers. The good work is defending the rule of law, not whatever cause happens to have majority approval at that moment in time.

Now imagine you are a judge.

- If plaintiffs' and defendants' lawyers get carried away at times, we can chalk it up to our desire to be zealous advocates for our clients.

- The judge has no such excuse or expectation. Among all lawyers, we expect judges to be the most impartial, literally and figuratively above it all. At its most fundamental level, our courts determine the very validity of our laws.

## What happens when judges take it personally?

What then would you say about a judge who decides a case because she identifies with one side more than the other, or has strong personal feelings about the morality and not legality of conduct?

What would you say about a judge who can be counted to vote in line with their racial or gender preferences, or their political affiliation, no matter the law? These are all easy questions.

- The lawyer who defends only free speech for those he agrees with?
- The lawyer who refuses any objectionable clients?
- The judge who decides cases by personal feeling and party affiliation?

Bad lawyers all. Bad because they undermine the rule of law for nothing more than fickle emotion and public sentiment.

I had these thoughts when seeing the uproar over the leaked US Supreme Court draft opinion overturning *Roe vs. Wade*. By the way, the leaker themselves: Bad lawyer, for the same reason that they undermine the rule of law.

Is the benefit of putting pressure on a Supreme Court justice in any case worth undermining the legitimacy of the entire court?

## Be careful what you expect of your lawyer

What does it say about us and the rule of law that we think it matters who nominates our Supreme Court justices or what their political affiliation might be? Or that their skin color, gender, or ethnic background, is even part of the discussion?

Bad lawyers these days are sadly easy to spot. Let's make an effort not to join their ranks.

The way to do this is to remember the rule of law must benefit everyone equally or it is meaningless. And the time for us to be especially wary is when we feel most strongly about a cause.

Be well.

Chapter Twenty-Eight

# How In-house Counsel Reinforce the Rule of Law

## We must support freedom of expression, which includes dissenting opinions

In-house counsel are quick to agree to the principle that all people and institutions should be subject to laws that are fairly administered. We are vital links in defending the rule of law because it falls to us to adopt policies and enforce them fairly.

In practice, this means that we must apply the rules equally to everyone, regardless of their performance or position in the company. It means we respect employees' fundamental rights, including the right to privacy, freedom of expression, and due process.

Throughout history individuals worried most about intrusion by governments because they held asymmetrical power over citizens. Today, corporations play a much greater role in enhancing, or weakening, the rule of law.

Consider the following examples. As a condition to selling their product in a local market, a company may be asked to:

- Provide a version of their product that gives a government back-door access rights to private communications in their country.

- Allow governments to prevent certain groups from using the platform at all, or from discussing certain topics on the platform.

- Comply with government requests to censor disfavored individuals and limit the spread of their ideas.

A company's own employees may also create pressure on management and in-house counsel. For example, employees may demand the company cease doing legal business with disfavored customers. Employees may expect the CEO to make a public statement on controversial topics, which is guaranteed to alienate potential customers either way.

What's our fiduciary duty as in-house counsel when our companies come under government pressure or employee pressure?

## Censorship and cancellation requests

Here I'll focus on just one particularly harmful practice: Requests to suppress disfavored speech and to promote only consensus narratives. Whether on controversial topics or from controversial actors, how should in-house counsel respond to censorship or cancellation requests?

Giving in to these requests can seem like the path of least resistance. When we consider the effect our actions have on the rule of law, however, our choice becomes clearer: We must support freedom of expression, which includes dissenting opinions.

Here is a pledge you can commit to in defending freedom of expression within your company. If you follow these steps, you will be leading by example.

From this point forward, we will:

- Only say things in public and in private that we believe to be true, and will resist speech being forced upon us by protestors, employees, or the government;

- Not support isolated examples of someone's speech or thoughts can be used as an excuse to silence a person whose ideas challenge the orthodoxy; and

- Not participate in any training, lecture, or speech where the speaker promotes policies that divide us on the basis of immutable characteristics like skin color.

This is just a partial list of ways for you to reinforce freedom of expression. If you start to follow these habits, you will no doubt apply them well in additional settings.

Your resistance will be met with resistance, and some will fall prey to the ravages of the mob and be canceled. **There is no exception to upholding the rule of law.**

## Hold fast to the rule of law

No matter your position, no matter your political leaning, no matter your past support, you will be confronted with the choice to give in to cancellation requests. Your decision shapes your character each time and helps set your company's fate.

Even this simple step of holding fast to the rule of law is hard if you have become used to going along to get along. But holding fast is not as hard as the alternative that awaits if we give in too often.

Holding fast to the rule of law is not an easy path, but it is the least difficult of all other alternatives. Already today there are those demonstrating what it means to stick to their principles. Join your voices to theirs and neither of you stands alone!

The more people that embrace the evenhanded application of the rule of law, the quicker we will put an end to the tyranny of the cancellers. If we are not one or two, but hundreds or thousands, their power will evaporate.

Be well.

Chapter Twenty-Nine

# When the Best Course of Action is Inaction

By spending precious resources to improperly or only partially deal with problems, we can easily make things worse

Have you noticed there is an incredible bias toward action at work? Just consider what happens when we identify a problem. The single correct response is to craft a solution. We are so motivated to do something, anything, that we overlook one of nature's great problem-solvers: Doing nothing.

This is no paean to procrastination for the sake of being lazy. No, let me tell you why our desire to intervene, to meddle, and to change things is so often counterproductive. In brief, it's because crafting effective solutions to real problems is hard. By spending precious resources to improperly or only partially deal with problems, we can easily make things worse.

Our desire to tackle problems is admirable. We should celebrate the mindset that says "We can do this," and does not shy away from hard work. But let us not mistake good intentions for good outcomes. Just because we have our hearts in the right place, we get no free pass from accountability for results.

**Practical and pragmatic**

I had these thoughts after writing an article about how often government spending to achieve societal outcomes not only fails to achieve the desired outcome but rather worsens the very situation politicians want to improve.

Although the desirability of the policy objective cannot justify failed policies, it is depressing how often we hear only about the goals and never about the results.

Now to be fair, I thought it would be appropriate to shine the spotlight instead on corporations. How well do we do in solving the problems we set out to tackle? I admit I'm biased when I say that I believe corporations are pretty good at solving problems, at least compared to governments.

One key reason for better business performance is that we have skin in the game. That is, we're spending our own money, and we can't print more when we need it. This means we are more attuned to prioritizing solutions that may be practical and pragmatic, and much more wary of waste.

## Pausing and problem-solving

But that's not to say companies are perfect at solving problems, are we? I explained several reasons why employees in corporations also fail to solve problems well in the earlier chapters Identifying Problems Worth Working On and Identifying Solutions That Will Work.

I recommend you have another look at these chapters before we get too confident about our problem-solving abilities.

- In short, we are distracted by pressing but non-strategic problems, which means we waste our time.

- And we underestimate how hard it is to implement good solutions by failing to account for the full costs our solution requires and the world's stubborn resistance to change.

Now let's consider what happens when we pause instead of jumping immediately into implementing solutions. The pause gives us precious time to spend thinking about our problem.

By considering my earlier advice about how to both choose problems worth solving and design solutions most likely to succeed, we increase the odds we can craft a better solution than if we jumped in with well-meant but misguided action.

And here's something else to keep in mind about waiting. When you wait you will be amazed how often your problem turns into something different than it first appeared. Sometimes what looked like a massive problem turns out to be just a few anecdotes that got blown out of proportion.

Because humans are such great pattern-recognition machines, we see connections where none exist. My favorite problems were the ones that simply evaporated when we left them alone. This happened often.

## Sitting with the problem

Or maybe you realize upon reflection that what looked like the root cause of the problem isn't the only cause or even the main one. Difficult problems typically have multiple causes, and focusing too quickly on one increases the likelihood your solution will be partially effective at best.

When you give yourself time to sit with a problem, you can spend some time thinking about the foreseeable but unintended consequences of any proposed actions. Is what you want to do entirely consistent with your company's values? Could someone seeing only part of the problem or part of the solution reasonably misunderstand or criticize your actions?

The pause also provides you time to conduct a pre-mortem, in which you forecast the future and brainstorm all the ways your solution could fail to address the problem. Anticipating why your solution may fail is so helpful to good problem-solving that you should never embark on a costly solution without first wallowing in its likely failure.

For all these reasons, I say the next time you're facing a problem at work, take a deep breath and ... do nothing, at least for a while.

And if anyone asks why you're not doing something, tell them you're doing the hardest thing: thinking.

Be well.

## Chapter Thirty

# If We Are What We Eat, Be Worried

## We seem indifferent to the impact of the ideas we consume because we assume we can control what we think

Most people believe they are directly affected by the food they eat. Hence the successive panics resulting in regulating various components of and micronutrients in food: salt, fat, sugar, lactose, gluten, genetically modified organisms (GMOs), hormones, and much more.

It's as if we assume our body is just a physical machine, and so the food we put into our body is going to have a clear impact on how the machine works. It's just chemistry!

In contrast, people act as if their mental processes have a master governor overseeing everything in the form of our minds or consciousness. As a result, we seem indifferent to the impact of the ideas we consume because we assume we can control what we think.

Consider how badly nutrition science has performed in understanding how our bodies operate — mere machines.

- The consuming public suffered repeated gross errors from scientists underestimating the body's complexity.
- By focusing on just a small piece in a carefully controlled lab environment, they thought they could explain the whole system and failed badly.

Is it possible we have similarly underestimated the mind's complexity?

Maybe there's more going on in our heads than the conductor in our consciousness we imagine is carefully and logically orchestrating our lives. Why is the prevalence of mental illness among adults higher than it's ever been? Why are more children depressed than ever before?

Can we say anything about how the mind works and how people come to form their ideas? In some ways, psychology has been much more successful than nutrition. If we still cannot say exactly what we should eat to maintain a healthy weight, we have learned a lot about how to influence and manipulate people.

## We're affected by propaganda

The science of propaganda has a long and dark history, but that's because it works and repeatedly has been put to nefarious purposes. Here's an excerpt from a foundational 1930 text:

> ... Propaganda means an effort deliberately to manufacture popular opinions and attitudes and thus to control popular conduct; and usually the implication is that the aims of the propagandists are concealed. The objects of propaganda do not know the purposes of the makers of the propaganda. Propaganda then is the propagation of ideas, opinions and attitudes, the real purpose of which is not made clear to the hearer or reader. – Social Psychology: An Analysis of Social Behavior, Kimball Young

I've been thinking recently about the prevalence of propaganda in the West. We are by no means exempt from people trying to deliberately manufacture popular opinions and attitudes. In some ways, because of our democratic systems, we are even more routinely subject to such campaigns.

Our politicians gain power in part by detecting the winds of popular opinion and then riding along, but also in part by seeking to shape popular opinion in ways they think will be to their advantage.

Every time you hear a complex topic reduced to a catchy slogan you are being propagandized. It happens to us so frequently that we scarcely notice.

Look at how any significant legislation is described by both sides in a debate. You will see almost no substantive discussion of the actual law because laws are complex and it takes time to discuss them accurately. Instead, you see a scramble to label the law with a slogan that the media will then repeat.

## When smart, educated people ignore facts

Since I retired, I've been traveling around and meeting with people across the country. I'll tell you what's both shocked and frightened me. Not that people have different ideas and beliefs on hot-button topics. That's to be expected.

It's rather that people I know to be smart and assumed to be well-informed had obvious and serious gaps in their basic information. They held opinions in good faith but were acting without all the facts.

I don't want to give specific examples of my conversations, because I would send a number of you into cognitive dissonance. That is, you'd say, "I never heard of that. What's James talking about? I know my sources are good. He must be crazy." And you'd dismiss my whole argument as flawed.

It's easy, though, for you to recall times when someone — a clueless someone — disagreed with you on a basic point. They were so obviously wrong: They either ignored facts or simply didn't know fundamental things. That's what I'm talking about.

## How much can we control what we think?

Come back now to your faith in the idea that you have a mental governor (or mind or consciousness) that regulates how you think about the world.

You can consume any media and make up your own mind about what your values and beliefs are, right? Well, if that's so, how do you explain the wide disparity in what your fellow citizens believe? Surely you don't think their minds work fundamentally differently than yours.

Not to stretch the analogy, but there is every reason to believe modern media is feeding us a diet of junk food. Blatant propaganda that, because we're force-fed it, we come to accept.

- Much of what we think we know is wrong.

- People are missing vital nutrients from their diet of information and ideas.

- As a result, we don't know what we don't know.

Is there any solution to this problem? I am not sure. My advice is to keep an open mind to the idea that you may be misinformed. Be less sure about what you think you know.

Allow for the possibility that you cannot so easily control what you think and that you may be influenced by what you consume. That chances are good none of our media is impartial, even though I know you think yours is.

If we are being propagandized, even a little, remember that consuming poison is never going to make us healthy.

Be well.

Chapter Thirty-One

# How Being Humble Can Help You Be Wrong Less Often

## A person can be smart, well-intentioned, and sincere while also being dangerously wrong

Let me teach you how to disagree with yourself. That is, if you want to improve the quality of your thinking and decision-making. One way to do so is to regularly challenge your thinking.

I assume no one wants to fail at what they set out to do. I also understand that few people like to be reminded of their failures. But, if by studying our failures we can improve our odds of future success, I say the study is well worth the discomfort.

Even better, when we get into the habit of considering what could go wrong before we act, we can improve our odds of future success without having to first personally experience failure. In this chapter, I explore how being humble can lead us to make better decisions.

### Shooting from the hip is for the foolhardy

Johnny Mercer wrote the lyrics in 1940 to what could be the unofficial decision-maker's anthem: Fools Rush In (Where Angels Fear to Tread).

But I prefer the earlier formulation by Alexander Pope in An Essay on Criticism:

*Foolish people are often reckless, attempting feats that the wise avoid.*

(N.B. This could also serve as the rallying cry for every technical writer preparing warning labels for consumer goods products.)

While avoiding reckless behavior is a worthy goal, inaction is no answer. To make progress in business, relationships, and life, we must act.

I recall our CEO frequently exhorting us to have a "bias for action." Analyze as necessary, but make sure not to be paralyzed by wanting to perfect your analysis. Sooner than you feel ready, plan to take concrete action. Even if the original plan is not perfect, we can also make corrections while we're implementing it.

The ideal mix of analysis and action comes about when we plan to increase our odds of success while simultaneously contemplating how our plans could be frustrated. That is, identifying what are the things that could go wrong and derail us.

Planning for success while also contemplating failure is not intuitive, and most people can't do it reliably. In my experience, we like to focus on the pleasant daydreams of success rather than the ways we might flop.

Daydreaming of success is necessary and healthy, to a point. Taken too far, we risk falling into cognitive dissonance.

We fall in love with our plan and see all the ways that it will be great. But then we tend to filter new information to fit our view of the world. We easily disregard contrary indications and ignore warning signs.

We have two potential countermeasures to this blindness:

## 1. Conduct a pre-mortem

When working alone, we can ensure our personal project plans include a "pre-mortem" step. It's usually helpful to do this sometime after starting your planning, but before you get too near the end. Say halfway through your planning as a good rule of thumb.

The purpose of the pre-mortem is to daydream again, but this time you imagine all the ways your project could be frustrated. Nothing goes according to plan. Why is that?

Be broad in spinning out your disaster scenarios and try to come up with a lengthy list. Only once you've prepared a good list, rank your future obstacles in terms of likelihood, magnitude, and addressability.

- Focus some of your planning attention on more likely risks of consequence that you can pragmatically do something about.

- Ignore small risks, unlikely risks, and risks that you cannot reasonably plan around.

- But be creative in considering potential mitigation before dismissing a risk as too hard to plan around. Even if you can't think of a solution, if the risk is real and not unlikely, you might get some advice from others before moving on.

## 2. Make sure to invite a spoiler to the team

Our second countermeasure is available when we are working in teams: Assign a person specifically to think of the various spoiler scenarios while the rest of the team does its work.

When the spoiler has a good list, bring the team together for a brainstorming session. This serves to review and expand the list and then discuss possible countermeasures.

The benefits of the pre-mortem review go beyond identifying weaknesses and improving your plan. A good pre-mortem includes asking *"How will we know* if things are starting to go badly? What types of information will we collect, and who will review it?" This helps shield you from ignoring negative data after you've started to implement your plan.

## We improve our vision by remembering our fallibility

We humans value the things we invest time and effort into. The harder you and your team work on a project, the more difficult it is for you to objectively identify and assess warning signs.

Knowing this, you can get help from people who are close to, but not directly involved in, your project. Have them monitor the data and assess for you whether you are on track or need to correct course.

A person can be smart, well-intentioned, and sincere while also being dangerously wrong. Relying on your good intentions to confirm the validity of your actions is risky indeed.

One way to improve our chances of being wrong less often is to be humbler.

When planning our initiatives and implementing them, use the pre-mortem process to identify how our plans might go awry. This includes designing processes for collecting good data, objectively reviewing that data, and adjusting course if results aren't coming in as hoped.

Doing so is no guarantee against being a fool rushing in, attempting feats the wise avoid, but it will make you more effective than most.

Be well.

# Chapter Thirty-Two

# Disagree Without Being Disagreeable

Ideas spread and become influential because they win over new adherents. If you want your ideas to gain traction you must expose them to people who do not yet agree with you

Because I believe continuous improvement principles can aid us in many areas, I am always looking for opportunities to do better. A good indication for such an opportunity is when I've had a setback or failure. My natural instinct is now to say, "Well, that sucked. How can I do better next time?"

Treating a painful experience as an opportunity for learning is useful for multiple reasons. It helps you get over the sting of disappointment, because you hope to learn something new. It keeps you focused on the future and away from dwelling on past mistakes. And you often do learn how to perform better, which helps you get better over time.

This is by way of introducing a change I've noticed in how people interact: People are emotional train wrecks, and many don't know how to have a civil discussion. When it comes to any topic people feel strongly about, rational and reasoned discussion is rare. Emotions drive the rules of engagement and emotions often carry the day.

Why is this hard for me? After all, I know from my psychology studies that humans are ruled more by emotions than reason, and that we all justify our emotional decisions with supposed reasons after the fact. I think it's due to my further education in law and business, and then a couple decades working as a business lawyer. This made me a rationalist to the core.

That means I like to discuss and agree on premises, apply logical reasoning, and explore reasonable conclusions, of which there may be more than one. There are almost always pros and cons, and costs and tradeoffs associated with every proposed solution.

Being a rationalist also means I often change my mind. Maybe I learn new facts, or the other person raises an argument I hadn't considered. Sometimes I take the opposite side of an argument just to make sure I understand it correctly. I try to be only weakly committed to my starting position.

This process worked well not just with like-minded business colleagues, but also with negotiation partners and opposing counsel. It was rare for someone to take a business discussion intensely personally, or to view an exploratory sally as anything other than a discussion.

Thus, I am still struggling with the fact that, increasingly, reasoned discussion is no way to win an argument, and introducing nuance is like bringing a skunk to a garden party. No one wants to see it, and if you try to stick it under their nose they shy away.

If my habitual method of expounding logical positions is ill-suited to discussing issues, I can tell you another method that doesn't work well: What everyone else is doing, namely giving free run to emotions and shouting at each other. Let me explain why, looking at both in-person interactions and those occurring remotely on-line.

In-person interactions appear more civil, and I think they are more civil. This is partly because social conventions still prevent a certain amount of direct hostility. But only in small part. My observation is that face-to-face conversations are more civil primarily because most people avoid controversial topics.

The first few minutes' conversation with a new person represents a kind of exploratory dance. Can I discern from this person's statements whether they are a (fill-in the blank for your appropriate measure): Progressive menace, liberal idiot, ultra-MAGA Trump supporter, hard-right conspiracy theorist, semi-fascist, etc. If you detect enemy sentiments, the conversation usually turns to safer, bland, and non-controversial topics. If, however, you hear sentiments similar to your own, you can spend time agreeing with each other and laughing at how clueless supporters of the other party are.

Contrast this with on-line interactions. Although many posts are superficial and unobjectionable, whenever a substantive topic is introduced, there is no tentative probing. The initial volley is more likely to be inflammatory, because people are usually trying to make a point. Also, there's no one to check your inner dialogue, where your every thought is positively genius. Of course, you're right!

The return volleys to your post are either (a) wholly in agreement, confirming your brilliance, or (b) from someone who is apparently attacking everything you stand for and your inherent worth as a person. The proper response to such a challenge is to counterattack. By not immediately agreeing with you, your commenter deserves to be punished, ridiculed, misquoted. Whatever serves to get them to apologize, acquiesce, or go away, and right quick.

When did we get so fragile? Since when does a question or a comment, indeed anything other than slavish agreement, represent an attack on our personal integrity? It could be because the primary purpose of social networks is not to engage in reasoned debate, but to identify like-minded persons.

My mistake seems to be in assuming that people who post ideas are open to discussing those ideas. Rather, people behave as if all they want is reinforcement or silence. In my old world of legal wrangling, silence can be taken as assent. This makes it hard for me to scroll by glaring logical errors. Or even to resist adding another perspective to a topic. Hey, do you think this could lead to unintended consequences? Or, I agree the societal objective is valid, but are there better ways to achieve the desired outcome?

Remember that ideas spread and become influential because they win over new adherents. If you want your ideas to gain traction you must expose them to people who do not yet agree with you. How should you deal with their questions and overcome potential objections?

Here's a tip that is supported by all my learnings in psychology, economics, law, and business: Personal insults are remarkably poor persuaders. Insults in an exchange signal failure, not that you're winning.

When I see someone resort to personal insults, I take it to mean their idea cannot withstand criticism. Moreover, you are all but guaranteeing that your counterpart will dismiss what you have to say further. This makes it that much harder to achieve a common understanding.

Disagreement does not have to be disagreeable. When you make an exchange personal, you not only lose the argument, you lose the chance to gain a convert to your idea.

If you find yourself shouting at strangers, stop and ask yourself why. It's unlikely to be changing anyone's mind. And I bet you don't feel better after doing it. If your method is ineffective, and makes you bitter and unhappy to boot, why are you still using it?

I don't expect everyone to be Spock-like in their reasoning. But I'd be happy to see reasonable minds disagree reasonably more often.

Be well.

# Chapter Thirty-Three

# The World's Worst Persuasion Tactic: Insults

## If you're tired of political insults, take the no-insult pledge with me

President Trump is a giant bully and an ass for insulting his opponents. His violation of norms shocked the world and pushed a great many people into horrified opposition.

What's baffling is how ready his opponents are to resort to the precise tactics they deplore. (*We must destroy democracy to save democracy.*) The last decade presents a truly depressing spectacle to see who can most comprehensively violate norms.

To pick just a simple example, let's look at name-calling. It's more dangerous than we might think. Because of this, I make a personal commitment below and invite you to do the same.

It's one thing to disagree with a person and everything they stand for. It's another to spend hours of one's life dreaming up pejorative names.

### When we resort to insults, we've already lost the argument

I've spent years learning how people think and how to get them to change their minds. My favorite lenses for understanding people and what motivates them have been psychology, economics, and law.

As General Counsel of a large public company for 20 years, I put these tools to good use in negotiating many thousands of contracts and deals with people all over the world. What they taught me is this: Personal insults are remarkably poor persuaders. Insults in an exchange signal failure, not that you're winning.

I wrote about this in Disagree Without Being Disagreeable:

> *When I see someone resort to personal insults, I take it to mean their idea cannot withstand criticism. Moreover, you are all but guaranteeing that your counterpart will dismiss what you have to say further. This makes it that much harder to achieve a common understanding.*

> *Disagreement does not have to be disagreeable. When you make an exchange personal, you not only lose the argument, you lose the chance to gain a convert to your idea.*

> *If you find yourself shouting at strangers, stop and ask yourself why. It's unlikely to be changing anyone's mind.*

## If insults win no arguments, why do we hurl them at each other?

Here's where things get scary. Insulting an opponent (say, a politician) or a group (like their supporters) is not meant to change anyone's mind but to bolster opposition. That is, I want you to feel both righteous anger and a vicarious thrill when I insult our common enemy.

In other words, these insults are tools to divide citizens and dehumanize our enemies.

Reading history, I used to wonder how it is that so many seemingly enlightened and civilized societies found themselves turning on each other. How is it that neighbors could not only willingly, but happily, round up neighbors to imprison, torture, and even kill them?

I wonder no more. It starts with ceasing civil discussion in favor of bullying, shouting, and insulting. It's no joke, even if we find ourselves laughing.

## The way to stop insulting people we disagree with...

I'll paraphrase Chief Justice John Roberts: The way to stop insulting people we disagree with is to stop insulting people we disagree with.

I will take the first step. Although I disagree with many people on politics, I hereby commit to the following no-insult pledge:

- I will never insult you personally for your political beliefs
- I will not personally insult a political figure I disagree with
- I will not become that which I despise to defeat that which I despise
- I will engage respectfully and in good faith, even when my political opponents do not

Fellow citizens, it's up to us. If our leaders won't serve as role models, let us do so ourselves. Take the no-insult pledge with me.

Be well.

# Chapter Thirty-Four

# How Not to Be a Sloppy Second Guesser

## A short explanation of how risk management actually works

Join me on a simple thought experiment to understand how risk management works. You can then apply these principles to your own life to make better decisions.

**The umbrella decision**

Let's imagine you're heading out for a walk. How do you decide whether to take an umbrella with you? Under what circumstances would you second-guess your decision?

How you feel about your decision depends on two things: What you knew before you left the house, and what happened outside until your feet once again cross the threshold of your door.

If it's a sunny day with a clear forecast, you have no trouble leaving the umbrella at home. The idea of taking it never crosses your mind.

Similarly, if it's already pouring out your decision is easy. We call it a no-brainer because you don't have to think.

Seen this way, it's clear all the magic happens amidst uncertainty. It's not raining now but it *might* rain later. You make a judgment call in the face of not knowing whether you'll need the umbrella or not.

## Amidst uncertainty, we emphasize the downside

Let's say you decide to take the umbrella. Then if it rains, you feel good about your decision. You decided correctly!

- And if it doesn't rain, you are happy not to have needed your umbrella.
- You took reasonable action to mitigate a risk that didn't occur. You feel OK about it even though it was, in one sense, a "wasted" effort.

Now let's say you decide to take your chances and leave the umbrella at home. If it rains, you feel bad about your decision.

- To save yourself a small inconvenience (carrying the umbrella), your clothes were soggy all afternoon.
- But if it doesn't rain, you don't celebrate too much because you don't take an umbrella every day it doesn't rain.

When you mitigate risks, you are happy if they occur and fine if they don't occur. Remember you didn't know what would happen. It was a risk, not a certainty.

## Second-guessing based on outcomes is common ... and wrong

The whole point of risk management is making decisions when the outcome is uncertain.

Thus, we properly judge such decisions based on the conditions when they were made, not on the ultimate outcome.

After events have played out, it is worse than useless to say "Knowing what we know now, you should have done X, not Y."

People do this all the time, however. Worse, they fall prey to hindsight bias and falsely remember what they thought and knew at the time.

## Hindsight bias is widespread

You will hear people saying things like the following:

- "I could see the housing crisis forming. Anyone with half a brain knew the market was unsustainable."

- "Well, it's obvious that all that money printing and deficit spending was going to cause inflation."

- "I knew the vaccine wouldn't work. It was developed and rolled out in record time. It was a no-brainer not to put that unknown substance into my body."

To the sloppy second-guesser, taking steps to mitigate risks that occur is no big deal because the risk was obvious (in hindsight). And it was a wasted effort to mitigate risks that did not occur.

*The sloppy second-guesser*

Similarly, the sloppy second guesser thinks they made a good call when a risk they did nothing to mitigate does not occur and suffered from bad luck when it does.

## It is no mistake to plan for risks that do not occur

Just as it is no mistake to plan for risks that never happen, it is no victory to hope for the best and get lucky. At least not from a risk management perspective.

The proper way to think about risk management under conditions of uncertainty is as follows:

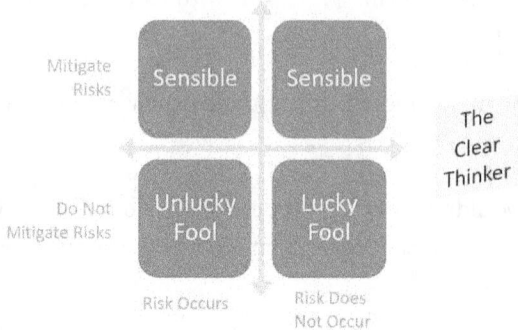

*The clear thinker*

It is sensible to mitigate against risk amidst uncertainty regardless of whether the risk occurs or not.

As a corollary, you are a fool not to mitigate risks, also regardless of outcomes. You are unlucky if the risk does not occur, and lucky if it does, but a fool either way.

Don't let what everyone knows after the fact turn you into a sloppy second guesser.

Be well.

# Chapter Thirty-Five

# I Think, Therefore, You're Wrong

If you disagree with something I've written the odds are quite good that I'm right. While I came to my approach accidentally, you can do it purposefully

I'm more likely to be right, not because I'm unusually smart, although that's part of it. It's rather because of another quirk in my personality. I'll start with the role of intelligence before turning to the quirk that makes me right annoyingly often.

You can use my method to be right more often, but it probably won't come naturally.

**Smart people work best with other smart people**

Oh, how I envied Charlie Munger!

It's not because he lived in good health to almost 100, although I think that would be great. Nor is it due to his billions in wealth, even though I too daydream about such riches.

No, the reason I envy Charlie Munger is that, as intelligent as he was, he worked with an equally smart business partner. Charlie described handling his disagreements with Warren Buffett by simply reminding him, "I'm right and you're smart."

What a wonderful phrase. A smart person knows they're right and knows why. When they're dealing with other smart people, they can count on those people to eventually get the point.

## I'm smart… and I'm extremely grateful for it

It's become taboo to discuss intelligence across societies. I understand why and while I find the taboo counterproductive, that's another topic. I'll limit myself to direct observation and first-hand experience.

Tested by educators in grade school and again 15 years later before heading to graduate school, my IQ appears to be in the top 1%. This is nothing I can take credit for, just the vagaries of nature. Not taking moral credit doesn't make a high IQ illusory, though.

Being in the top 1% of intellectual ability makes one 25 times more likely to earn a doctorate-level degree than the general population. This is where you find many successful doctors, lawyers, and business executives.

Not surprisingly, one's earning power is linked to IQ as well. I've no doubt being smart put me in a position to earn well. I have a JD and an MBA, and I worked as a lawyer in an executive role at a public company for many years.

A while back, I asked readers what their preference would be if they could choose between intelligence, attractiveness, and wealth. It was one of my most-commented articles and those comments were revealing.

I'm tempted to say smart readers chose the intelligent answer (intelligence), while ugly, stupid people chose one of the other options. But that would be both incorrect and unkind—the sort of thing some writers do for cheap laughs.

Readers' answers were nuanced and thoughtful and I saw valid arguments made for each of the three choices. At the same time, while I understand what led readers to choose beauty or wealth, I could see those choices were much more likely driven by emotion, not cool rationality.

That is the key to the quirk that's made me an annoying debate partner.

## I am low on empathy … and I don't care how that makes you feel

I am not some psychopath completely lacking in empathy. Nor am I a sociopath, who has some understanding of what others feel but chooses to ignore it.

Too bad, or I could have leveraged my intelligence to become CEO of my company. It's also clear to me I could have had a fine criminal career had I further lacked morals and a value system.

No, thankfully I have feelings, and I am aware that others have feelings. I rarely consider others' feelings intuitively, however, or without consciously reminding myself to do so.

Unlike high intelligence, I find having low empathy decidedly less advantageous. I hurt people's feelings by accident, I'm needlessly callous, and I am slow to pick up on social cues obvious to others.

Amidst these negatives, I've identified one significant positive: Most people make most decisions on an emotional basis and then rationalize them (if at all) afterward. I consider most situations analytically and dispassionately and only secondarily (if at all) consider the emotional implications.

This, it turns out, is a superpower. At least it's a superpower if one's goal is to avoid being **passionately wrong**. Incidentally, that is the name of the podcast I host with my friend, Randall Surles

## Clear seeing is immensely helpful to clear thinking

My education and my career honed my appreciation for this point: Successfully navigating the world requires an accurate perception of it.

From my psychology degree, I learned that people are a mess of emotions and of predictably irrational behavior. From my economics degree, I learned that incentives directly drive behavior, both positive and negative. From my legal degree, I learned the power of dispassionately analyzing facts and applying a system of rules (the law) to those facts.

Entering the business world, I was amazed to see people confused about why events played out the way they did. Couldn't they see the connection between the inputs and the outputs? Didn't they realize that the design of systems not only predicted certain outcomes but virtually guaranteed them?

Apparently not. The reason, I came to understand, is that many people are led astray by their emotions. They live in the land of wishful thinking. This is what happens when you see what you want to see rather than the world as it actually is.

Wishful thinking applies both positively and negatively, so it'd be more accurate to call it delusional thinking. For example, some perceive slights where they do not exist. Others mistake a systemic advantage for anything but the gift it is.

I seem to dwell in delusional states less often than many people. My hypothesis is that I'm merely lucky to be low on the emotive scale. Together with above-average intelligence, that makes me more inclined to focus on the facts and consider what frame of reference is most useful for analyzing them.

## Cogito ergo erras — and it's not your fault

*I think, therefore, you're wrong.* This sounds arrogant as hell, but now you know why I say it this way.

There are plenty of smart people in the world. A disproportionate number of them are here reading this — after all, who is likely to be attracted to reading and writing like this? I don't fool myself that I'm smarter than many of my readers.

But what is less plentiful are people who can, by disposition like me or via practice like Zen masters, put their emotions to the side and dispassionately look at a situation. That's my default mode.

Thus, when I've written something you find yourself disagreeing with, the chances are good you're wrong. It's your wonderful human emotions that have led you astray.

If you find yourself incredibly annoyed with me right now, I understand. Really, I do.

If you think you can master your emotions enough to put them in the background while debating tough topics, you can take advantage of my method.

Be well.

# Chapter Thirty-Six

# Thriving In A Low-Trust World

## You can, too, by adopting the lawyer's mindset

Many people are angry and confused because the world doesn't make sense.

Our politicians lie and while that's disappointing it's no longer shocking. Worse, each month brings the revelation that another institution has engaged in shading the truth, censorship, or fraud: Universities, scientists, the media, government agencies, corporations, doctors, nonprofits, and the list goes on. Is there no one we can trust?

Among this muddled mess, one group is happily unaffected. You may not have noticed but lawyers are doing just fine. Our worldview is the same as in years past. And our methods of navigating the world work just as well as ever.

Here's what differentiates lawyers and how you can adopt their mindset to maneuver more safely in a post-truth world.

### How lawyers see the world — What, not why

One of the best outcomes of a legal education is honing your judgment. By that, I don't mean coming to any moral conclusion about a situation but being able to perceive it accurately.

A person with good judgment can observe a situation objectively, which is the key that unlocks good decision-making. Clear observation starts with simple facts: What happened? Who did what to whom?

Notice I did not include "Why?" as in "Why did this happen?" That's because it's a mistake to ask "Why?" too early. The why is rarely evident up front, which means suggesting a why puts your emotions into the game.

Emotions are like sulfuric acid to clear thinking. Emotions eat away at what's really there and leave you with a burning mix of what you added. Who knows why people did what they did?

A second reason to be wary of the "Why?" is something that every experienced lawyer knows: People lie. They lie blatantly and frequently, whenever it suits them. The most reliable prediction a lawyer can make is that people always lie when they believe it's in their interest to do so.

The sad follow-up is it's almost always in someone's interest to lie. I wish it weren't so, but the legal profession wouldn't exist otherwise.

A more useful question than "Why?" is "So what?" as in "What are the consequences of individuals' actions?

- John punched Fred in the face. So what? Did the police get involved? Did Fred punch John back? Did anyone get it on camera?

- Mary pilfered $1,000 from the petty cash fund. So what? Did she pay it back before anyone found out? Did it come up in our internal audit?

Answering the "So what?" questions requires more than knowing the facts. We also must know the potential consequences of actions. And not hypothetical consequences but practical ones. Can you prove it? If what you say is true, would it matter? What can we do about it?

"I follow you, James, but none of this makes me feel better. People are liars and we can't trust them. We need to look at actions and the consequences of individuals' actions. How does this help me navigate the world?"

## How lawyers behave —What can we count on?

Good summary, dear reader, and take heart. Knowing that what people say is untrustworthy means we can give their statements the proper weight: zero. Instead, we look for ways to protect ourselves when it's important. This comes in the form of a handful of contracting principles.

I spent 30 years drafting and negotiating contracts. Millions and millions of them. The primary reason for most contracts is to answer the "So what?" question.

You agreed to buy my car next week for $10,000, which I've told you has 50,000 kilometers on it. A good contract will specify what happens if

- You don't come up with the money in time
- The car has 150,000 kilometers on it
- You decide six months later you don't like it anymore
- And usually a bunch of other things

You can think of contracts this way: Contracts exist to add consequences to otherwise empty statements. "If you lie or fail to keep your promises, there will be consequences, and here's what they are." Contracts turn untrustworthy people (the default) into reliable ones or at a minimum enable us to work together.

Thus, a key rule of thumb is you can count on statements or actions where the person making them is exposed to clear consequences for lying or failure. The corollary is that when there are no consequences for lying or failure, you should not blindly trust the person's statements or actions.

This drastically reduces the scope of what you safely take seriously. That's because people rarely face consequences for mistakes of fact, shading the truth, or outright falsehoods designed to mislead or propagandize.

Just to mention it, the answer is not to surrender trust to people who say things you agree with. They're just as unreliable if they face no consequences for getting it wrong.

## Checklist for thriving in a low-trust world

1. Accept that people are untrustworthy and will mislead you when it suits them. It always suits someone.

2. Apply healthy skepticism to claims made when the person faces no consequences for misleading. (Legacy media and publications, social media)

3. Be especially wary of people who want your action or agreement while paying no price for lying. (Politicians, regulators, nonprofits)

4. Seek ways to attach consequences to statements or promises that are important to you. Have explicit "So what" conversations and, yes, sign a contract when the stakes are high.

5. Don't let the quirks of human nature get you down. It's true that skepticism is safer than blind trust, but you needn't become jaded. Forewarned is forearmed and you are now set up for safely making your way.

Be well.

Chapter Thirty-Seven

# How To Win an Argument

Effective communication is a joy to behold. Here's a virtuoso display of the method, if we're willing to look past the messenger to the message

What do pennies and plastic straws have in common? Some uncommonly good ways to win an argument. If you're open to learning how to use the methods, you will be amazed at how powerful you'll feel.

**Important: This post is not about politics.** I am using examples provided by President Trump to illustrate the communication and persuasion principles.

### Appreciate the skill, if not the practitioner

President Trump has an unusual set of talents, including effective communication. His words are always vivid, emotional, and tangible. They are correspondingly quite persuasive.

It's not just how he creates pictures in our heads. It's the purpose behind those pictures that make them powerful. Two recent examples illustrate what I mean.*

### 1. Back to black, er plastic, same thing

In a Truth Social post, Trump wrote this:

> *I will be signing an Executive Order next week ending the ridiculous Biden push for Paper Straws, which don't work. BACK TO PLASTIC!*

The first sentence sets the stage by highlighting what we disagree with in disagreeable terms. To begin, "ridiculous Biden push" is so strong, calling on fully three levels of emotional reaction:

- No one likes to feel they are behaving foolishly because it subjects them to ridicule. "Ridiculous" thus has us on high alert.

- Biden was singularly unpopular, having been ousted by his own party in favor of a historically unpopular Vice President. Who wants to be associated with that?

- We hate being told what to do, which is exactly what a push does. If we wanted to do it, we wouldn't need a push.

In three words, Trump primes us to expect something foolish, unpopular, and imposed on us by force. He nails it by then naming the culprit, Plastic Straws.

Did you notice the final three words of the first sentence? Devastating, in light of the setup:

- which don't work.

Don't underestimate the power of those words. They underline the frustration much of the population feels about many government policies. Politicians keep pushing stuff on us that doesn't work.

With this, he's tapped into a deep pool of existing, powerful emotions: Anger, confusion, and resentment.

The final words are where the argument is decisively won. The first sentence would be devastating enough but it's negative and leaves a bitter taste (sort of like a disintegrating paper straw on your lips).

Trump ends with an all-caps declaration BACK TO PLASTIC! that is every bit as emphatic as his raised fist after getting shot at the Butler rally.

The tactic he's using: Reframing the argument, taking away your opponent's advantage

- If the argument is about the environment (clean water, happy turtles, pollution), there's no possible way an appeal to plastic could ever win

- In a beautiful judo move of a few words, Trump reframes the argument into (i) not acting foolishly, (ii) resisting yet another push from a government we don't trust, (iii) acknowledging what works and what doesn't, and (iv) taking back individual freedom

As a student of logic, rhetoric, and persuasion, I say this is effective communication. As a psychologist, lawyer, and manager, I say he's won enough hearts and minds that the old argument is effectively dead. Only zealots and fools will now push for paper. Simply masterful.

## 2. For want of a penny...

What's the President doing worrying about the cost of a penny? Consider this post of his:

> *For far too long the United States has minted pennies which literally cost us more than 2 cents. This is so wasteful! I have instructed my Secretary of the US Treasury to stop producing new pennies. Let's rip the waste out of our great nations budget, even if it's a penny at a time.*

I'll give you a hint: It's not about the penny. This is about cutting off his opponents' argument at the knees without them even realizing it.

The first two sentences set the scene.

- Note the words "For far too long" (how long has it been?), drawing the reader into the narrative from the first words

- "minted pennies" is a strong, visual image — we can almost see the shiny copper coins dropping into the collection vat at the end of the belt

- When making something costs more than twice what it's worth, "This is so wasteful!" is the immediate, visceral reaction. Of course, he's right.

With that setup, no longer producing new pennies is eminently sensible.

What follows, though, is a real kill shot: "Let's rip the waste out of our great nations budget, even if it's a penny at a time."

- "Rip the waste" is a powerful image. We get the sense that the waste won't go willingly. That we'll have to pry it out of the resisting hands of those who benefit from it. That's exactly right.

- "Our great nations budget" reminds us that it is our country and our money we are fighting for. Personal and patriotic at the same time.

- "Even if it's a penny at a time" is wonderful. We all know how hard it is to save money. Many of us had piggy banks as children, into which we faithfully deposited our coins, seeing our small fortunes grow.

The tactic he's using: Taking the moral high ground, making it impossible for opponents to argue against the principle you're championing

- What clueless, arrogant, cold bastard can stand up and say "It's only $40 billion of fraud and waste. There are better things to focus on?" or "It's only 1% of the budget. Why is this important?"

Trump just claimed the moral high ground. The highest officer in the country just reminded Congress and the bureaucracy that every penny counts. It's the citizens' money and not a penny of it shall be wasted.

That's it. The fight over how much fraud, waste, and abuse is OK for Americans to tolerate is over. We don't want a single penny of it lost to grubby theft and malfeasance.

## Effective communication is a superpower

Many people struggle to understand how President Trump continues to bounce back from every setback. His rhetorical skills are off the chart. That's contributed greatly to his resilience.

He communicates emotionally, visually, and viscerally. When used together with persuasion tactics like those I've described here, it's a great way to win arguments.

Be well.

* The sharp-eyed among you will have noticed Trump makes typos in his posts and his grammar is often errant. That's the case for both the posts I discussed today. I admit it offends my publisher's eye. But the mistakes are a red herring and we must not get distracted by them.

# Chapter Thirty-Eight

# How To Get What You Want

## Five common mistakes waylay us, but you can avoid them

Individuals often sabotage their progress toward their stated goals. They act in ways that reduce the odds they'll get what they want. Understanding the common reasons for failure can help us avoid them.

Say young Johan desires to become wealthy. He sees wealthy people spending money on expensive houses, cars, and vacations. Johan does the same, although he is not yet wealthy. While he earns a good salary, he does not save or invest but rather incurs substantial indebtedness.

Johan's mistake is obvious to all observing him: One cannot spend their way to wealth. Why isn't it obvious to Johan himself?

### 1–3. Basic reasons we fail

Possible reasons for Johan's suboptimal behavior include:

1. He is unaware that his spending will have significant consequences, i.e. preventing him from becoming wealthy (**unaware**, *like a baby*).

2. He is aware his financial habits are relevant but is ignorant of better approaches, i.e. keeping his spending modest, investing his savings, and being patient (**uninformed**, *like a child*).

3. He knows of better approaches but is unwilling to take the necessary

steps to implement them (***unrealistic***, *like a young adult*).

## Wishful thinking: The unaware, uninformed, and unrealistic

A great deal of self-defeating behavior takes place in these three domains. It is a consequence of willful ignorance and wishful thinking.

Are some people genuinely unaware that smoking dramatically reduces one's life expectancy and is a direct cause of lung cancer? If so, they are keeping themselves ignorant.

How about people who maintain a balance on their credit cards for more than a short period? Have the usurious rates charged by banks escaped their attention? Do they not see how rapidly their balances grow when they make only the minimum payment?

Knowing one's approach is counterproductive to achieving stated goals does not mean one is aware of better alternatives. Think of everyone who fiddles with their eating habits only to see themselves inexorably gaining weight each year.

We keep ourselves ignorant and uninformed because the truth of how we make progress is harsh: It requires patience, discipline, and control to achieve desired outcomes. One must invest time and effort to attain what one wants.

The new employee who proclaims their desire to become CEO in five years while also expecting to depart at 5:00 p.m. and enjoy their work-free vacations is guilty of wishful thinking.

The only antidote for the consequences of willful ignorance and wishful thinking is being confronted with reality. When one's plans go awry and one's goals are frustrated, some are motivated to find a new approach.

To achieve better outcomes, a person must genuinely desire to improve. Wallowing in any of the first three domains thus represents a lack of motivation.

Because we get better results in helping those who wish to help themselves, let's turn to the final two categories.

## 4. We cannot progress when we lack clear direction

Assuming Johan is acting in good faith, a fourth potential reason he takes actions that appear inconsistent with his goals is this: He may have ill-defined or unstated goals. (***ill-defined goals***, *the mark of a superficial thinker, a person who takes the headline for the news*)

That is, Johan says he wants to become wealthy. But what does "wealthy" mean to Johan? Financial security? The trappings of success? Being able to attract a suitable life partner?

**Dangerous waters: The peril of ill-defined goals**

This case is at the heart of much of what appears to be flawed thinking and decision-making.

People do things that are demonstrably inconsistent with their *stated goals*. Their actions become understandable when we examine individuals' unstated goals and motivations, which they may not have consciously acknowledged.

The path to improving outcomes for those of us who genuinely want to improve lies in spending more time understanding our motivation and our desires.

Success comes from probing beyond the first answer because it represents superficial thinking. Rather, look to the underlying motives and ask follow-up questions: And why do I want that? Continue to ask the question as many times as necessary to arrive at the fundamental motivation.

You might recognize this as embarking upon asking the Five Whys to gain a deeper understanding.

Johan has realized that his stated goal of becoming wealthy is inconsistent with his behavior of borrowing to fund a rich lifestyle. So he sits himself down for an honest conversation, starting with this question: What is it I truly want? What is motivating me?

- Perhaps Johan realizes that he is insecure about whether he's good enough for his spouse.

- Or he wonders whether the career path he's chosen is the right one for him or whether he's wasting his life.

- Maybe he is so deeply pessimistic about climate change that he believes humanity is doomed.

- Or for Johan, it's none of that, he just wants to enjoy life now while he's young and he's confident he has time to save in a few years.

The point is twofold: Only Johan knows his true goals (which may be inconsistent with his stated goals), and Johan's actions appear differently when measured against his true goals.

If you don't understand your motivation, your actions appear inconsistent with your goals.

Moreover, when you do clearly define your goals, you are (finally) in a position to improve your chances of getting what you want.

## 5. Critical thinking and decision-making are hard

There is a fifth case, which describes the rest of us most of the time: A person willing to put in a sincere effort to achieve their goals, but who is inexperienced in the available methods or lacks expertise in their implementation (***the inexperienced non-expert***).

This includes everyone who's tried to lose weight by dieting or employed the services of a financial advisor.

The inexperienced non-expert is at risk of the following stumbles:

- Choosing a suboptimal approach
- Implementing a suitable approach in a flawed manner
- Taking further decisions that undermine or undo their progress

Using Johan again, knowing that savings are important,

- A *suboptimal approach* would be keeping his savings in cash under his mattress or in a checking account
- A *flawed implementation* would be buying individual stocks that his brother-in-law recommends
- And *further decisions* that undermine his progress would be cashing in his early investment gains to buy a Ferrari

While avoiding mistakes does not guarantee successful outcomes, committing mistakes guarantees failure.

Thus, we can get what we want more often by avoiding the mistakes I've outlined here.

Be well.

www.ingramcontent.com/pod-product-compliance
Lightning Source LLC
Chambersburg PA
CBHW061922220426
43662CB00012B/1769